A DISTANT THUNDER
Michigan in the Civil War

RICHARD BAK

Huron River Press

3622 W. Liberty

Ann Arbor, MI 48103

www.clocktowerpress.com

10 9 8 7 6 5 4 3 2 1

Library of Congress Cataloging-in-Publication Data

Bak, Richard, 1954-

A distant thunder : Michigan in the Civil War / Richard Bak.

p. cm.

Includes bibliographical references (p.) and index.

ISBN 1-932399-03-8

1. Michigan – History – Civil War, 1861-1865. 2. Michigan – History – Civil War, 1861-1865 – Pictorial works.

3. United States   History – Civil War, 1861-1865 – Pictorial works. 4. Soldiers– Michigan–History–19th century.

5. Soldiers–United States–History–19th century.

I. Title.

E514.B355 2004

973.7'09774--dc22

2004006497

Printed in Canada

To Carrol Ann Stankovitz and Fay Dutka-Zavitz
and the memory of school days in Detroit

John Rock was one of 90,000 Wolverines to answer his country's call during the Civil War. The private from Rockland served in the 27th Michigan Infantry.

Foreword

Standing on Little Round Top in Gettysburg, Pennsylvania, I was absolutely convinced someone was watching me. Dawn was breaking after an all night drive from my home in Michigan. A light, summer rain was falling through the trees. Not a tourist in sight. And yet, I wasn't alone.

For those who've never been to a Civil War Battlefield, it's a little like stepping into a cathedral. There's a presence. A sense of being surrounded. Someone was here before you and they haven't left yet. With only days before *Gettysburg* began filming and my head swimming with anything having to do with Joshua Lawrence Chamberlain, I had an inkling as to whom it might be.

I had spoken with scholars. Seen his grave. Touched his boots. Studied his letters. I even tried to match his handwriting. I knew the accent, how he stood, how he spoke, even how he thought. It may have been a hundred thirty years ago, but I knew him like it was yesterday. And now, finally, I was where he was, standing in what had to be the very place where, in the face of certain death, Chamberlain held at all costs. I looked up through the rain and promised him I would do everything in my power to make him proud.

After my pilgrimage, I wandered up the hill. Past the handmade rock walls. Past the trees that had replaced those which surely must have been shot to pieces. I heard muskets firing, soldiers screaming, and a distant rebel yell that kept coming and coming and coming. And then, as I stepped out of the woods and onto the crest of the ridge, I saw it. A simple slab of marble. Wet with rain. Looking west out over Devil's Den.

16TH MICHIGAN

I read the names. Without knowing one, I knew them all. I knew from where they had come, where they had been, what they had loved. I was one of them. I wanted to thank them. I wanted to tell them what they did mattered more than they would ever know.

Through tireless research and a great knack for storytelling, Richard Bak has created a monument to all who served our great state during the Civil War. Throughout this wonderful history, you will come to know the brave and the foolish, their widowed wives, their orphaned children, their songs, their poems, their prayers. They will sound very familiar. They will tell you why they have to enlist and you will hear their goodbyes and watch them march off to war, waving their hats, and you will find yourself wanting to wave back, silently praying they return safely because these were our sons, our brothers, our fathers, uncles, nephews, cousins, and friends, but they were not strangers. They were from our city, our town, our street, our home. And now, because of this book, I am honored to say they make me proud.

Jeff Daniels
Chelsea, Michigan
March 16, 2004

Andrew Noah Guyor was 25 when he mustered into the 4th Michigan Infantry on June 20, 1861. The Monroe private posed with two familiar martial props—a knife and a revolver. In reality, pistols were too expensive to be issued to all soldiers as a standard firearm.

Table of Contents

Chapter 1

WAR IS HELL

War was hell for Lieutenant John Clark of the 7th Michigan Infantry. The 21-year-old officer from Monroe was killed at the Battle of Antietam in 1862 and buried in a shallow grave (opposite page). A dead Confederate lies in the foreground.

William Tecumseh Sherman was a no-nonsense man of forceful language, making him a natural for *Bartlett's Familiar Quotations* as well as the American military. "Hold the fort! I am coming!" is just one of several memorable utterances the general entered into the English language. "War is cruelty, and you cannot refine it"—a message issued during his army's devastating march through the Confederate homeland in the closing stages of the Civil War—is another. Sherman, one of the first "modern" military commanders, had no illusions of what war was really like—as the inaugural graduating class of the Michigan Military Academy was about to find out.

It was June 19, 1879, and Sherman—who a decade earlier had succeeded U. S. Grant as commander-in-chief of the army upon Grant's move into the White House—had been invited to address the cadets and their families. The Michigan Military Academy in Pontiac was just two years old, having been established by Captain Joseph Sumner Rogers, a wounded Civil War veteran from Maine. The private academy, whose buildings and grounds today comprise the schools of Orchard Lake St. Mary, was modeled after West Point. The institution would enjoy a brief but distinguished life. Before closing its doors in 1908, it would graduate such luminaries as Sewell Lee Avery, the future chairman of Montgomery Ward, and Edwin Baruch Winans Jr., the future superintendent of West Point. It also would be cited in an 1889 U. S. Army report calling it "the leading military institution of the country, outside of West Point."

The turnout was estimated to be in the several thousands, with at least one newspaper claiming the number exceeded 10,000. Some of the middle-aged men in attendance were proud to say

The eminently quotable William Tecumseh Sherman addressed the inaugural graduating class of the Michigan Military Academy, which operated from 1877 to 1908.

they had been among Sherman's "bummers" in 1864-65, torching and looting and generally helping to "make Georgia howl," as the general had so expressively put it. Those who had come with the expectations of hearing the army's top man "wave the bloody shirt," however, were to be disappointed.

"I am tired and sick of war," Sherman told the assemblage this late spring day. "Its glory is all moonshine. It is only those who have neither fired a shot nor heard the shrieks and groans of the wounded who cry aloud for blood, more vengeance, more desolation."

At this point Sherman delivered what was to become the most enduring of his many familiar quotations.

"War," the old general said, "is hell."

Like most combatants in the fratricidal conflict, Private John Houghton, who endured years of tough campaigning with the 4th Michigan Infantry Regiment, understood war to be hell—right down to the licks of flame that consumed foes and comrades as if in some sort of Biblical holocaust. In his journal he described the following scene at the Battle of Chancellorsville, Virginia, in the spring of 1863:

> soon after this the woods caught afire burning over the principle part of the battlefield. and it was thought that a good many of the wounded was burnt up alive we could plainly hear the poor fellows scream and yell. we thaught from the agonys of being burnt the bodies of the dead men was completely roasted. their clothing burning on them helped to roast their Bodys beyond all Recognition. Some of them had layed in the sun for four days this and the fire made them swell up till they were as big as two or three common men their mouths were Swelled wide open. Their tongues protruding from their mouths full length. No Human being could be made to look any wors than they did. They were so chared up that we could not tell a white man from a Negro. nor a Union man from a Rebel.

Houghton was just one of some 90,000 Michiganians to serve in the national conflagration known as the Civil War—and one of the 75,000 or so to survive it. Individually, the motivations and experiences of these citizen soldiers from St. Joseph, Alpena, Fowlerville, Lansing, Bay City, Cross Village, Detroit, Hancock, Kalamazoo, Calumet, Albion, Green Oak, Galesburg, Constantine and numerous other communities from across the state varied greatly. Almost without exception they were proud Union men, eager to restore the number of lost stars in the flag while teaching the "secesh"—shorthand for secessionists—a thing or two about loyalty. Some saw the war as a crusade to end slavery. Others simply wanted to leave a nagging wife or a boring job and see a bit of the world. Their ranks included heroes, opportunists, adventurers, patriots, cowards, glory hounds and fools…volunteers, draftees and substitutes…whites, blacks, immigrants, Indians and at least one Filipino…old men, young men, boys and even a few women. There were strapping farmers who dropped their rifles and hid in the opening moments of combat; mild-mannered store clerks who literally lost their heads charging enemy cannon; well-educated attorneys who could never master the manual of arms; God-fearing shoemakers who smote the enemy at

A slave auction, where families were torn apart and prospective purchases were examined and sold like livestock.

the rate of three minie balls a minute; rambunctious teamsters who brought venereal disease home to their unsuspecting wives; venturesome schoolboys who died feverishly in hospital beds while calling out for their mothers. Although each Michigan soldier's contribution to the bigger picture was extremely limited and often insignificant, the collective weight of their sacrifice—added to that of the more than 2 million others under Union arms—ultimately helped to keep one great nation from splintering into two lesser countries. At the same time—though emancipation was not an original war aim—they lifted an entire race of human beings out of bondage. These twin results bore greatly on the future course of not only America, but of the world.

"That in view of the necessity of battling for the first principles of republican government and against the schemes of an aristocracy, the most revolting and oppressive with which the earth was ever cursed or man debased, we will cooperate and be known as Republicans until the contest be terminated."

Resolution of the Republican Party, formed "under the oaks"

at Jackson on July 6, 1854

If General Sherman and Private Houghton were among us today, they would repeat their warnings to a new generation that war is not glorious, war is not orderly, war cannot be refined. Nonetheless, wars are sometimes necessary—and theirs, they undoubtedly would insist, was one of them.

The separate issues of slavery and states' rights became hopelessly entwined in the decades leading up to the Civil War, as lawmakers representing divergent regional interests passed a series of unsatisfactory Congressional compromises. When Michigan entered the Union as the 26th state in 1837, its constitution prohibited slavery. As an economic system it was hardly worth preserving in cold-climate states in the North, anyway. Slavery had existed in Michigan when it was a territory—its first census in 1810 listed 24 slaves—but even these were principally house servants, not field hands.

Practical considerations aside, in the years following the American Revolution the idea of enslaving other human beings was viewed by an increasing number of people in all sections of the country as being morally repugnant. Slavery actually was dying out in the South—until the invention of the cotton gin in 1793 allowed domestic and European textile mills to use the short-staple cotton that could only be grown in that region of the country. This was a financial boon to such states as Virginia, Georgia, Mississippi and Alabama, and produced a great demand for cheap, unskilled labor. Despite the United States' ban on the importation of slaves from Africa and the

Sojourner Truth was born a slave in New York in 1797, but freed when that state passed its own emancipation act in 1827. A powerful speaker for abolition and women's suffrage who claimed she had personal conversations with God, Truth moved to Battle Creek in the 1850s and became the community's most famous resident. During the war she was received by President Lincoln, who appointed her counselor to Washington's freedmen. Her funeral in 1883 was described as the largest Battle Creek had ever seen.

West Indies in 1807, the trafficking continued illegally. While much of the rest of the civilized world was rejecting slavery, in the bottom half of the United States it was flourishing into a social and economic institution. On the eve of the Civil War, the 11 states that would comprise the Confederacy had a total population of 9 million, of which 4 million were slaves. Although three in four Southern families were too poor to own even a single slave, some 10,000 others had 50 or more slaves toiling on their plantations or farms.

It was an abominable system of human trafficking. Unlucky individuals, families and sometimes entire villages were captured (or purchased from tribal chiefs) by slave traders in Africa, put in chains, then herded onto filthy, overcrowded ships for a dangerous transatlantic crossing that ended with the survivors being sold and distributed like any ordinary shipment of cargo. Henry Bibb, an escaped slave who lectured in Michigan of his experiences, recalled the auction block:

> Another man was called up whose wife followed him with her infant in her arms, beseeching to be sold with her husband, which proved to be all in vain. After the men were all sold they then sold the women and children. They ordered the first woman to lay down her child and mount the auction block; she refused to give up her little one and clung to it as long as she could, while the cruel lash was applied to her back for disobedience. She pleaded for mercy in the name of God. But the child was torn from the arms of its mother amid the most heart-rending shrieks from the mother and child on the one hand, and bitter oaths and cruel lashes from the tyrants on the other. Finally the poor little child was torn from the mother while she was sacrificed to the highest bidder. In this way the sale was carried on from beginning to end.

In this painting by Charles T. Webber, fugitive slaves are assisted by abolitionists as they arrive at yet another "station" on the Underground Railroad.

Slave owners, looking to justify slavery to their critics, often pictured the South's "peculiar institution" as being a benevolent one, but mistreatment was the norm. Depending on how vengeful or sadistic a master was, a slave might have a finger or limb amputated, or even be killed, as punishment. But because slaves were considered very valuable "property"—a healthy field hand fetched as much as $1,800—whippings usually were employed to keep malcontents in line. Runaways were hunted with bloodhounds and large rewards were offered for their capture. Slave catchers routinely made forays into Michigan. Although they often were thwarted by abolitionists, slave owners regularly won judgments in civil cases requiring a fugitive slave's protectors to financially compensate the master for the loss of his property.

The extent of sexual abuse was appalling, to the point that the rape of a slave by her master was not considered a crime and miscegenation carried little social stigma. "Southern women often marry a man knowing that he is the father of many little slaves," wrote Harriet Jacobs, a fugitive slave. "They do not trouble themselves about it. They regard such children as property, as marketable as the pigs on the plantation; and it is seldom that they do not make them aware of this by passing them into the slave trader's hands as soon as possible, and thus getting them out of their sight."

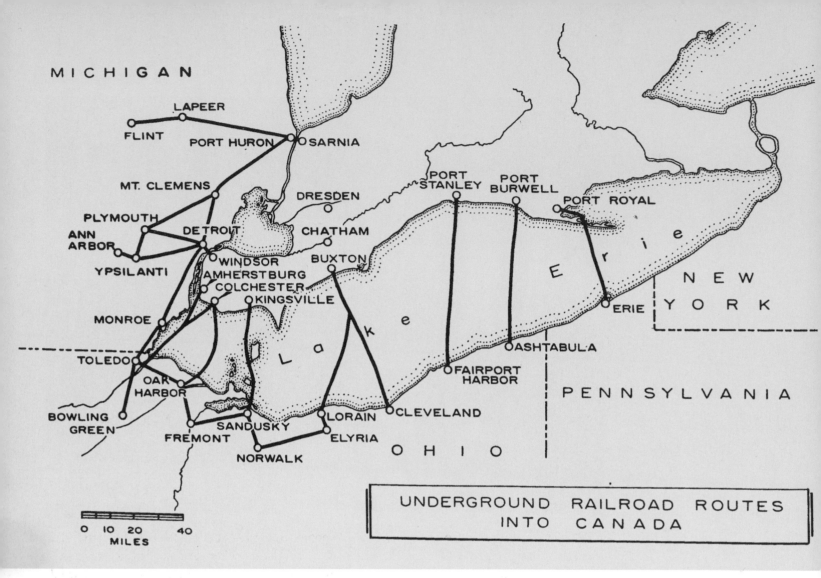

MICHIGAN

LAPEER
FLINT
PORT HURON   SARNIA

MT. CLEMENS   DRESDEN

PLYMOUTH   DETROIT   CHATHAM
ANN
ARBOR
YPSILANTI   WINDSOR
                  AMHERSTBURG   BUXTON
                  COLCHESTER
                  KINGSVILLE
MONROE

TOLEDO

OAK
HARBOR

BOWLING   SANDUSKY
GREEN   FREMONT
                  NORWALK   LORAIN   CLEVELAND
                                 ELYRIA

PORT
STANLEY   PORT
           BURWELL   PORT ROYAL

                                    E r i e

                                              N E W
                      Lake   Y O R K

                              ERIE

            ASHTABULA

        FAIRPORT   PENNSYLVANIA
        HARBOR

OHIO

0 10 20   40
      MILES

UNDERGROUND RAILROAD ROUTES
INTO CANADA

This map shows the various routes to freedom for runaway slaves heading north to Canada. Untold thousands settled in Michigan or passed through the state in the years prior to the Civil War.

"I was a slave, a prisoner for life," said Henry Bibb. "I could possess nothing, nor acquire anything but what must belong to my keeper. No one can imagine my feelings in my reflecting moments, but he who himself has been a slave."

Michigan had a very active anti-slavery movement, with communities like Albion, Marshall, Farmington, Wyandotte, Pontiac, Mount Clemens, Rochester and Birmingham providing way stations for what was known as the "underground railroad." The railroad was a secret network of churches, barns, haystacks, attics, cellars and other hiding places (known as "stations") over which several thousand escaped slaves fled the South between 1830 and 1860.

Today, a permanent exhibit at the Detroit Historical Museum, "Doorway to Freedom," traces the railroad routes that led to Detroit and across the one-mile-wide river into Canada. Most of the escaped slaves who passed through will always remain anonymous, but the identities of several of the underground "conductors" are deservedly highlighted. One is Seymour Finney, a white

"In all history there is nothing like it. With no external enemy to trouble us, with no internal oppression, with none of those visitations of pestilence or famine by which nations are often punished for their offences, we have recklessly put to hazard our inestimable blessings, and are entering that path of discord, and division, and border disputes, which, if there is any truth to history, must lead to the most disastrous consequences."

Lewis Cass, addressing supporters at a Detroit banquet in his honor, March 1861.

abolitionist who owned the Finney Hotel at Woodward and Gratiot Avenues. At the same time Finney was regularly housing slave catchers from Kentucky at his hotel, he was hiding the objects of their search inside his horse barn located a few blocks away at the corner of State and Griswold. Another is George DeBaptiste, a free black who came to Detroit from Virginia in 1846 as the ex-steward of President William Henry Harrison. During the day DeBaptiste ran a catering service; at night he clandestinely conducted a smuggling operation, spiriting escaped slaves to freedom aboard his steamship. Reflecting the community's often hypocritical views on race, DeBaptiste had to hire a white captain to pilot his craft because blacks were not allowed to hold a boating license.

Abolitionists were not afraid to resort to violence to frustrate slave catchers. In 1833, an angry crowd of Detroiters—many of them black, and some armed with clubs, rocks and revolvers—surrounded the jail where the sheriff was waiting to transport a pair of runaway slaves, Thornton Blackburn and his wife, back to their owner in Kentucky. Somehow a sympathizer was able to switch clothes with the imprisoned woman, allowing her to flee to Canada. The next day another mob freed Thornton himself, wounding the sheriff in the process. Similarly spectacular rescues occurred in Porter and Calvin Townships in Cass County, where sympathetic Quakers helped to resettle and protect blacks. On one occasion in 1847, a raiding party led by a slave owner-preacher attempted to return to the South after capturing a fugitive slave and her infant.

Cryptically worded notices alerted abolitionists that a new group of fugitive slaves had arrived. Seymour Finney's barn (pictured here several decades after the war), housed many runaways.

The raiders were foiled by a large group of free blacks and white sympathizers, who sank their wagon in a lake and forced the reverend to give up his horse to the woman. The preacher was then ordered to ignominiously carry the infant in his arms while neighbors "were called out to look at that child-stealer," recalled a witness. An abolitionist named "Nigger Bill" Jones "taunted him so much that he actually cried with vexation." Given this level of support, it's not surprising that the majority of Michigan's 6,800 blacks, who constituted less than 1 percent of the state's population in 1860, lived in Cass and Wayne Counties.

One of the state's most prominent abolitionists was a kindly Quaker named Laura Smith Haviland, known by many of those she aided as "Auntie Laura." Born in Ontario, Canada on December 20, 1808, her views were shaped at an early age by a book she read describing the evils of the slave trade. She married Charles Haviland when she was 15, and their subsequent involvement with a local anti-slavery society led to them breaking away from the Quakers, who were ambivalent in their approach to helping escaped slaves. Some members of the Society of Friends

STOCKHOLDERS
OF THE UNDERGROUND
R. R. COMPANY
Hold on to Your Stock!!

The market has an upward tendency. By the express train which arrived this morning at 3 o'clock, fifteen thousand dollars worth of human merchandise, consisting of twenty-nine able-bodied men and women, fresh and sound, from the Carolina and Kentucky plantations, have arrived safe at the depot on the other side, where all our sympathising colonization friends may have an opportunity of expressing their sympathy by bringing forward donations of ploughs, &c., farming utensils, pick axes and hoes, and not old clothes; as these emigrants all can till the soil. N. B.—Stockholders don't forget, the meeting to-day at 2 o'clock at the ferry on the Canada side. All persons desiring to take stock in this prosperous company, be sure to be on hand. By Order of the

Detroit, April 19, 1853. BOARD OF DIRECTORS.

thought the immorality of slavery justified committing occasionally illegal acts; more law-abiding members were content to sit back and do nothing while waiting for a sign from God. "We claim a higher law than the wicked enactments of men who claim the misnomer of law by which bodies and souls of men, women and children are claimed as chattels," declared the Havilands, who moved to Michigan in the 1830s.

In 1836 the couple started an unusual school called the Raisin Institute. Located a few miles northeast of Adrian, the institute began as a manual-labor school for boys from the local poorhouse. It soon grew into a normal preparatory school, admitting girls and blacks—the first such school in the new state. Charles Haviland died of rheumatic fever in 1845, leaving Laura to contend with the almost overwhelming tasks of raising seven children while also taking care of the school and running a farm. Although the term hadn't been invented yet, Laura Haviland was a model of 19th-century multitasking. Not only did she keep the school and farm operating smoothly enough, she became deeply involved with the clandestine activities of the underground railroad. Runaways, moving at night to escape notice, found refuge inside the Raisin Institute or the Haviland farmhouse while passing through Lenawee County on their way into Canada. Despite the passing of the Fugitive Slave Act in 1850, which made it a crime for anyone to protect or assist

"Gateway to Freedom," a monument sculpted by Ed Dwight and erected on the Detroit riverfront in 2001, portrays Underground Railroad "conductor" George DeBaptiste pointing across the water to Canada, where many fugitive slaves found sanctuary.

Albion abolitionist Laura Smith Haviland posed for this postwar photograph with iron shackles and other implements of the slave trade.

an escaped slave, Haviland fearlessly became one of the railroad's prime conductors. She provided food, clothing, shelter and money to an untold number of escaped slaves and often traveled to the South to escort them to safety. In later years she sold her school to the state, freeing her to establish an orphanage in Coldwater and to get involved in the temperance and women's suffrage movements. After she died in 1898, a statue of her was erected in front of Adrian City Hall. The inscription on it reads: "A tribute to a life consecrated to the betterment of humanity."

In 1854 Congress passed the controversial Kansas-Nebraska Act. The legislation allowed western territories in the process of drafting state constitutions to decide for themselves if slavery was to be permitted within their borders. This policy of "popular sovereignty" was pushed through by Stephen Douglas, the diminutive Democratic senator from Illinois. This latest compromise did not satisfy dissident leaders of the Whig and Democratic parties, who in the summer of 1854 organized a series of meetings with an aim to forming a new party "to concentrate the popular sentiment of this state against the aggression of the slave power."

In Michigan a statewide convention was organized at Jackson on July 6, 1854. As many as 5,000 people attended. This was too large of a crowd to squeeze into a hall, causing organizers to build a speaker's platform in a grove of oak trees near what is now the corner of Second and Franklin Streets in downtown Jackson. Out of this meeting "under the oaks" a state platform was established, a slate of candidates was chosen, and the Republican Party was unofficially christened. That fall Republicans swept to victory in state elections, pushing the once dominant Democratic Party into the shadows, where it would spend most of the next eight decades.

Elizabeth Chandler, a Quaker from New England, settled in Adrian in 1830 and started Michigan's first antislavery society two years later. Before dying prematurely from disease in 1834, Chandler had attained national prominence in the abolition movement through her poetry and other writings.

The paradox of race relations during this tumultuous period was that many whites who opposed slavery on humanitarian grounds still felt the Negro race to be genetically inferior. This opinion was based on a blend of pseudoscience, folklore and anecdotal evidence, which included the hard fact that nearly all blacks in bondage were illiterate—a condition slave masters rigorously enforced as a way of maintaining control. Abolitionists, while exerting an influence disproportionate to their numbers, were at the same time a distinct minority in the white population. Thus, while Northern blacks were ostensibly free, with rare exceptions they were denied the right to vote even in local elections. Other discriminatory practices kept them from buying property, posting bail, suing a white man, or having a white spouse.

One of those who thought that, all things considered, the country would be better off without Negroes was Abraham Lincoln, the tall, homely and melancholic frontier lawyer who, ironically, was destined to become known as "The Great Emancipator." Political correctness didn't exist then, either as an expression or in practice, so Lincoln felt free to tell bawdy jokes, including a favorite about a well-endowed slave whose phallus was used as a razor strop by his master.

Lincoln, a member of the Illinois legislature, had recently switched from the Whig to the Republican party. He made the one and only Michigan appearance of his life on August 27, 1856 in Kalamazoo. The occasion was a rally for John C. Fremont, the new party's first presidential candidate. Fremont would go on to carry Michigan but would lose to James Buchanan in November's election. At the time Lincoln was a towering public figure only in the sense of his remarkable height—at 6-foot-4, he stood eight inches taller than the

Lewis Cass, one of the leading Democrats of the 19th century, strove to find a balance between free and slaveholding states. He died in Detroit in 1866, having seen his beloved Union torn apart—and then restored– by war.

average American of the day. As one of the lesser known speakers featured on the bill, he delivered some rather moderate remarks, disappointing a large, fire-breathing crowd of abolitionists that had arrived from all over the state via special trains.

Among those present was Zachariah Chandler, a wealthy Detroit businessman contemporaneously described as "profane, hard drinking & eternally grim." A transplanted New Englander, Chandler had made his fortune in the mercantile business while also maintaining an active interest in public affairs. He impressed many citizens during Detroit's great cholera epidemic of 1834, helping to care for the sick and burying the dead. As a member of the Whig Party, Chandler "worked the polls on election days, and when opposing Democrats became hostile, was not slow to take off his coat and exchange blows when needed," recorded one admirer. In 1851, in his first political campaign, he defeated seven-term incumbent John R. Williams to become Detroit's mayor. The following year he lost the gubernatorial contest. The defeat caused him to become one of the chief organizers of the Republican Party, which he would serve in a rousing and distinctive manner during his four terms in the U. S. Senate.

Chandler was a colorful counterpoint to Michigan's other major politician of the 19th century, the venerable Lewis Cass. A dull, long-winded intellectual (he was the recipient of several honorary degrees, including one from Harvard), Cass had proved himself very capable during his half-century of public service. He had toiled for 18 years as Michigan's territorial governor before being appointed secretary of war by President Andrew Jackson in 1831. As he had in Michigan, Cass deftly handled the government's Indian affairs. After a six-year stint as

U. S. Senator Zachariah Chandler was no friend of compromise. This most radical of Republicans wanted Washington to abolish slavery, thus removing the decision-making from individual states.

minister to France, Cass represented Michigan in the Senate from 1845 to 1848. That year he won the Democratic nomination for president—the only major candidate from Michigan to run for the country's highest office until Gerald R. Ford in 1976. Cass lost the election to Zachary Taylor, however, when Democrats unhappy with his temperate approach to slavery broke away and formed the Free Soil Party. Cass personally thought slavery was wrong, but in his subsequent return to the Senate he was willing to negotiate compromises with legislators from pro-slavery states in order to keep the Union intact.

In 1857 Cass left the U. S. Senate to become President Buchanan's secretary of state. Chandler replaced him. As was the practice then in Michigan, Chandler was not elected, but rather appointed by the state legislature, which was now dominated by Republicans. In Washington the new senator quickly became known as a "radical among radicals," loudly and consistently advocating the freedom and social advancement of the black race. Blunt and physically imposing, displaying a booming voice and an inflexible morality, Chandler gave a taste of what he and the new breed of Northern politicians were all about in his maiden speech. "The race of Union-whiners, the old women of the North, who have been in the habit of crying out 'the Union is in danger,' have passed off the stage....They were ready to compromise any principle; anything to save the Union. Sir, the men of the present day will compromise nothing....they will sacrifice anything but principle to save the Union."

During the 1858 race for the U. S. Senate, Republicans backed Lincoln in his bid to unseat Stephen Douglas. The incumbent agreed to a series of seven public debates that clarified each candidate's stand on the issue of slavery. In front of crowds as large as 15,000 people, Douglas—a gifted orator who had married the daughter of a slave owner—declared that "this

No published work did more to inflame both anti- and pro-slavery passions than Harriet Beecher Stowe's 1852 novel, Uncle Tom's Cabin. It's been suggested that Stowe, a New Englander, based the character George Harris on the true story of Adam Crosswhite, a fugitive slave from Kentucky who had resettled his family in Marshall. In 1847, the Crosswhites were able to avoid being captured by slave catchers and escape to Canada when a mob of angry sympathizers intervened. In a subsequent lawsuit the court ruled against the Crosswhites' Michigan benefactors, assessing fines equal to the value of the slave family if they had been sold at auction.

government can exist…divided into free and slave states." Lincoln did not believe in black equality any more than his opponent. However, he passionately believed in freedom for all people, regardless of skin color. Lincoln called slavery a social and moral wrong.

Douglas won the election, but Lincoln was transformed into a national figure through the widespread press coverage of his spirited and rational attacks on slavery. He also caused a major split in Democratic ranks by cleverly maneuvering Douglass into making a statement that slavery could be excluded from a new territory before it drafted a constitution. Despite Lincoln's heightened stature, unequivocal anti-slavers like Zachariah Chandler, a key member of the Republican National Committee, would always be lukewarm about the man, correctly sizing him up to be more of a fatalist than a zealot. In fact, Chandler would be almost dismissive of Lincoln after his assassination, telling his wife, "I believe that the Almighty continued Mr. Lincoln in office as long as he was useful."

Abolitionist John Brown's failed raid on Harper's Ferry, Virginia in October 1859 panicked both planters and non-slaveholders in the South, who feared the consequences of an armed slave rebellion.

As a result of the Kansas-Nebraska Act, agitators on both sides of the slavery issue stepped up their rhetoric and terror tactics in order to influence the decision-making in the new territories. The most fanatic of them all was a wild-eyed, bearded, Bible-thumping abolitionist named John Brown, who in 1856 led a guerrilla raid into Kansas that resulted in the murders of five pro-slavery men. On the evening of March 12, 1859, Brown and another of the leading historical figures of the time, Frederick Douglass, met at the Detroit home of William Webb, a black active in the underground railroad. Brown had arrived earlier in the day with 14 fugitive slaves from Missouri. By either design or coincidence, the noted black orator Douglass also was in town to deliver a lecture. Afterwards, Douglass and several local black abolitionists rendezvoused with Brown, who outlined his plan to lead a series of armed slave revolts throughout the South.

Exactly what kind of support Brown received in Michigan is unclear, but he then crossed into Canada, recruiting supporters for his famous, failed occupation of the U. S. arsenal at Harper's Ferry, Virginia, that fall. Ten of Brown's supporters were killed, while Brown and several others were tried for murder, treason and inciting slave insurrection. After a sensational trial, Brown was hanged on December 2, 1859. His eloquent and dignified defense, coupled with the popularity of his cause, made him a martyr and folk hero in the North. To Southerners, whose greatest single nightmare was a slave rebellion on the scale of the bloodbath that had occurred a generation earlier in Haiti, Brown's divine call to action put a chill in their bones and further heightened sectional animosity. Although Brown was probably insane and had acted on his own, many in the South were willing to believe rumors that radical Republicans were behind the botched plot.

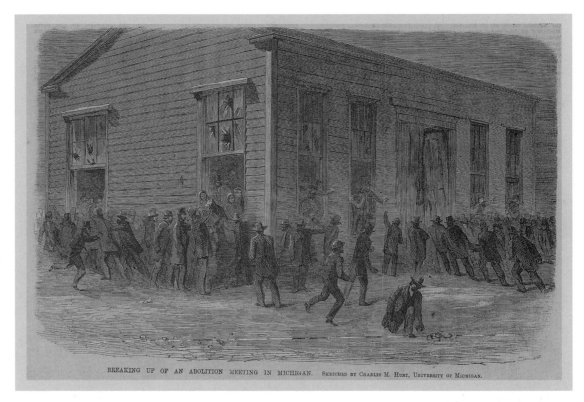

BREAKING UP OF AN ABOLITION MEETING IN MICHIGAN.   SKETCHED BY CHARLES M. HUNT, UNIVERSITY OF MICHIGAN.

On January 16, 1860, a meeting featuring Parker Pillsbury of the American Anti-Slavery Society was broken up by a mob of Ann Arbor citizens—including many students from the University of Michigan—who denounced Pillsbury's calls for immediate abolition as "radical anti-Unionism."

Shortly thereafter, when it came time for Democrats to select the party's presidential candidate in the 1860 election, Southern delegates refused to endorse the Northern wing's nomination of Stephen Douglas, who was now perceived to be "soft" on slavery. Instead they backed their own man, former vice president John C. Breckinridge of Kentucky. A hard-liner, Breckinridge ran on a pro-slavery platform. At the Republicans' equally riotous national convention in Chicago, Lincoln was nominated on the third ballot as a compromise choice. The Republican platform denounced popular sovereignty, denying territories the right to institute slavery, but stopped short of calling for abolition in states where it already existed. Lincoln's moderation didn't impress the legislatures of several Southern states, which were already debating the appropriate course of action should a Republican gain the White House. The Republicans, for their part, regarded any talk of a state leaving the Union as "contemplated treason."

The presidential election was held on November 6, with many continuing to warn of secession if Lincoln won. In Michigan, Lincoln received 88,445 votes to Douglas's 64,958 and Breckinridge's 805. Nationally the final poll results showed Lincoln receiving 1,866,000 votes, a half-million more than Douglas and a million more than Breckinridge. (A fourth party, the Constitutional Unionists, had nominated Tennessee's John Bell for president. Bell placed a distant fourth, though he took three border states that appreciated his noncommittal stance on the

Henry Bibb: "I Am Not Property Now"

An untold number of escaped slaves made new lives for themselves in Michigan in the decades leading up to the Civil War. Henry Bibb was one, fleeing a Kentucky plantation to become a renowned activist. In 1840 he and other abolitionists founded the Liberty Party in Michigan; soon Bibb was giving lectures on slavery throughout the state. While in Detroit he sent copies of an anti-slavery pamphlet to prominent slave owners in the South and one wound up in the hands of his former master, William Gatewood. The surprised Gatewood wrote Bibb, inquiring of his situation, and on March 23, 1844, Bibb responded in a letter.

Dear Sir:

I am happy to inform you that you are not mistaken in the man whom you sold as property and received pay for as such. But I thank God that I am not property now, but am regarded as a man like yourself, and although I live far north, I am enjoying a comfortable living by my own industry. If you should ever chance to be traveling this way and call on me, I will use you better than you did me while you held me as a slave. Think not that I have any malice against you for the cruel treatment which you inflicted on me while I was in your power. As it was the custom of your country to treat your fellow men as you did me and my family, I can freely forgive you.

I wish to be remembered in love to my aged mother and friends; please tell her that if we should never meet again in this life, my prayer shall be to God that we may meet in heaven, where parting shall be no more.

You may perhaps think hard of us for running away from slavery, but as to myself, I have but one apology to make for it, which is: I have only to regret that I did not start at an earlier period. I might have been free long before I was. But you had it in your power to have kept me there much longer than you did. I think it is very probable that I should have been a toiling slave on your property today, if you had treated me differently.

To be compelled to stand by and see you whip and slash my wife without mercy, when I could afford her no protection, not even by offering myself to suffer the lash in her place, was more than I felt it to be the duty of a slave husband to endure, while the way was open to Canada. My infant child was also frequently flogged by Mrs. Gatewood for crying, until its skin was bruised literally purple. This kind of treatment was what drove me from home and family, to seek a better home for them. But I am willing to forget the past. I should be pleased to hear from you again, on the reception of this, and should also be very happy to correspond with you often, if it should be agreeable to yourself. I subscribe myself a friend to the oppressed, and Liberty forever.

Bibb never was reunited with his family. In the course of a risky attempt to rescue them, he discovered his wife had supposed him dead and was now living with her new master. Bibb moved east, remarried, and in 1849 had his autobiography published by the Anti-Slavery Society. The following year Congress passed the Fugitive Slave Law, forcing Bibb to flee to Canada. There he helped organize the Refugees' Home, a colony for escaped

The Union eagle has to contend with several "fractured" eggs—secessionist states—in this lithograph published shortly before the outbreak of war.

issues.) Although Lincoln won only 40 percent of the popular vote and his name hadn't even appeared on the ballot in 10 Southern states, he easily gathered enough electoral votes to succeed Buchanan in the White House. However, the delicate political balance between North and South was now gone. The South's way of life, pro-slavery extremists declared, would soon follow.

On December 20, 1860, South Carolina—claiming it had no other recourse—announced it was seceding from the United States. "Can it be, can it be!" exclaimed Lewis Cass when a friend delivered the news. "Oh, I had hoped to retire from the public service, and go home to die with the happy thought that I should leave my children, as an inheritance from a patriotic man, a united and prosperous republic. But it is all over! This is but the beginning of the end. The people in the South are mad; the people in the North are asleep. The President is pale with fear, for his official household is full of traitors, and conspirators control the government. God only knows whatis the fate of my poor country! To Him alone must we look in the hour of darkness."

Cass, disgusted by President Buchanan's inaction, resigned as secretary of state in protest. The 78-year-old legislator, who as a child growing up in New Hampshire had watched the sky light up in fireworks in celebration of George Washington's inauguration, returned to Detroit, convinced he was witnessing the dissolution of his beloved country.

The shelling of Fort Sumter in Charleston Harbor created Michigan's first hero of the Civil War. Norman J. Hall of Monroe (opposite) was the fort's adjutant. When the pole bearing the flag fell during the bombardment, the 25-year-old West Point graduate rushed to save the national colors, burning his hands and face in the process. With the assistance of a sergeant and a civilian laborer, Hall fashioned a new staff and soon had the flag waving defiantly from the parapet. Soon after this the fort was surrendered and the entire garrison was returned by ship to New York. Colonel Hall went on to command the 7th Michigan Infantry and distinguished himself at Antietam, Fredericksburg and Gettysburg, where he helped repulse Pickett's charge. He died in 1867, having compiled one of the most outstanding records of any Michigan soldier during the war.

Three weeks later, Mississippi announced it was seceding. In short order five other states—Florida, Alabama, Georgia, Louisiana and Texas—also left the Union. Delegates from the seven states met in Montgomery, Alabama in February 1861 to create a new country they named the Confederate States of America. They drafted a constitution that called for a weak central government and forbade any law denying the right of a man to own slaves. On February 18, 1861, Jefferson Davis, a U. S. senator from Mississippi and a former secretary of war, was inaugurated president of the Confederacy.

Although there was nothing in the U. S. Constitution specifically preventing states from seceding, radical Republicans were adamant that the outlaw nation be dissolved—by force, not negotiation. To those who believed in the sanctity of

"Well, boys, your troubles are over now, but mine have just begun."

President-elect Abraham Lincoln to a group of friends before leaving Illinois for Washington

the Constitution and the Union, there simply was no compromising with traitors. When Austin Blair was sworn in as Michigan's new governor in January 1861, he declared "secession is revolution and revolution is the overt act of treason and must be treated as such." Zachariah Chandler was almost cavalier about the prospect of war. "Some of the manufacturing states think a fight would be awful," he wrote Blair from Washington. "Without a little bloodletting this Union will not, in my estimation, be worth a rush."

When Lincoln took the oath of office on March 4, 1861, his sole objective was preserving the Union. The cornerstone of the emerging Confederacy may have been slavery, and the industrial North and the agrarian South had long squabbled over such issues as tariffs and immigration, but at the core of the acrimony was the question of the expanding power of the federal government. As the states collectively pursued a common destiny—their "manifest destiny," one that most Americans thought was guided by Providence—how much of each state's autonomy should be surrendered to Washington in the process? The current debate revolved around slavery, of course, but there were larger implications contained in the answer to that question. A strong central government had been anathema to the framers of the Constitution. Lincoln himself was determined to work within the perimeters of that document, having called slavery "an evil not to be extended but to be tolerated and protected" until a reasoned and level-headed solution could be found. While extremists on both sides made the regional split appear insoluble, many Americans in the spring of 1861 still held out hope that "a little bloodletting" could be avoided, that the rebellious states might somehow be brought back into the fold.

In the early morning hours of April 12, 1861, secession officially became an armed insurrection. Shore batteries manned by South Carolina militia opened fire on Fort Sumter, a federal fortification in Charleston Harbor that Lewis Cass had futilely urged President Buchanan to reinforce months earlier. Following 34 hours of relentless bombardment, a Confederate flag flew over the ruins of the surrendered fort, emboldening four more states—Virginia, Arkansas, Tennessee and North Carolina—to throw in their lot with the pugnacious Confederacy.

The faint hopes of a peaceful resolution ended with the shelling of Fort Sumter. Now there was war—and it would be hell. ●

Chapter 2

THANK GOD FOR MICHIGAN

In the aftermath of Fort Sumter's fall, Detroiters gathered in front of the U. S. Post Office to pledge an oath of loyalty to the Union.

The Confederates' shelling of Fort Sumter electrified the North. Newspaper posters on Michigan street corners told the ongoing story in screaming headlines: "Latest from Charleston—Sumter on Fire!!—Rebels Firing on the Burning Fort!!" The fort had not yet fallen when the citizens of Lansing, then a community of fewer than 3,000 people, organized a mass meeting at the state capitol building to discuss their appropriate response to the unfolding events.

Among those present that evening of April 13, 1861 was Charles T. Foster, a 23-year-old clerk in the dry goods store of A. Turner & Co. According to his younger brother, Seymour, Charles was "a young man about 5 feet, 10 inches in height, light complexion, big blue eyes, high forehead, and a very becoming moustache. He was a fine singer, a member of the Presbyterian church and choir, and with genial disposition and agreeable manner, he was a general favorite with all who knew him." Charles Foster also was a patriot, and for that reason he was anxious for the opportunity to demonstrate his sentiment for the Union.

"At this mass meeting practically the whole town turned out, excitement and patriotic fever ran high," recalled Seymour Foster. "So dense was the crowd that hundreds could not get within hearing distance of the speakers and we younger boys climbed up from the outside and sat in the windows."

Vigorous, fiery, patriotic speeches were made…and at the conclusion of each the excitement ran higher and the cheers were louder and longer, but it was when Judge

Most of the men in the state's regiment of three-month volunteers, the 1st Michigan Infantry, were drawn from existing militia units, such as this unidentified member of the Detroit Light Guard.

Tenney finally came forward with a series of eloquent patriotic resolutions, and askedtheir adoption, the closing sentence of which was—"The Union, one and indivisible must and shall be preserved"—it was then, that the cheering, so loud, and so long, went up, that as I sat perched in my window seat, I thought that surely the rebels of South Carolina must have heard it.

After a short lull in the proceedings, evidently from pure exhaustion, Judge Tenney announced that a roll had been prepared, and that an opportunity would be given anyone who desired to tender his services in defense of the Union to come forward and sign the roll.

Upon that announcement, a profound silence pervaded that great gathering, not a soul moved; in fact, I doubt if they even breathed, and I verily believe you could have heard a pin if dropped on the floor, so deathly still was it—until, after a few moments there was a slight shuffling of feet, and movement of those on the other side of the hall, and I could see that some one was trying to work his way through the crowd and toward the front, but from my perch in the window, I could not distinguish who it was. By this time he had reached Judge Tenney's desk, and was signing that roll. In the meantime that deathly silence still prevailed—until Judge Tenney announced—"Charles T. Foster, tenders his services, and his life if need be to his country and his flag."

Then a great cheer broke forth, and before this had died away, Allen S. Shattuck and John T. Strong had come forward and signed, and in quick succession followed John Broad, E. F. Siverd, Jerry TenEyck, Homer Thayer, James B. TenEyck, and a score of others (to the total of 31 as I now remember it) had signed the roll pledging their all in defense of their country.

Wearing forage caps of the Mexican War era, the Hardee Cadets leave Adrian for Detroit, where they will be mustered into federal service as Company K of the 1st Michigan Infantry Regiment.

Because the United States had always maintained a small standing army, Lincoln was forced to issue a call for 75,000 Northern men to volunteer three months' service. Michigan was asked to provide one fully equipped regiment of infantry. This quota was easily met by mustering into Federal service 10 of the 28 militia units around the state, such as the Detroit Light Guard and Adrian Hardee Cadets. Although peacetime had made these units more fraternal than military in nature, members had a distinct advantage over the thousands of volunteers like Charles Foster who desperately wanted their chance to "Crush the Infamous Rebellion," as the recruiting broadsides urged. The militiamen were already organized, had several West Point graduates and Mexican War veterans in their ranks, and even the youngest members had at least a rudimentary understanding of military drill and discipline. With the state legislature unable to meet for an emergency session until May 7, public-spirited citizens donated a total of $81,020 to fund the regiment.

May 11, 1861: The 1st Michigan Infantry is presented with its regimental colors during a ceremonious send-off at Detroit's public square, Campus Martius.

"I pass my time very pleasantly under the circumstances. In the morning I read Baltimore and Washington papers, and in the afternoon I amuse myself killing secession flies."

Lieutenant George C. Mogk, 1st Michigan Infantry, in a letter to his sister, October 13, 1861

The 2nd Michigan Infantry Regiment in formation at Fort Wayne in Detroit in June 1861. The war forced volunteers, civilians and reporters to learn a few basics of military organization. Each company of 100 men was commanded by a captain and was identified sequentially by a letter (Company A, Company B, and so on). Each regiment was comprised of 10 companies (called "batteries" in artillery units), carried a state name (such as the 5th Michigan Infantry or 3rd Michigan Cavalry), and was commanded by a colonel. Between three and six regiments (taken from two or more states) made up a brigade, which by definition was commanded by a brigadier general but was often led by a colonel. There were three or four brigades to a division, with several divisions making up an army corps. It was at the brigade level that an individual state's identification (with rare exceptions such as the Michigan Cavalry Brigade) usually was lost. During the course of the war, many regiments were reduced by disease, desertion and battle casualties to little more than company size.

There were no yellow ribbons tied around trees in 1861, but there was plenty of red, white and blue to go around. In those days it had yet to become customary for flags to be flown from every government and commercial building. But in Detroit, as a sign of loyalty to the Union, Ol' Glory was hoisted at the Board of Trade Building, followed in short order by flag raisings at the Custom House, the post office and Firemen's Hall. "Flag-raising now became general," wrote the city's capable 19th-century historian, Silas Farmer, "and churches, schools, stores, and residences displayed the Stars and Stripes."

"The Star Spangled Banner rages most furiously," noted the *Detroit Free Press*. "The national anthem…is whistled by juveniles…hammered on tin pans by small boys, and we had almost said barked by the dogs." One day 3,000 schoolchildren gathered in the heart of Detroit, Campus Martius, to sing the anthem.

The First Battle of Bull Run (opposite) turned into a Union rout, but no blame could be placed at the feet of Colonel Orlando B. Willcox, who was wounded and spent the next year as a prisoner. After his release and a triumphant return to Detroit in August 1862, Willcox was promoted to brigadier general and spent the rest of the war commanding on the division and corps levels at such battles as Antietam, Spotsylvania and Cold Harbor. As a field commander he was wounded four times and had four horses shot out from under him. He returned to his law practice after the war but, citing boredom, went into the regular army. He retired in 1887 and eight years later received the Medal of Honor for his actions at Bull Run. He died at age 84 in 1907 and was buried in Arlington National Cemetery.

By late April all 10 companies of Michigan's three-month regiment had assembled at their rendezvous point, Detroit's Fort Wayne. They were commanded by Colonel Orlando B. Willcox, a 38-year-old Detroit attorney who had graduated eighth in the West Point class of 1847. Under Willcox's direction the men practiced battle formations, worked on their marksmanship, and were issued new Federal uniforms to replace their gaudy militia attire. On May 11, the 1st Michigan Infantry received its regimental colors in a splendid send-off ceremony on the Campus Martius, then embarked via steamship and railroad connections to the East. The 798 men arrived in Washington on the evening of May 16, causing Lincoln—anxious for reinforcements to secure the area around the nation's capital—to reportedly exclaim "Thank God for Michigan!" The 1st Michigan had the distinction of being the first western regiment to arrive in Washington.

On May 24 the 1st Michigan was one of two regiments sent to secure Alexandria, Virginia, which sat across the Potomac River from Washington. As the Wolverines marched past a plantation, some muffled cries were heard. Investigating, soldiers found several slaves locked inside a pen. Before fleeing, the overseer had hid the large brass key. Sergeant Eugene Robinson searched around, found the key inside a nearby well, and released the frantic prisoners. It reportedly was the first emancipation of a slave pen during the war.

Michigan's "Fight" Song

Music was an integral part of American life during the Civil War, with both sides expressing feelings of melancholic loss and fierce patriotic pride in song. Not long after the battle of Fredericksburg in 1862, a young Detroit woman named Winifred Lee Brent composed the words to what was to become Michigan's unofficial state anthem. "Michigan, My Michigan" borrowed the melody of a popular period song, "Maryland, My Maryland," which itself was sung to the traditional German Christmas carol, "O Tannenbaum." Brent came from a military family—her late father had been a career army officer, her brother was a West Point cadet during the war, her brother-in-law was the colonel of the 2nd Michigan Infantry, and she later married Henry F. Lyster, a surgeon in the regiment. Despite its haunting tune, "Michigan, My Michigan" was as martial as it was nostalgic, with references to Antietam, Shiloh, and other battles where Michigan troops had recently distinguished themselves. After first seeing limited distribution in a leaflet, the song was reprinted in the *Detroit Tribune* and soon found itself being sung by homesick soldiers at the front. In 1902, Douglas Malloch and William Otto Meisner revised "Michigan, My Michigan" with all new lyrics and a slightly different melody. The changes rankled more than a few gray-haired veterans, who fondly recalled singing the original version around camp fires and on the march:

Home of my heart, I sing of thee!
  Michigan, my Michigan,
Thy lake-bound shores I long to see,
  Michigan, my Michigan.
From Saginaw's tall whispering pines
To Lake Superior's farthest mines,
Fair in the light of memory shines,
  Michigan, my Michigan.

Thou gav'st thy sons without a sigh,
  Michigan, my Michigan,
And sent thy bravest forth to die,
  Michigan, my Michigan.
Beneath a hostile southern sky
They bore thy banner proud and high,
Ready to fight but never fly,
  Michigan, my Michigan.

From Yorktown on to Richmond's wall,
  Michigan, my Michigan,
They bravely fight, as bravely fall,
  Michigan, my Michigan.
To Williamsburgh we point with pride –
Our Fifth and Second, side by side,
There stemmed and stayed the battle's tide,
  Michigan, my Michigan.

When worn with watching traitor foes,
  Michigan, my Michigan,
The welcome night brought sweet repose,
  Michigan, my Michigan.
The soldier, weary from the fight,
Sleeps sound, nor fears the rebels' might,
For "Michigan's on guard tonight!"
  Michigan, my Michigan.

Afar on Shiloh's fatal plain,
    Michigan, my Michigan,
Again behold thy heroes slain,
    Michigan, my Michigan.
"Their strong arms crumble in the dust,
And their bright swords have gathered rust;
Their memory is our sacred trust,"
    Michigan, my Michigan.

And often in the coming years,
    Michigan, my Michigan,
Some widowed mother'll dry her tears,
    Michigan, my Michigan,
And turning with a thrill of pride,
Say to the children at her side,
At Antietam your father died,
    For Michigan, our Michigan.

With General Grant's victorious name,
    Michigan, my Michigan,
Thy sons still onward march to fame,
    Michigan, my Michigan.
And foremost in the fight we see,
Where e'er the bravest dare to be,
The sabers of thy cavalry,
    Michigan, my Michigan.

Dark rolled the Rappahannock's flood,
    Michigan, my Michigan,
The tide was crimsomed with thy blood,
    Michigan, my Michigan.
Although for us the clay was lost,
Still it shall be our broadest boast:
At Fredericksburg our Seventh crossed!
    Michigan, my Michigan.

Winifred Lee Brent.

And when the happy time shall come,
    Michigan, my Michigan,
That brings thy war-worn heroes home,
    Michigan, my Michigan,
What welcome from their own proud shore,
What honors at their feet we'll pour,
What tears for those who'll come no more,
    Michigan, my Michigan.

A grateful country claims them now,
    Michigan, my Michigan,
And deathless laurel binds each brow,
    Michigan, my Michigan;
And history the tale will tell,
Of how they fought and how they fell,
For that dear land they loved so well,
    Michigan, my Michigan.

Public officials address the returning members of the three-month regiment that had been rushed to Washington in the opening weeks of the war. While most of the men in the original 1st Michigan Infantry chose to return to civilian life after their commitment expired, others enlisted for an additional three years of service in one of the newly organized regiments.

Later that summer the regiment was part of the Union force headed toward the Confederate capital of Richmond, Virginia. Richmond lay just 100 miles from Washington, and over the next four years that strip of land would become the bloodiest stretch of earth in American history. By June 25 the 1st Michigan had been joined by three more infantry regiments from the state, the 2nd, 3rd and 4th Michigan, which had been quickly raised after Lincoln's request for 42,000 more Union volunteers. These and all subsequent regiments (including a reconstituted 1st Michigan after the original unit returned to Detroit) were mustered in for three years. They joined General Irvin McDowell's army outside Washington.

Lincoln initially had asked for 90-day enlistments because he figured—or more precisely hoped—he could quell the rebellion with one quick, major battle. It turned out he was overly optimistic and that the war would become a long and drawn-out affair. While the Confederacy had a population of only 5 million free whites, compared to 22 million northerners, and also lacked the North's industrial capacity, it fielded resourceful armies commanded by a more competent officer corps. Moreover, the southerners would surprise the Yankees with their robust fighting spirit, consistent with a people defending their home land. For their part, southerners also thought the war would end with one showdown that would reveal the Yankees for the cowardly bullies they were.

James H. Wheaton fought as a private with the three-month 1st Michigan Infantry Regiment at the First Battle of Bull Run. The 25-year-old volunteer from Manchester re-entered service as a sergeant in the 1st Michigan three-year regiment and was wounded at Second Bull Run. Promoted to captain of Company F, Wheaton was killed in action near Poplar Grove Church, Virginia on September 30, 1864.

After taking several weeks to organize and train, the Yankee and Confederate armies had their first major encounter on the morning of July 21, 1861 near Manassas, Virginia, 25 miles south of Washington. Hundreds of civilians packed picnic baskets and lightheartedly went off in buggies to watch. The Union army attacked the rebel force positioned along the south bank of a meandering stream called Bull Run. Both armies were green, so confusion and panic reigned on this hot, sticky Sunday. At first the Confederates were beaten back, but by early afternoon they stiffened, led by the example of General Thomas J. Jackson, who stood "like a stone wall" while rallying his troops. While "Stonewall" Jackson picked up a nickname, Colonel Willcox of the 1st Michigan earned the Medal of Honor, having his horse shot out from under him as he led his men into a withering fire trying to recapture some seized Union artillery. Willcox was wounded and captured and, as was the practice then, later returned to his unit in a prisoner exchange.

By the close of the day the rebels had counter-attacked and literally chased the Yankees off the field. Soldiers threw away their rifles, canteens and packs as they joined the mob of politicians, reporters and picnickers already fleeing the countryside for the safety of Washington. "Turn back! Turn back!" they yelled. "We are whipped!"

It would have been almost comical, except for the casualties. Roughly 3,000 Yankees and 2,000 Confederates were dead, wounded or missing. Neither side was equipped to handle the flow of casualties. "It was a terrible sight," one Michigan foot soldier recorded the following day in his diary, "to see the wagons coming in last night with dead, cut, torn and mangled in every possible manner and the wounded running or hobbling along with arms & legs dangling or hanging by shreds or crawling on the ground dragging their limbs slowly after them crushed, broken, or torn off entirely."

The regimental flag of the 2nd
Michigan Infantry bore the motto,
"At the Union's sacred call, her
Patriot Sons Will Peril All." Two
of those patriot sons were Captain
August Goebel, (above) who
returned from the war to become
a noted Detroit brewer, and
Timothy Fish (right) of Battle
Creek, who was wounded five
times and rose from corporal to
captain during his four years
of meritorious service.

9/11 had a different meaning for George B. Race, who answered his country's call on September 11, 1861 by enlisting in the 2nd Michigan Cavalry. The 19-year-old private from Greenville went on to serve three years and was discharged at Nashville, Tennessee on October 22, 1864.

William B. McCreery of Flint enlisted in May 1861 as a sergeant in the 2nd Michigan Infantry and was soon commissioned a captain. He was wounded three times at the Battle of Williamsburg, Virginia in 1862 but survived to become the colonel of the 21st Michigan Infantry. At Chickamauga he was wounded three more times and taken prisoner. He was able to escape from Libby Prison but his many wounds forced him to retire in September 1864.

It was early, but some disillusion was already seeping into the ranks. Robert Brethschneider had served for a dozen years in the Prussian army—seven as an officer—before settling in Niles. Now the 32-year-old German immigrant was the captain of Company E, 2nd Michigan Infantry. "It is sad to see thousands slaughtered through the ignorance of their leaders," he wrote his wife not long after Bull Run, "but the Americans have to learn and pay for it. All our fancy officers here are sick or not worth the powder it would take to shoot them."

This early in the war the North, while disheartened, was still far from discouraged. Eager Michigan men quickly filled up regiments, then marched determinedly to the front. Throughout the war, nothing could stop those who really wanted to go. One sawed-off private in the 1st Michigan Mechanics & Engineers, William Simms, met the minimum height requirement by standing on an anthill. Philip Vahue, a 54-year-old farmer from Allegan, was rejected by a cavalry regiment because his teeth were so rotten he couldn't bite off the end of a cartridge. Undeterred, he successfully enlisted in a battery of the 1st Michigan Light Artillery, where bad "choppers" were no detriment.

In the summer of 1861, just a few weeks after the news of Bull Run had reached his neck of the woods, Ira Gillaspie of Sturgis recorded how he went about enlisting in a company being raised by a local merchant, Calvin C. Hood.

August 20, 1861—I come to the conclusion that I would volunteer my cirveses to my country....I talked with my wife on the subject and she did not want me to enlist but she feared I would be drafted for thare was a goodeel of talk about drafting. She said I

Harmon Wise, an 18-year-old from Ypsilanti, fought at Bull Run with the three-month 1st Michigan Infantry. After that unit mustered out on August 7, 1861, he enlisted in the first U. S. Sharpshooters. He was killed at Chancellorsville, Virginia, on May 3, 1863. On the reverse of this portrait, housed in the State Archives, is the inscription, "Dearest Harmon… may we meet in Heaven to part no more…Mother."

might do just as I saw fit. I explained to her the state of our country that it is in need of all true patriots to sustain her government but all did not convince her that I aught to enlist. I went to my employer told him my intentions. He said you are write Ira for your country needs you. Saturday evening I went out to my fathers on a viset. He lived in the town of Sherman about seven miles from Sturgis. My father and mother was very much aposed to my enlisting. They admitted that our country needed men but their plea was that there was anuff without me but I had fully made up my mind to enlist so thare was no stoping me.

August the 22—My wife said all she could to me to convince me that it is not my duty to go to war. Next day when Capt. C. Hood's Company was marching about town in the afternoon they was collected in front of the recruiting office. I went over opened the dore went up to the desk and told Henry Plat that I had been to see Mr. Falkner. He had told me the termes of enlisting as followes said he if you enlist you will draw 26 dolars every two months and you wife will draw 12 dolars every 2 months and said he at the end of the war you will be entitled to 160 acres of unoccupied land and one hundred dollars. Now Henry is this fact or not. Said he it is. I told him to hand me his pen. He done so. I put my name to the muster role. I was a soldier. I then went back to my work until the company was formed in line to be mustered into the cirveses when I went over to the offices agane and fell in and was mustered in with the rest.

Bombs Away

The home front in Michigan had more than a few old-timers who enjoyed playing armchair general around a cracker barrel or dining room table. At least one citizen, C. G. Birbeck of Jonesville, was so bold as to make suggestions directly to the Secretary of War. Why not, Birbeck asked, blast artillery shells filled with cayenne pepper at the Rebs? These would descend on the infidels like a "destroying angel," he claimed. Secretary Edwin Stanton said no, thanks. However, Birbeck's other idea for an alternative weapon was, in retrospect, not nearly as far-fetched. He suggested explosives be dropped on enemy positions from high-altitude balloons—a tactic that, while also rejected, eerily foreshadowed the massive aerial bombardments of the next century.

When I got home I found that the news had got thare before me. My wife was acrying. I told her to console herself that the war would soon be over and our country at peace but she thought I had aughtnot to have enlisted. I told her that the drafted men was not used as well as volunteers and in battle they was shuved write ahead and used for brestworks for volunteers.

Private Gillaspie proudly served out the war as a member of Company C of the 11th Michigan Infantry, one of the 45 regiments the state would end up providing the Union. These included 31 infantry regiments, 11 cavalry regiments, and one each of artillery, engineers and mechanics, and colored infantry. An undetermined number of Wolverines enlisted in about 50 different units raised in Missouri, Ohio and other states. Several hundred more volunteers served in the U. S. Navy and the much smaller regular army.

"Stirring times were those when the army of the North was gathering for the fray," recalled one Detroiter. "Soldiers paraded the streets of Detroit in new uniforms, gaining the admiration of their wives, mothers and sweethearts. They drilled zealously, and had their mad pranks when off duty. War songs were sung and whistled about the streets at all hours of the day and night….When the boys were recruiting, or when a number of them were home on a furlough, street fights were frequent, for the soldier is loaded with patriotism and very touchy about national honor. If a southern sympathizer made invidious remarks about 'Lincoln's hirelings, or mudsills,' or 'nigger equality,' or delivered himself of any disparaging phrases, he would be instantly attacked by the soldier boy, and usually got the worst of it."

EXCURSION PARTY
FOR THE
SUNNY SOUTH!

1776 !   1862 !

NINE MONTHS' Volunteers Received up to
the 16th instant, for the Second and Eighth Michigan Regiments and for a new company of Sharp Shooters.

Don't let the 30th of December find you still EXPOSED TO THE DRAFT !
☞ Go at once to the General Recruiting Office, No. 8 Noble's Block, BATTLE CREEK, and enlist.   Choice of Regiment and Company given as far as practical.

☞ Unless the quota is filled by the 30th, the Draft will certainly be made.
CAPT. C. BYINGTON and LIEUT. J. G. SMITH,
RECRUITING OFFICERS.
No. 8 Noble's Block, Battle Creek, Mich.

Recruitment posters like this one helped influence many Michigan men to take up arms.

In a string of battles fought in the spring and summer of 1862, the Union army, now under the command of Major General George B. McClellan, made a major move on Richmond from the east, but ultimately was turned back. Michigan troops were heavily involved in the Peninsula campaign, fighting and falling at such places as Yorktown, Williamsburg, Seven Pines and Gaines Mill. For a man who privately considered himself the second coming of Napoleon, McClellan was a remarkably cautious commander. He exasperated Lincoln by constantly overestimating the enemy's strength and always asking for more time to maneuver his troops. Some of his timidity may have had to do with the weaponry, which had improved dramatically since older officers on both sides had fought together in the Mexican War of 1846-48.

Infantry tactics had traditionally centered around opposing troops, lined up shoulder-to-shoulder, firing inaccurate smoothbore muskets at each other from close range. By 1861 the rifled musket had become standard issue for infantrymen. Instead of a bullet basically being pushed out of a musket's barrel, it now picked up speed, distance and accuracy as it was "spun" through

John Boughton of Constantine enlisted in the 2nd Michigan Infantry and rose from sergeant to command of the regiment by war's end.

the spiraled grooves of a rifled barrel. The minie ball—the cone-shaped lead bullet that was the standard infantry projectile of the war—packed a terrible wallop and accounted for the vast majority of battlefield deaths. All-out frontal assaults against entrenched riflemen led to horrible Union losses at Cedar Mountain and Fredericksburg in 1862 before tactics began to change to emphasize flanking movements and defensive positioning. Field artillery also was more accurate and murderous, with scores of massed cannon creating a physically and psychologically devastating effect known as "rolling thunder." Most terrifying to attacking troops were anti-personnel shells like canister, which cannoneers switched to when the enemy closed in on their battery. Its cousin was grapeshot ("they're not the kind of grapes you like to eat," one Michigan soldier wryly observed). Both projectiles unleashed an annihilating spray of iron balls, scrap metal, even nails. They acted like giant shotguns and were capable of chopping down rows of men with a single blast. The heaviest weapon of the war was the 17,000-pound mortar, capable of hurling a 220-pound bomb more than two miles, which Union forces used to pulverize Vicksburg and Petersburg.

Charles Foster, the patriotic clerk from Lansing, feared neither musket, canister nor mortar. Following his dramatic signed pledge of allegiance, Foster and many other men from the Lansing area were ordered into camp in Grand Rapids and designated as Company G of the newly formed 3rd Michigan Infantry. Soon the regiment was in Virginia. Just prior to the beginning of the Battle of Williamsburg on May 5, 1862, the color sergeant gave out and a major called for a replacement. Nobody volunteered—until, finally, Sergeant Foster stepped forward, saluted the major, and informed him that he would carry the regimental flag until a regular color bearer could be found. Then he "took the old 3rd flag and bore it through that terrific fight, in a most gallant manner, and to the satisfaction of all who witnessed his conduct."

Union skirmishers in the Virginia woods during the Peninsula campaign of 1862. At the Battle of Malvern Hill that summer, the 4th Michigan Infantry's killed in action included Sergeant Ambrose Easton of Lima (opposite, top) and Colonel Dwight A. Woodbury of Adrian (bottom). Woodbury was shot through the head while trying to rally his men; his last words were "Good bye, boys."

Foster explained his decision afterwards in a letter to his mother: "When the major called for volunteers and none of the sergeants seeming to want to take the responsible and dangerous position, I felt it was my duty to do so, for some one must do it, and if none would volunteer, a detail would have to be made, and the lot might fall on one who had a wife and children at home, or a dependent father or mother, and could not be spared, whereas, I was single and free, and would not be missed if I should be killed."

On May 29, 1862, at the Battle of Fair Oaks, the major once again called on Foster to take the colors into the fight. Many years later, Seymour Foster addressed an assembly of

veterans, telling them what happened next—and reminding them why the Charles T. Foster Post of the Grand Army of the Republic came to be named after his courageous older brother.

"Evidently believing his duty again called him there," said Seymour, "he assented and once again he bore the flag into a terrible battle, and through charge after charge, and always with the flag well to the front, and until he was stricken by a minie ball through the neck. He went down   but not the flag—for here again we see a manifestation of his keen sense of duty to keep the flag aloft—for as he fell, he drove the flag staff into the ground; still grasping the staff with both hands he called to his comrades, 'Don't let the colors go down.'

"And they did not go down, for, when the color guards sprang forward to take the flag from his hands, they found they could only release the staff from his death grip by pulling each finger loose from the staff—and Charles T. Foster had fulfilled the pledge he had made to the citizens of Lansing a little more than a year before, when he had signed that roll in the old capitol, pledging his services, and his life if need be in defense of the Union and our flag."

In the early stages of the war, each side viewed the other with a mixture of contempt and curiosity, certain that they were fighting heathens. Edward H. C. Taylor, a Wolverine serving in the Peninsula campaign, informed family members that the rebels cut the throats and chopped the ears off of wounded Yankees. The rebels' courage also was suspect. "We have to Corner them before they will fight and then they wont fight if they can find any possible Chance to escape," insisted William

The aftermath of battle, as sketched by a survivor of Shiloh. The repulsive task of collecting and burying thousands of dead men, horses and mules, many blasted apart by artillery projectiles, was the same on every Civil War battlefield. A disheartening number of the dead were never identified, leaving the family of a soldier declared "missing" to agonize for months, even years, over his fate.

N. Barnard of the 13th Michigan Infantry, which fought in the western theater under General Ulysses S. Grant's overall command. Barnard's comment is interesting in that he evidently missed his regiment's participation in the Battle of Shiloh a few days later.

Joseph Ruff of the 12th Michigan Infantry didn't. He was there at that first great bloodletting of the war, a two-day slugfest that produced nearly 24,000 casualties—a figure that astounded the public. Coming a little less than a year after Fort Sumter's fall, in which only one soldier had died (and that in an accidental explosion), the number of men killed in this remote corner of Tennessee exceeded the combined battle deaths of America's three previous wars. The raw recruits of 12th Michigan, for example, suffered 245 casualties. To their eternal credit, they tenaciously held their ground during a critical juncture of the battle while other regiments around them sprinted like rabbits.

The confusing and incredibly bloody Battle of Shiloh (also known as Pittsburg Landing) on April 6-7, 1862 doomed the Confederacy in the western theater. When the first waves of rebels came howling out of the Tennessee woods in the opening hours, one of the few regiments to stand firm was the untested 12th Michigan Infantry. Pictured here are four of the regiment's officers. Clockwise from lower left are Colonel William Graves, Adjutant William Stewart, Major Phineas Graves and Lieutenant Colonel Dwight May.

As Ruff explored the churned, blood-soaked ground afterwards, he came across three Confederates, "two of them wounded so sorely that they were just breathing their last," he recalled in a postwar manuscript.

One was a beardless boy, not more than 14 or 15 years old. He was sitting leaning up against a tree and as I approached him he called out in a clear voice:

"Well, if you are going to kill me—kill me."

I said, "Why do you think I want to kill you?"

He answered, "Our folks say that you kill all the prisoners."

I replied, "Yes, your people have told you many things. They would make us out savages."

"But what are you going to do with me?" he asked.

"Why," said I, "the ambulances are out picking up all the wounded and they will come for you too."

A piece of shell had shattered his hip and he could not rise upon his feet. Just then an ambulance came near and I called their attention to this severely wounded boy. He continued saying like all the people did down there:

"What you'se come down to fight we-uns for? If you want the niggers I wisht you had all of them. I haven't got any."

Ruff and the defiant youngster had no way of knowing that Lincoln was contemplating the timing of a declaration intended to ensure that no member of the Confederacy would ever own slaves.

September 17, 1862 was the most murderous day in U. S. military history, with more than 26,000 men killed, wounded or missing at the Battle of Antietam, Maryland.

On September 22, 1862, Lincoln issued his preliminary Emancipation Proclamation, which would take effect January 1, 1863. Its practical effect was to offer any slaves who could make it to Union lines their freedom. Unwilling to upset loyal slave-holding states like Missouri and Kentucky, Lincoln specified that the document referred only to those slaves held in Confederate territory. Privately, Lincoln thought the legality of his proclamation, issued under the vaguely defined "war powers," was doubtful. It wouldn't be until the passage of the 13th Amendment in 1865 that the ideas expressed in the document gained constitutional legitimacy. Nonetheless, on New Year's Day of 1863 the president issued his final Emancipation Proclamation. It asked liberated slaves to "abstain from all violence" while also declaring they would "be received into the

One of those mortally wounded at Antietam was Major General Israel Bush Richardson, a Pontiac farmer who had organized the 2nd Michigan Infantry and subsequently been promoted to division command. At Antietam, the West Point graduate and veteran of the Seminole and Mexican wars directed an assault on the rebels in a sunken road that history remembers as "Bloody Lane." Demonstrating the tenacity that earned him the nickname "Fighting Dick," Richardson hung onto life until November 3, 1862. His body was returned to Pontiac for burial.

armed service of the United States." Emancipation served its purpose in many ways. It helped win crucial European support for the North, broadened war aims by making the conflict a struggle for human freedom, and provided the depleted Union army with tens of thousands of Negro soldiers, all eager to demonstrate their race's adulation of "Father Abraham."

Freeing the slaves was an extraordinary humanitarian gesture by Lincoln, as well as an astute political move. The president, listening to his advisors, had waited to release his controversial proclamation until after an important Union victory at Antietam forced General Lee to leave Maryland for Virginia. At a combined cost of 4,710 dead, 18,440 wounded and 3,043 missing, the Battle of Antietam remains the single bloodiest day in the long history of the American military. As the North attempted to digest the ungodly casualty rolls, it also wrestled with the consequences of Lincoln's proclamation. Many people howled over the thought of suddenly liberating millions of blacks. Edward H. C. Taylor was one. He wrote his sister Anna: "When we cease to fight for the Union and begin to fight for Negro equality I am ready to lay down arms and will." True to his word, the Michigan soldier didn't re-enlist after his original three-year term expired.

But thousands of other Michigan soldiers, for moral or pragmatic reasons, agreed with emancipation. John B. Kay of Woodhall, a sergeant in the 6th Michigan Cavalry, was one who approved. "It is against the constitution to take life," he wrote thoughtfully, "but life has to be taken to preserve the Union; it is against the constitution to abolish slavery, but slavery has to be abolished to preserve the union." Captain John T. Pierson wrote his daughter from the Deep South, where he was supervising a confiscated plantation. "I have been among Slavery for over 10 months," he observed, "and most of the time among the large Slave[owners] and I am satisfied that if you want to strike the Rebelion in a tender place, hit the Negro on the Shins. There is no Species of Property that they seem to lament over looseing Except the Negro." ●

"The course pursued by the President, although under other circumstances would not only be questionable but even adverse to the principles of the Republican Party, in the present state of affairs I heartedly endorse for the very reason that the course which has been pursued by the South has been such as to forfeit to them all rights of protection whatsoever."

Lieutenant George W. Laurence, 3rd Michigan Cavalry, expressing his opinion of emancipation to his uncle

A classically heroic painting of the Great Emancipator. Prior to freeing the slaves, Lincoln had seriously weighed the practicality of returning them to Africa. "I don't know what to think of the President's Emancipation scheme," one Michigan cavalryman admitted. "That slavery is a curse to the country, I can see all around me. That if it is not crushed in this struggle and annihilated, it will rise again to subjugate us; but in crushing this monster, there is danger. Who can foresee the consequences?"

Captain Henry Albert Potter, a schoolteacher in Ovid before joining the 4th Michigan Cavalry, was one of many soldiers conflicted by Lincoln's Emancipation Proclamation. "I am not willing to fight one moment for Slavery," he wrote his father. "Whenever they [the Confederate states] are ready to come back, then I say stop fighting, for Gods sake, and let reason once more be heard on both sides." Potter survived the war and lived to the ripe age of 93, dying in 1933.

We Are Coming, Father Abraham

Corporal Preston Helman, a farmer from Leoni, was one of more than 200 Michigan blacks to serve in the 54th Massachusetts, a regiment made famous by its charge on the Confederate works at Fort Wagner, South Carolina (opposite). Ironically, Helman moved to South Carolina after the war.

To abolitionist Frederick Douglass, Lincoln's decision to arm free blacks was what many members of his race had been waiting for. "A war undertaken and brazenly carried on for the perpetual enslavement of colored men," he declared, "calls logically and loudly for colored men to help suppress it."

The most renowned Negro regiment of the war, the 54th Massachusetts, recruited widely throughout the North. Thus many Michigan blacks were among those who fought—and died—in the 54th's gallant assault on Fort Wagner, on Morris Island, South Carolina, on July 18, 1863. Advancing in the twilight along a narrow strip of sand, the ocean on one side of them and a swamp on the other, the 54th led an assault column of several other regiments on the Confederate earthworks. Cannon and musketry cut them to pieces. The failed attack, which cost the regiment 272 of its 650 men, was made famous in the 1989 movie *Glory!*, starring Denzel Washington and Morgan Freeman. In the film the black soldiers of the 54th are depicted for the most part as being illiterate former slaves. But in reality the majority of the members were educated professionals who had grown up free in the North.

The tenacity of colored troops at Fort Wagner convinced a skeptical North that Negroes could fight. Their example helped recruiters fill the ranks of the 30 regiments of black troops then being raised, including one in Michigan. Like all black units, the 1st Michigan Colored Infantry was commanded by white officers—in this case, Henry Barns, editor of the *Detroit Tribune Advertiser* and an ardent abolitionist. When it came to discrimination, the new recruits found little difference between army and civilian life. They initially were paid less than their white counterparts (an act of Congress remedied that injustice), and their food, equipment and camp facilities were inferior.

At the regimental headquarters, Camp Ward (today the site of Duffield Elementary School in Detroit), men lived in a half-dozen barracks that were judged to be "unfit for human habitation…there is not a barn or pig-sty in the whole city of Detroit that is not better fitted for human habitation than Ford Ward." Nonetheless, morale stayed high, and by the end of 1863 the regiment embarked on a tour of several Michigan cities. At Jackson, Governor Austin Blair addressed the troops. "This is the first time I ever saw Negro troops," he said, "and I am very proud of your general bearing."

Artis Kinchen, a 37-year-old Battle Creek resident, was one of the 895 men who left the state for the East in late March, 1864. "He was a family man who had basic values that served him well," his great-great granddaughter, Eleanor Austin, said in a 2001 newspaper interview. "Here we have an individual who lived in a time when the rights of blacks were limited. He made a commitment to serve for a cause he truly believed in." Before the regiment left for the front it was officially mustered into Federal service. On February 17, 1864, the 1st Michigan Colored Infantry was re-designated the 102nd U. S. Colored Infantry Regiment. It was the only Michigan unit to lose its state name during the war.

"Abe," a runaway slave from Kentucky, was befriended by the officers of the 23rd Michigan Infantry Regiment, who employed him as a camp aide.

Sylvan S. Hunting served as chaplain of the 27th Michigan Infantry from 1863 to 1865. Writing from Tennessee, Hunting declared, "This country will begin to be regenerated as soon as the Devil of Slavery has been cast out."

The 102nd acquitted itself well, doing everything asked of it. Owing to the prevailing pseudoscientific theory that blacks were better able than whites to handle tropical climates, they principally served in the Carolinas and Florida. Battling heat, humidity, mosquitoes and alligators, the men helped build fortifications, guarded supply lines, and saw their share of combat. The 102nd returned to Detroit in the early fall of 1865 and was disbanded on October 17, 1865.

As many as 200,000 blacks served in segregated regiments like the 102nd, comprising roughly 9 percent of the Union army. They suffered an appalling death rate—one in three died, the overwhelming majority from disease. Of the 1,673 men who served in the 102nd, a dozen were killed or mortally wounded and another 118 died of disease.

For the last couple of decades, the memory of these black soldiers has been kept alive through the efforts of Company B, 102nd U. S. Colored Troops Black History Group, a nonprofit organization of living history buffs from the Detroit area. Many of its members, such as Ross Fowler, had ancestors in the Union army. Some are among the 16 black Civil War veterans buried at Detroit's Elmwood Cemetery.

Fowler's great-grandfather, Alfred White, was with the 102nd during a bloodbath at Honey Hill, South Carolina on November 30, 1864. That afternoon, the regiment rescued several cannon from behind enemy lines. It was one of the few bright spots in an otherwise resounding Union defeat.

"He had enlisted five days before his son was born," Fowler said of White. "This is a man who was making a better life for his family. He left a wife with child and went off to preserve their freedom."

53 THANK GOD FOR MICHIGAN

This portrait of five members of the 24th Michigan Infantry includes Charles McConnell (center) and Robert Gibbons (second from right), two Detroit printers who enlisted as corporals on July 24, 1862 and made it through some of the regiment's toughest fights. McConnell, who was born in Ireland in 1841, was one of nearly 4,000 Irish immigrants to fight in Michigan units.

Private Francis Miller was just one cog in the mighty Union war machine. The patriotic farmer from Brownstown was 18 when he volunteered for the 24th Michigan Infantry Regiment. He was wounded at Gettysburg and again at the Wilderness, then was trampled when a false alarm about approaching Confederate guerillas caused a panic inside the hospital he was recovering at. He died a short while later, one of some 325,000 Union men who paid the ultimate price during the war.

Chapter 3

HARDTACK AND GRAPESHOT

The Michigan men who shouldered arms were a variegated bunch, their ranks including thousands of foreign-born (including the only Filipino to fight in the war) and nearly 150 Indians, some of whom carried Bibles printed in Ojibwa into battle. Migratory patterns could be seen in a unit's composition. In one company of the 8th Michigan Infantry Regiment, for example, New Yorkers actually outnumbered native Wolverines, 47 to 37. Another 26 volunteers in the unit hailed from neighboring states. The muster roll also included a large number of immigrants: seven Canadians, five Englishmen, four Germans, two Irishmen, one Dutchman and one Scotsman, as well as an enigmatic fellow whose nationality was listed as "the ocean."

The democratic makeup of the Union army was reflected not only in the many different nativities of the volunteers, but also in the wide range of ages and professions. Of the 1,030 men who formed the 24th Michigan Infantry, 322 members of the regiment—more than 30 percent— were first-generation Americans. The 24th's ranks included a 22-year-old tinsmith from Switzerland, a 45-year-old physician from Prussia, a 38-year-old ropemaker from Scotland, a 44-year-old clockmaker from Germany, and a 19-year-old silversmith from France. Roughly half of all Michigan soldiers were farmers, a percentage that held true for the Union army overall. The balance of occupations represented a true cross-section of society: mechanics, clerks, teamsters, shoemakers, lawyers, printers, foundry workers, sawyers, carpenters, bookkeepers, waiters, butchers, engineers and furriers, as well as a considerable number of day laborers and unemployed.

Corporal Jonas Richardson of Washtenaw County enlisted in the 4th Michigan Infantry in 1861. He and many other members of his regiment were photographed next to this tree by Mathew Brady for his "Illustrations of Camp Life" series.

Whatever a man's nativity or occupation, it wasn't too long in uniform before he had mastered the common soldier's universal language—complaining. "It nothing but fall in and March again all the time and it will be now till we meet the Rebels," one volunteer in the 24th, weary of the never-ending marching and drilling, wrote from camp. A disillusioned private in the 19th Michigan Infantry instructed the folks back home to "tell Martin that if he feels as though he would like to be a soldier to take a bushel of corn and travel twenty miles some day and see whether he likes it or not. I tell you what we have to carry we have a knapsack in which we put our clothing consisting of two changes of underclothes, a heavy blanket dress coat and some little trinkets that to a soldier are indispensable and then we have our gun weighing about ten pounds and a cattridge box containing 40 rounds of cattridges and a haversack containing three days rations of hard crackers and meat and a canteen filled with water…." Another disconsolate recruit, this one in the 14th Michigan Infantry, attempted to discourage his son from enlisting. He wrote his wife: "Tell him i don't want him to enlist as it is a real dogs life which he will find out after it is to late….i had rather see him go to his grave then to enlist." John Ryder, a young farmer from Livonia, had been a soldier for less than five months when he moaned, "I have got just sick of war….this soldiering is a big thing, but I can't see it."

As anyone who has spent any time in uniform knows, bellyaching is a time-honored, chronic and mildly cathartic condition of soldiering. Michigan volunteers weren't shy about sharing their complaints with newspapers back home, which were eager to publish any news from the front. The quality of foodstuffs, much of which arrived moldy and spoiled after spending months in storage and transport, was a favorite topic. One

"Picket again. Very cold today. Some officers went off near Lookout Mountain for the view. Wonder if there is one for the privates."

Diary entry of Private Edward A. Raymor, 24th Michigan Infantry,
January 4, 1864

Davis M. Richards was 23 years old when he enlisted as a sharpshooter in the 16th Michigan Infantry on December 14, 1861. Richards, a resident of Wayne County, was killed at Bethesda Church, Virginia on June 1, 1864.

correspondent to the *Detroit Free Press,* identified only by the initials S. D. G., told of his regiment receiving "boxes of bacon which became so habituated to moving that it had commenced to crawl of its own inherent powers."

The Civil War was the first in American history to feature the widespread use of preserved food, particularly canned beef, commonly known as "embalmed beef." The principal bread ration was hardtack, a thick oversized cracker with the taste and consistency of a roof shingle. The crackers were delivered to camp in barrels stamped "B. C.," which stood for "Brigade Commissary." Soldiers were convinced it was the date of manufacture—"Before Christ." In order to be edible, hardtack typically was boiled in water or fried in grease, which made things hot for the flour worms crawling around inside. One of these crackers can be viewed today at the historical museum in Manistee. The 140-year-old hardtack remains in perfect shape, with nary a crumb missing—a testament not only to its remarkable durability, but to the common soldier who regularly risked his teeth and digestive system attempting to eat one.

A diet heavy on meat and lacking nutritional variety could lead to scurvy, as well as boredom, recalled Lieutenant Samuel C. Hodgman of the 7th Michigan Infantry. "Our living is generally hard bread, pork and bacon, beans and rice and occasionally beef," he told folks back in Climax, where he had worked in his father's shoe store before the war. "When we want a change we reverse the order." Although foraging was usually forbidden, soldiers regularly combed the countryside for fruits and vegetables as well as for any chickens or turkeys in need of "liberating." Pies, cheese, butter, cakes and other treats could be purchased from the ubiquitous sutler or a roadside stand. Fresh milk and eggs were luxuries, which made a tethered cow or hen a real prize. To help keep one's energy level up, coffee—gallons of it—and tobacco in all its forms (except cigarettes, which hadn't been invented yet) were important staples of everyday life in the army.

Another favorite topic of griping were the officers, the common soldiers' so-called superiors. With their horses, aides, and oversized tents and trunks, they inevitably were the focus of much resentment by the men in the ranks, whose notions of democracy were severely tested every time they saw the quartermaster make room for a captain's valises while they struggled under the

Another photograph in Mathew Brady's series of camp portraits included this group of 4th Michigan Wolverines with a young "contraband," who helped out with chores.

weight of a full pack and rifle. In the surviving diaries and correspondence of ordinary enlisted men, some officers are routinely referred to as "the Presiding Genius," "the worthless drunk," or "that d---d fool." Robert Findley, an ace grumbler serving with the 26th Michigan Infantry, described his officers as being "no more fit to take charge of a lot of men than a hog is fit to superintendent a soap and candle manufactory."

Many officers deserved the abuse and scorn. Some were pompous, egotistical martinets who got their commissions through connections or public office. Even worse for those men marching under their orders, they often proved to be grossly incompetent as well. There was, for instance, Colonel Francis Quinn, a political appointee whose lack of military and

Lieutenant Oscar Davis of the 23rd Michigan Infantry (right) was one of 185 Jewish soldiers from Michigan to serve in the war—a disproportionately high number for what was then one of the state's smallest ethnic groups.

leadership skills while commanding the 12th Michigan Infantry at the Battle of Shiloh bordered on the criminal. Even Governor Austin Blair had to concede that Quinn was "the worst colonel I ever saw" as he accepted the embattled officer's resignation. Quinn returned to Niles, where he had been prominent in business, civic and political circles, and was shunned. After a few years of failing to restore his name, he moved to Chicago. There were several other cases where discredited officers in the field returned to Michigan and fought to redeem their reputations through newspaper rebuttals, self-published pamphlets, and even lawsuits. But often the offending officer was just quietly cashiered, his position of authority assumed, it was always hoped, by someone of superior mettle and competence. As the fighting went on, more and more officers were promoted from the ranks.

Three hundred and fifty-eight Michigan officers died during the war. A good number of them did so under extraordinarily brave circumstances, inspiring their men and gilding the state's war record. The example of one such officer, Colonel Thornton F. Brodhead, will serve for many.

Brodhead was the 40-year-old postmaster of Detroit when war came. He helped organize the 1st Michigan Cavalry and was its commander when it left for the Potomac in September 1861. The following August he distinguished himself at the Second Battle of Bull Run, a debacle that cost 16,000 Union casualties and paved the way for Lee's invasion of the North. While leading his troopers in a near-suicidal charge in defense of the retreating Union forces, Brodhead had his horse shot out from under him and was struck twice in the chest. Meanwhile, the support Brodhead had been promised, in the form of two New York cavalry regiments, never materialized, leaving the

Idling away in winter quarters in Virginia, Heber Woodruff of the 16th Michigan Infantry mused over the soldier's life in a letter to some relatives back in Gibraltar. "Perhaps you wonder how I like a Soldiers life how I stand it….very little comfort and pleasure is there in it but any amount of privations Hunger, thirst, Weariness Exposure to wet cold and bullets—lack of society of the right kind no females to refine no one to nurse you to speak a kind word if you are sick nothing but military law which obliges an inferior to be an absolute slave to a Superior."

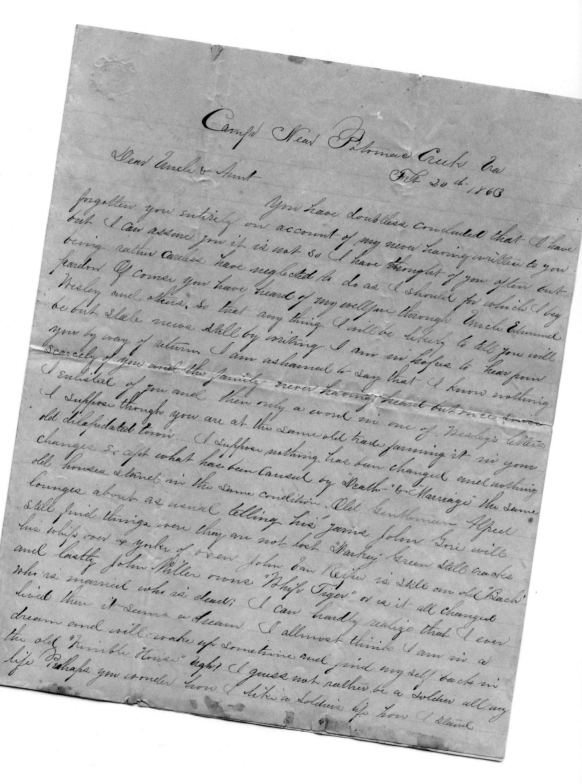

Nineteen-year-old Joseph Benton Sawyer of Kent County served three years with the 2nd Michigan Cavalry, which fought more than 100 battles and skirmishes.

Wolverines to fend for themselves. In the opinion of Captain E. L. Negus, whose company was practically annihilated fighting this rearguard action, Brodhead and his inspired troopers bought valuable time and "saved Pope's bleeding army."

Brodhead was evacuated but the wounds were judged mortal. Published accounts had the colonel dictating several farewell letters, including one to his brother: "I am passing now from earth; but send you love from my dying couch. For all your love and kindness you will be rewarded. I have fought manfully, and now die fearlessly. But the old flag will triumph yet. I had hoped to have lived longer, but now die amid the ring and clangor of battle as I would wish." This message inspired a popular song of the Civil War period, "The Old Flag Will Triumph Yet."

Interestingly, even Brodhead had some unkind words for his field commanders as he lay breathing his last. According to a postwar interview with Negus published in the *Detroit Saturday Night*, "while weltering in his life's blood on that disastrous field [Brodhead] wrote these lines to his wife in Detroit: 'I die a martyr to my country through [General John] Pope's imbecility and [General Irvin] McDowell's treason, but the old flag will triumph yet.' This letter was published in the Detroit papers at the time and created a great deal of excitement at the war department at Washington. Every means was taken to suppress it."

Felix Baldberry was born in 1842 in the Philippine Islands and as a young man spent two years sailing the Atlantic and Pacific Oceans as a crew member of an American merchant ship. When the ship's captain retired to a farm in Leonidas, Michigan, he took Balderry with him. On December 7, 1863, the Filipino farm hand joined the 11th Michigan Infantry and subsequently saw action in Georgia and Tennessee. After the war Balderry married and worked as a tailor in Colon. He died in 1895, having literally seen the world.

To be sure, enlisted men often acted in ways that earned their officers' contempt. Stephen W. Haydon, a lawyer-turned-lieutenant with the 2nd Michigan Infantry, was sickened by the looting and vandalism his men routinely exhibited. In his diary, Haydon—who would not survive the war—wrote of their mindless desecration of a historic church in Virginia.

Pohick Church is a brick building built in 1773. Gen. Washington contributed to building it & was a frequent attendant. It has a very ancient look & one would suppose that it might be sacred enough to be secure. I have long known that the Mich. 2nd had no fear or reverence as a general thing for God or the places where he is worshipped but I hoped that the memory of Gen. Washington might protect almost anything with which it was associated. I believe our soldiers would have torn the church down in 2 days. They were all over it in less than 10 minutes tearing off the ornaments, splitting the wood work [off] the pews, knocking the bricks to pieces & everything else they could get at. They wanted pieces to carry away.

I do not believe there is a civilized nation on the earth which has so little appreciation of the beautiful & sacred as ours. In the madness of the French Revolution mobs not one in a hundred of whom could read or write, not a man of them was known to injure a work of art or violate a place sacred by association. A more absolute set of vandals than our men can not be found on the face of the earth. As true as I am living I believe they would steal Washington's coffin if they could get to it. What else can you expect of men who will steal even from an enemy family pictures, daguerreotypes, family bibles, records and such like articles.

Camp entertainment included everything from checkers and card games to elaborate skits and company-wide snowball fights. This musical club of the 1st Michigan Engineers & Mechanics included six officers and one enlisted man.

Drunkenness was a continuing problem. Although liquor was banned in camp, it wasn't a difficult matter to procure a bottle of whiskey or a jug of applejack. For those who enjoyed "putting on a toot," no form of punishment seemed effective. Private Lawrence Banks of the 19th Michigan Infantry, for example, spent four days in the guardhouse and was forced to wear a barrel labeled "The Price of Whiskey" for his first offense. A second offense resulted in him being locked up for five days, freed only to be drilled in the manual of arms for one hour each morning and afternoon. He also forfeited one month's pay. All this did little to curb his thirst for alcohol. Banks continued to cause his outfit grief until he died in Virginia.

In the fall of 1862, Private James Greenalch, a teetotaling carpenter who had recently joined the 1st Michigan Engineers & Mechanics, wrote his wife and parents from camp in Kentucky, describing his experiences handling drunks while on guard.

> Our first tower [tour] was the worst, it was in the first part of the evening, some fifteen or twenty drunk and some not, and fetching them in all the time holering and swaring, some of them the officers, two or three of them, would pitch on one man and knock him down and pound him all up, some of them handcofed and some tied down to the benches groaning and yeling. They made so much disturbance and noise that one of the oficers went out and got a revolver and pointed it at two or three of them and told them if they did not sit down and be still he would give them the contence [contents]. Last night two men were shot by the goard. They were told to stop and did not and they fired. They were drunk I sopose. One was shot dead, the other was brought in to the hospital this morning, and another was shot the night before. They were our men and shot by our men, that was their orders….I tell you it was a leson to me, did I not see the evel of sin and the beauty of religeon.

John H. Brainard, a "voluntier" with the 25th Michigan Infantry, carried this creatively painted canteen through three years of campaigning.

Expressions of Christian faith regularly appeared in soldiers' writings, especially as battle, with its many terrors and uncertainties, seemed imminent. A God-fearing infantryman in Virginia presciently wrote his wife that, should he not return to Michigan, she should bring up their infant daughter "in the way she should go and when she gets big enough to Run around whatch her....keep an every watchful eye on her and if God spare her life that she may grow up a true Christain is the sincere Prayer of her Father." He was killed three months later.

❧

Although combat comprised but a tiny fraction of a soldier's time in uniform—and many men never fired a shot in anger during the entire war—the experience of two groups of strangers trying their utmost to murder each other could sear indelible impressions upon one's psyche. Treetops bursting into flames. A fence exploding into a hundred lethal splinters. An eviscerated horse kneeling dumbly in its harness. A bouncing cannon ball shearing off a drummer boy's leg at the knee. A single blast of grapeshot lifting the scalp of one soldier, shaving the jaw off the man to his right, and blowing the lungs out the back of the soldier to his left. Desperate men swinging rifles like clubs and hurling rocks like snowballs. Soldiers called it "seeing the elephant," a reference to a similarly awe-inspiring experience many had shared as boys, when a youngster could get into the circus for free by agreeing to wash down the elephants.

Colonel H. S. Roberts of the 1st Michigan Infantry described the "infernal" noise of dueling artillery and the frightful apprehension of waiting under fire, sometimes for hours on end. "It is the most trying position a soldier has to endure, to stand these horrid missiles, crouched low, seeing them strike all

"Here an incident occurred that I will never forget. I was riding along with my bugler by my side—his name was O'Keefe, and he was a typical Irishman—when he said to [a captured Confederate], 'Johnny, you don't wear very good clothes.' At once there came back the sharp and not over delicate retort, 'When we go out to kill hogs, we don't put on our best clothes.'"

Captain E. L. Negus, 1st Michigan Cavalry, recalling the Second Battle of Bull Run

E. L. Negus.

about him, hearing them burst all around him, and yet unable to move or do a thing but wait in that awful suspense. Now a pause, and your heart beats quicker, for youknow they are getting a new range. Zim! and now it comes, and they have got a cross fire on you—grin and bear it—shut your teeth and swear and beg for a chance to move on them—anything but this. But no faltering, not a bit of it; occasionally, yes, frequently, some young fellow picks up his leg or his arm, and hobbles off to the rear; then some fellow, less fortunate, has to be picked up."

The randomness and illogic of combat could be maddening to anyone inclined to ponder it—and most men did. A few inches here or a couple of seconds there could spell the difference between a man siring a half-dozen children and enjoying another 60 years back in Michigan or being prematurely sent to oblivion. A Union officer remembered a terrible bombardment during the Battle of Chancellorsville. "As I stood looking down the line I saw a shell strike an officer of the 1st Michigan as he lay upon his back reading a paper. It passed directly through his stomach, scattering his entrails on those around him." Private John Houghton of the 4th Michigan Infantry, also present at Chancellorsville, wrote of "one fellow in co. G that had ben out

The men of Company I of the 6th Michigan Infantry in Baltimore, Maryland in September 1861. The regiment would suffer the most deaths of any state regiment, 528, but only 78 were killed in action. The rest were the result of accidents and disease.

on duty came in throwed off his knapsack and sat down on it to rest he did not set there two minutes til he was shot in the head and instantly killed." Conversely, Houghton was saved from his own untimely demise when the Confederate bullet "that was intended for me struck into a white oak tree throwing splinters into my face....if the tree had not stood, there I should stood there myself."

A Michigan cavalryman recalled the experience of being shot. "The first sensation of a gunshot wound is not one of pain," he said.

> The feeling is simply one of shock, without discomfort, accompanied by a peculiar tingling, as though a slight electric current was playing about the site of injury. Quickly ensues a marked sense of numbness, involving a considerable area around the wounded part....the panorama of life—described by many as having appeared to them when apparently near to dissolution—was here presented to the mental vision. Various conjectures respecting this phenomenon have been broached, mostly influenced by religious views. The most plausible explanation is believed to be that which assigns it to the same process of retrospection, as when, after a pleasant journey, or visit, the end is nearing, the mind turns backward in review of that which has been delightful and all too brief. The mind, however, was probably not occupied more than an instant in the consideration of any thing other than the matter of being able to hold out against the foe until fate of some sort should furnish honorable extrication.

Lyman Colby (left) was one of the 300,00 more men called for by President Lincoln in the summer of 1862. Colby enlisted in the 17th Michigan Infantry at the age of 24. The 17th, nicknamed the "Stonewall Regiment," saw nearly continuous action from South Mountain, Maryland to the siege of Petersburg. Private Colby was there every step of the way.

Private Isaac W. Lucas (right) of the 7th Michigan Cavalry contemplatively chews on a cigar in this tintype. He was 24 when he left Grand Rapids for the war. Although taken prisoner at one point, Lucas survived and became one of many Michigan veterans to settle in California. He rests in the national cemetery at Los Angeles.

The concept of "honorable extrication" was lacking in the 278,000 cases of desertion (including 6,525 from Michigan) the Union army officially recorded. Soldiers deserted for a variety of reasons—boredom, homesickness, family troubles, infrequent pay—but the most detrimental to morale were those "leg cases" whose courage failed them in battle. At first, most Union soldiers convicted of desertion or cowardice were subjected to some sort of corporal punishment and public humiliation before being discharged. But by the midpoint of the war offenders were being hanged and shot by firing squads. A total of 141 were executed, including several from Michigan. Many more were pardoned on personal appeal to President Lincoln, who disliked the death penalty but hoped it would serve as a deterrent. It didn't. The spectacle of troops throwing down their arms and running away, ignoring the shouted curses and threats of their commanders, was common throughout the war, as was the sight of men huddled behind trees and under bridges or drifting to the rear. "Some men cried like babies, others acted like maniacs, others showed promptness, coolness and courage, whilst a few showed contemptible humiliation and cowardice," Lieutenant Samuel Hubbard said of the 19th Michigan Infantry in battle. "Some

Life in the navy, as in the army, was filled with mundane but essential tasks. The constant loading, shipping and delivery of men, animals and supplies was a huge logistical undertaking that consumed far more of the navy's time and resources than actual combat.

Several hundred Michiganians served in the U. S. Navy during the Civil War, including Russell Arnold of Monroe. Arnold survived the war but later died when he was crushed between boxcars while working for the railroad.

2541. Gunboat "Mendota," in James River, near Deep Bottom, 1864.

A stereocard of the kind of Union gunboats many Michigan sailors served on. These light-draft fighting vessels penetrated the numerous rivers and inlets of the Confederacy.

This unidentified Union sailor was photographed inside a Detroit studio. If he was a recruit seaman (a "landsman"), he received $12 a month; if he was an ordinary seaman he was paid $14. Able seamen received $18 a month. No matter what their grade, in the first couple years of the war all seagoing sailors over 21 were issued a daily ration of wine or grog. This was replaced by a cash payment of $1.50 a month.

Panic at Second Bull Run.

Colonel Thornton Brodhead.

feigned illness, others that their guns were out of order and useless, others had to undergo a change of linen, the next day." The problem of keeping a command together under fire would only grow worse over time, as draftees, substitutes and bounty jumpers replaced many of the original volunteers.

Even the best units were not immune to outbreaks of panic. The 1st Michigan Sharpshooters, to cite just one of numerous examples involving state regiments, degenerated into "a howling mob" at the Wilderness, their colonel found cowering behind a tree. "Rout is the worst of all conflicts," said Captain Negus of the 1st Michigan Cavalry, recalling the scene at Second Bull Run. "Friends slay each other in their mad flight. The artillerymen rush off with their horses and the guns are left to the care of themselves. The soldiers of the wagon train unhitch and take their animals for escape. Wagons are upset

Marcus Satterlee enlisted in the 3rd Michigan Infantry on August 22, 1864, but lasted less than five months in the reorganized regiment. On February 16, 1865, the 22-year-old corporal from Hart died of disease at Knoxville and was buried in the national cemetery there.

James Harvey Self, along with his brother John, served in Battery D of the 1st Michigan Light Artillery. Both Ann Arbor volunteers died of disease in Tennessee—John, at Nashville on March 9, 1864, and James, at Murfreesboro on May 18, 1865.

with their four wheels in the air, blocking the road and helping the massacre. As they crush and crowd they trample on the living and the dead alike….Knapsacks, muskets, cartridges, boxes and belts are cast away. No more officers, no more generals." Just chaos and confusion replacing the calm and order of the parade grounds.

The landscape of battle was a sight never to be forgotten. In a letter to his sister, S. L. Loving of the 3rd Michigan Infantry recorded what he saw as he wandered the battlefield at Williamsburg, Virginia in the spring of 1862. "In one instance a Michigander and an Alabamian [who had] thrust a bayonet through each other lay dead, [each] still grasping his bayonet….Another had undone his knapsack and taken out his Testament and died with it grasped in his hands." Others had died clutching rosaries, a cross, or letters from home, "as though loath to part with the last messengers from loved ones." Roscoe Dix of the 2nd Michigan Infantry had images of the immediate aftermath of the Battle of Fredericksburg stamped in his memory, and they contained far too many bodies for his liking. The sergeant from Berrien Springs remembered one soldier being brought into a temporary hospital, the top of his head gone, whose only words until his death the following day were "Jesus, have mercy on me." Doctors equipped with hacksaws and unsterilized instruments performed amputations by the dozens, the removed limbs piled in stinking heaps in an adjacent garden for days until they were finally burned. Bodies that were hastily buried in the frozen ground were dug up by ravenous dogs, who finally were chased away with musket shots.

Time was slow to eradicate the signs of struggle. Herman Lowe of the 1st Michigan Engineers & Mechanics arrived at Shiloh weeks after the battle. He "went through the Battle ground which shows plainly what an awful fight occurred…. large trees cut off entirely & some with holes through the

A week after celebrating the second Christmas of the war, the 21st Michigan Infantry was mauled at the Battle of Stones River, Tennessee, suffering 147 casualties. "For two full hours we were in the midst of this lead and iron hail, until two of our flag-bearers were shot down, and 26 bullet holes torn in our banner," reported Lieutenant Marcus W. Bates. "Scarcely a man in the regiment came out of that wood without bearing marks of the bullets on his person or clothes. You can form some idea of the terrible searching character of the fire, when I tell you that the very rabbits in their nest were killed by it."

center made by cannon balls, small trees & bushes mowed off with musketry & grape shot." In October 1863, when the 118th Pennsylvania bivouacked on ground where Second Bull Run had been fought a year earlier, the ghoulish evidence of the slaughter that had taken place was still everywhere. "The dead had been so carelessly buried that among the uncovered remains, that of an officer of the 1st Michigan who had been killed here was recognized by the formation of his teeth," observed a captain in the 118th. "Time was taken to more properly cover his bones and to mark his grave." The remains of a cavalryman, possibly that of a Wolverine, were found nearby. "The flesh had entirely disappeared from his bones but his uniform was still in fair condition and his sword was still belted around his waist. He had evidently been wounded and crawled to this spot in search of water. The bones of his legs protruded well beyond his pants, which were much shrunken, and his shoes were still on his fleshless feet. In attempting to lift his remains by the sword belt it all fell apart, so gathering them together as compactly as possible a little earth soon hid them from view."

"They have had a new Colonel appointed. His name is Poe. He is from the regular army. The boys don't like him much. He puts on too many airs to take with volunteers, and he will find out he is not in the regular army."

Private Perry Mayo, 2nd Michigan Infantry, commenting on the appointment of Colonel Orlando Poe

Barely five feet tall, Rufus W. Jacklin initially was rejected for service because he didn't meet the minimum height requirement. By war's end, however, the little Detroiter had organized and commanded a special battalion of hand-picked sharpshooters and was promoted to major. At Gettysburg he was adjutant of the 16th Michigan Infantry. During the second day's action, he recalled, a Confederate cannon ball "took off the top of my horse's head, at the moment he was in the air, and fell a mass of quivering flesh, and I partly under him." Jacklin's injured leg would bother him for the rest of his life.

The phenomenon of post-traumatic stress syndrome had yet to be identified. But the condition certainly existed and undoubtedly contributed to countless nightmares and accounted for some aberrant behavior. "Dreams of Fredericksburg continue to haunt me and I can not sleep," confessed one diarist with the 24th Michigan Infantry. "Dead men parade before my eyes. Cannonading rings in my ears. Always there is the dead Reb. I took his tobacco. It was shameful to do but he did not need it. I have killed men."

Given the horrific nature of combat, the wonder, perhaps, is not that so many men behaved dishonorably at the sound of guns, but that all of them didn't hurriedly retrace their steps back to Fowlerville and Tawas City once lead and loud noises filled the air. What kept the feet of most stalwarts pointed in the right direction was a genuine sense of duty to cause and country, of course. Of greater importance, perhaps, was the obligation a soldier felt he owed comrades who were equally frightened but determined to work through their own fears of impending death or dismemberment. "I dared not look at my knees," admitted one officer with the 1st Sharpshooters, "for I could feel them shaking like a twig in the breeze and I was afraid that the others would notice it."

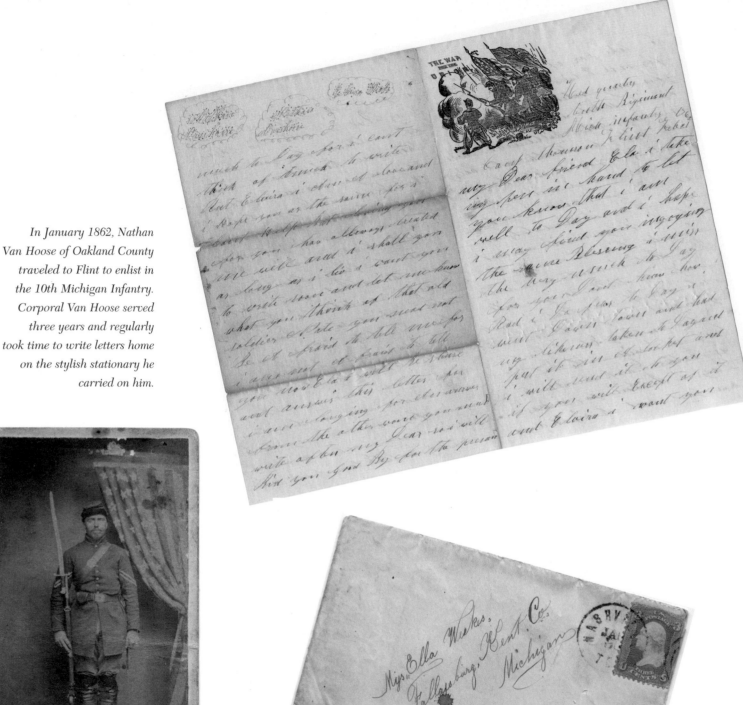

In January 1862, Nathan Van Hoose of Oakland County traveled to Flint to enlist in the 10th Michigan Infantry. Corporal Van Hoose served three years and regularly took time to write letters home on the stylish stationary he carried on him.

Benjamin Franklin Richards (right) and Adelbert Dickinson, both of Tuscola County, enlisted in Company E of the 7th Michigan Infantry on August 18, 1861. The two friends had this photo taken on March 11, 1862. Richards was discharged for disability that winter while Dickinson re-enlisted and wound up serving nearly four years.

Samuel Kittring, from Hartford, served in Company D of Birge's Western Sharpshooters. The multi-state unit was originally mustered into service as the 14th Missouri and later redesignated the 66th Illinois Infantry.

This turn-of-the-century work by artist Gilbert Gaul is a generic but accurate depiction of a Union skirmish line in the grip of combat. One Wolverine, speaking for combatants on both sides, declared, "May the curse of God light on the men who caused the war which brought us here."

Courage was a point of personal honor, a factor often mentioned in diaries and letters. "They isent many but what would choose death, rather than to have such everlasting disgrace," Private John Ryder wrote his family one day in 1863 after watching several "skedaddlers" get their heads shaved and drummed out of camp. Corporal John Pardington, in describing the same incident to his wife back in Trenton, suggested that the disgraced men should have "the finger of Scorn" pointed at them when they reappeared in their communities. "Sarah," he promised, "before I would under go the same as they did I would sooner be brought home in my coffin....I never could Bring such disgrace on you and my little darling [daughter]." Ryder and Pardington belonged to the 24th Michigan Infantry. Although the war was lasting longer than either had anticipated, they were determined to finish what they had started. Both would die at Gettysburg.

A Kurz & Allison lithograph of the Battle of Chancellorsville, Virginia, in May 1863, in which several Michigan regiments were heavily engaged. "No man can give any idea of a battle by description nor by painting," insisted Alpheus S. Williams, Michigan's most capable general of the war. "If you can stretch your imagination so far as to hear, in fancy, the crashing roll of 30,000 muskets mingled with the thunder of over a hundred pieces of artillery; the sharp bursting of shells and the peculiar whizzing sound of its dismembered pieces, traveling with a shriek in all directions; the crash and thug of round shot through trees and buildings and into the earth or through columns of human bodies; the 'phiz' of the Minie ball; the uproar of thousands of human voices in cheers, yells, and imprecations; and see the smoke from all the engines of war's inventions hanging sometimes like a heavy cloud and sometimes falling down like a curtain between the combatants; see the hundreds of wounded limping away or borne to the rear on litters; riderless horses rushing wildly about; now and then the blowing up of a caisson and human frames thrown lifeless into the air; the rush of columns to the front; the scattered fugitives of broken regiments and skulkers making for the rear…you may have some faint idea of a…scene so terrible and yet so grand."

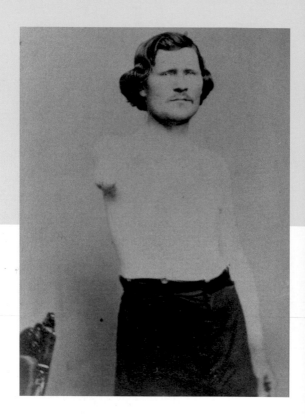

*The wounds of war.
Sergeant James Harris of the
19th Michigan Infantry had
parts of his face sliced off while
Charles Dunn of the 5th
Michigan Cavalry lost his
entire right arm.*

For all the terror that combat engendered, the odds of a soldier actually being killed or mortally wounded in a battle were comparatively low. Statistically, he was far more likely to succumb to diarrhea, dysentery, pneumonia, malaria, measles, smallpox, tuberculosis or some fever than to a bullet, bayonet or shell. In fact, one of every nine Michigan men who served in uniform would be carried away by disease—nearly 10,000 victims overall. This figure represented an astonishing two-thirds of the 14,343 Michigan men who died in the conflict, a percentage that roughly matched that of the Union army overall.

George F. Grather was an early contributor to this morbid calculus. In a fit of enthusiasm he had joined the 11th Michigan Infantry to help teach the upstarts in the South a lesson, but had fallen ill during training camp in White Pigeon. Diagnosed with typhoid fever, he finally died on October 19, 1861. At Private Grather's funeral, wrote an observer, "all seemed to feel the

George W. Fox enlisted in Company I of the 1st United States Sharpshooters on November 18, 1861 at the age of 27. Michigan supplied the Union with one full regiment of sharp-shooters, the 1st Michigan Sharpshooters, as well as 10 individual companies attached to various regiments. Sharpshooters were expert marksmen who were deployed as snipers and light infantry.

mournfulness of the occasion. He enlisted with us at Centreville to share in the dangers and privations of a camp life, but alas he has fallen before he met the enemies of his country."

The regiment's first death was a sobering introduction to the consequences of crowded, unsanitary conditions and lax attitudes regarding vaccinations and personal hygiene. Within a year of its formation the 11th Michigan would bury another 115 volunteers because of disease, most of them victims of measles, pneumonia, smallpox and typhoid fever.

Dysentery. Hardtack. Rats. Grapeshot. Mud. Blisters. Flies. Bullets. Fever. Boredom. Marching. And more marching. The misery of sharing a cramped tent with a half-dozen high-smelling men, all afflicted with body lice and chronic diarrhea, could test the resolve of the most ardent patriot, as could the heartache of gathering the parts of friends and neighbors on some broken field far from their Michigan home. Despite the onerous physical and psychological toll exacted from them, most members of Mr. Lincoln's army gamely soldiered on. For those fortunate enough to survive, the simple satisfaction of making it through the grandest—if most harrowing—adventure of their life would usually prove enough to offset the memories of all the hazards and hardships endured. As Barden M. Hicks, a veteran campaigner in the 11th Michigan Infantry, would declare upon his discharge: "No money consideration could buy my experience during that term of service, and no amount of money would induce me to again undergo it." ●

The Union army had one doctor for every 134 men, a ratio two and a half times greater than that of the enemy. Professor Moses Gunn was nearly 40 years old in 1861 when he left the University of Michigan's medical school to become surgeon of the 5th Michigan Infantry. The former dean left the regiment the following year, resuming his distinguished career in Ann Arbor before moving on to Chicago.

James Rundell, a 27-year-old doctor from Niles, joined the 12th Michigan Infantry as an assistant surgeon less than a week after the Battle of Shiloh in April 1862. Each Union regiment was assigned a surgeon, two assistant surgeons, and a hospital steward. Rundell finished the war as chief surgeon of the 2nd Division.

Illustrator Tom Nast produced this behind-the-lines sketch for Harper's Weekly. As the opposing armies do their best to murder each other, battlefield casualties stream in and are attended to as best as possible at a makeshift field hospital. Note the bottle of "cure-all"—typically whiskey or brandy—on the table where a harried surgeon is preparing to amputate a wounded soldier's limb. Field hospitals, initially set up on a regimental basis, were by 1862 being organized on the brigade and division levels. In addition, an ambulance corps was established. Each infantry regiment had a detachment of 10 men plus three ambulance wagons with drivers whose sole task was to evacuate the wounded; musicians also assisted.

Captain Augustus Chapman of St. Joseph enlisted in the 6th Michigan Infantry when the regiment was organized at Kalamazoo in the summer of 1861. Three years later he died of wounds in Louisiana. Despite the many inadequacies of military medical practice, roughly 87 percent of all wounded Union soldiers receiving treatment survived.

*A familiar scene during the Union draft: The random selection of names
is held inside the local provost marshal's office. The Confederacy resorted
to a draft in 1862.*

Chapter 4

HOME FIRES

A postwar portrait of George Purdy, who served in the 1st Michigan Infantry as a substitute for Henry Hess— and lived to tell of his experiences.

By the spring of 1863, as the fighting dragged on into its third and darkest year, it was clear that only continued sacrifice—not rhetoric nor proclamations—would wear down the rebellion. Morale flagged as the survivors of Shiloh, Antietam and Fredericksburg, many missing limbs or eyes, trickled back to their villages and farms. Large numbers of men didn't return at all. "Little children had their share of grief in those dark days," remembered Florence Marsh of Detroit. "Some morning, a companion's seat would be empty. Then, after several days absence, a little figure in black would be sitting at her desk. Her dress told the sad story. Her father lay dead on a southern battlefield."

Military and political leaders came under savage attack for a string of catastrophes that was bleeding the army dry. The fight many idealistic men had signed on for seemed almost doomed to fail, causing one disillusioned Michigan soldier to admit to his wife that he'd "disert in a holey minet" if he could. Another infantryman, this one in the 24th Michigan, wrote his wife that he "wish[ed] this cursed Civil War was over. Only the thoughts of you and the children keep me at my duty."

For Captain John T. Pierson, worries over a cold-hearted creditor back home in Pontiac added to his stress. Helpless and angry, he assailed those who would dare dun his ailing wife, Joanna, while he was serving the cause with the 10th Michigan in Alabama. "Those left at home in the quiet pursuit of their business can well afford to wait," he fumed in a letter to his daughter in early 1863. "The business I am engaged in is a game of heads and I may loose mine and his is in no danger unless they chose to get up a war at home…."

John Litogot (right) and the man he substituted for,
Andrew Threadgould.

There *was* a war at home, and it was the source of much bitterness. It centered around the draft, which was as divisive and controversial a practice as the one that would split the country a century later during the Vietnam war. The first draft was instituted by presidential order in August 1862, with Michigan asked to provide 11,686 of the 300,000 men Lincoln requested. On March 3, 1863, Lincoln officially signed into law the country's first true conscription act—legislation that had been approved by Congress and was filled with holes.

The draft worked as follows. Each state's designated quota was divided among Congressional districts, numbers which were further broken down by county and then town. In large population centers like Detroit, quotas were broken down into wards. Each district had to muster into service its assigned number of men. It was preferable that they be volunteers, of course, but if a ward or town did not meet its quota by the appointed deadline, a lottery of all local men between the ages of 20 and 45 was then held. Most communities considered it a mark of shame to have to resort to a lottery to place men in uniform, so it was common for local governments or groups of public-spirited citizens to offer cash bounties to induce enlistments. In time the federal government added its own bonus, swelling the financial enticement. The cash was paid after a recruit produced proof of his enlistment. The amounts varied, but often totaled several hundred dollars—not a bad haul at a time when the average worker made about $500 a year. Sometimes the bounties amounted to more than $1,000.

As the war became less popular, the bonuses increased, with the result that a new breed of criminal opportunist flourished. "Bounty men" would enlist in one district, collect their bonus, then desert and enlist in another district, usually under assumed names. Some were known to enlist and desert several

An unidentified member of the 5th Michigan Cavalry and his family. A corporal in the regiment tried to reassure his wife: "I can't understand why you worry so much. Try to believe that I'm safe. Do you suppose I'm foolish enough to get killed? I enlisted to kill Rebels and not to get killed....You must remember I'm small, and the bullets find more room around me than on me."

"You wanted to know what I would say if you should reenlist again for three years. I really hope if any such thoughts are passing your mind you should banish them at once....I fear my wrath would rise a little and might tell you to enlist for life while you were at it."

Melissa Wells to her husband, Benjamin Wells,
11th Michigan Infantry, July 8, 1864

times before being caught; even then, the punishment rarely fit the crime. Placed under guard and forced to actually join a unit, most simply bided their time until another opportunity to desert presented itself. Hundreds of unscrupulous Canadians found Michigan ripe for the plucking, snatching their bounties and easily dashing back across the water, protected by an officially neutral government that made only a half-hearted attempt at stopping the practice.

Lincoln knew the conscription act was unfair and possibly unconstitutional, but these were perilous times. He was, above all else, a brutally pragmatic politician who believed the preservation of the union justified the occasional suspension of civil liberties. Although he wasn't eligible, the commander in chief paid $500 to a Pennsylvania man to act as his substitute. Lincoln's symbolic gesture underscored the draft's chief inequity—the ability for a man with money to let a man without money do the fighting for him.

As a "delegate" of the Christian Commission, Elmina Brainard of Lapeer cared for the sick and wounded and distributed Bibles to soldiers.

There were clauses for reasons of health or hardship, but a strapping young man with soldiering potential could buy a one-time exemption by paying the government $300. Technically, the exempted man was eligible to be drafted again during the next call-up; practically speaking, when that happened he could be expected to just pay $300 again for another temporary exemption. All the while there remained a quota to meet, which meant each time a temporary exemption was granted, another member of the community who lacked the financial resources would be conscripted in his place. Hundreds of affluent Michiganians (as well as more than a few ordinary citizens who scraped together the required amount from family and friends) paid a collective $594,000 to go this route.

There was a better way for a reluctant warrior to stay home. He could hire a substitute, in which case he earned a permanent exemption. The price was whatever the market would bear. In the case of John Litogot, the price was $1,000—and his life.

Litogot, a 27-year-old farmer from Brownstown Township, reportedly received that amount from Andrew Threadgould, a middle-aged gentleman with an unrecorded livelihood. There was no cry of "Rich man's war, poor man's fight," from Litogot, as the surrogate soldier happily posed for a photograph with his benefactor shortly after enlisting in the 24th Michigan Infantry on August 14, 1862. Just as nothing of Andrew Threadgould can be found in the city directories or census rolls of this period, in four short months the man he sent off to fight for him similarly ceased to exist. On December 13, 1862, Litogot was killed by artillery fire at Fredericksburg. John's younger brother, Barney, also was wounded during the battle. At the time their sister, Mary Litogot Ford, was carrying her first child. The following July the boy, Henry Ford, was born inside a Dearborn farmhouse. Ford's birth came on the heels of the Battle of Gettysburg. Because of the entwined nature of all these events, the creator of the Model T always believed he was the reincarnation of a dead Civil War soldier. Whether he really was or not, his uncles' sacrifices, especially the death of Private John Litogot, helped explain the auto tycoon's lifelong pacifism.

Charles Scribner was a 33-year-old farmer who enlisted in Company F of the 22nd Michigan Infantry at Utica on January 24, 1864. He was exposed to measles in camp and died after spending just five weeks in the army. He left behind his wife, Minerva, and two young sons.

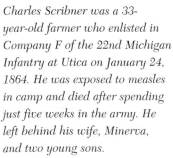

For all the contentiousness the draft produced, its impact appears comparatively minimal. By war's end only 6 percent of the Union force had been conscripts and substitutes, including 4,281 from Michigan. However, the number of men who "voluntarily" enlisted to avoid the stigma of being identified as a draftee or because they couldn't afford an exemption is unknown, but probably was considerable.

In the main, the people of Michigan stood solidly behind the men in uniform during these trying times. Across the state, civilians and local governments pitched in whenever and wherever they could. Debts often were reduced or canceled, relief funds for soldiers' families were subscribed, and charities were created to look after the needs of orphans and widows. Wayne County alone paid out $547,000 in relief and another $660,554 in bounties to its soldiers and their families, a total of more than $1.2 million.

As a group, the women of Michigan stepped up admirably. They already were hardier and more independent than their eastern counterparts, the result of the exigencies of frontier life and the state's more enlightened views regarding their legal status. While there were no co-ed universities in the East, in Michigan females could choose from a half-dozen colleges. They also enjoyed guardianship and property rights that were liberal for their time. While it was still overwhelmingly a man's world, and would remain so well into the next century, members of the "fairer sex" did their fair share in advancing the national cause. For most it was assuming the role of the traditional head of the family while a husband or father went to war. For others it was actually risking death and disease on battlefields and in hospitals.

Sex in the Civil War

Domestic bliss: Sergeant Major Thomas Canburn of the 9th Michigan Cavalry and his wife had their portrait taken inside an Adrian studio one day during the war.

Because of its sensitive nature and the relative scarcity of first-person accounts, one aspect of the soldier's life during this period remains largely unexplored after all these years: sex. But if sex is hard to find on the pages of most memoirs and unit histories, it was easy enough to find for any man looking to "storm a masked battery," which was soldier-speak for sexual intercourse.

The average Civil War soldier was in his twenties and temptations were everywhere, as one diarist remembered. In visiting Washington, D.C., Charles Haydon of the 2nd Michigan Infantry observed three "great classes" of people. One was the soldiers and the other two were "politicians and prostitutes, both very numerous and about equal in numbers, honesty and morality." By the midpoint of the war an estimated 5,000 prostitutes in Washington were servicing soldiers inside Madam Russel's Bake Oven, the Devil's Own and hundreds of other brothels. Another Michigan soldier, this one in Georgia, wrote his wife that "some of the women…have been convinced that the Yankees have hornes but not horns on top of the head. I should have hesitated to of believed that men or those pretend to be men would become so demoralized and void of all decency or respect."

Some men who couldn't buy a woman took one by force. Several Michigan soldiers committed rapes during the war, including George Hakes, a corporal in the 6th Michigan Cavalry. Hakes was found guilty of ravishing "the wife of one Cornelius Robinson, a loyal colored citizen of Frederick County, Virginia." Largely because he was white and the victim was black, Hakes escaped capital punishment. Instead he was sentenced to a dishonorable discharge and two years at hard labor. In nearly every case where the skin colors of the rapist and victim were reversed, the offender was hanged.

Aside from these relatively few court-martial cases, sex was overwhelmingly consensual. Soldiers in the field who couldn't wait for their next pass to a nearby urban area satisfied their

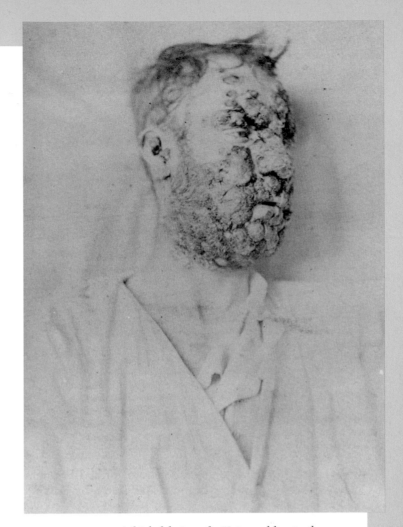

urges in the bushes with one of the many women who regularly prowled camps searching for a "cousin" or "brother." There often was a steep price to pay beyond the money or goods that exchanged hands, however.

In his diary, Charles Haydon admitted many men in his regiment had been "injured"—a euphemism for contracting a sexual disease, usually syphilis or gonorrhea. These diseases were rampant in both the Union and Confederate armies and were characterized by measles-like rashes, high fevers, crusty pus-filled blisters and massive ulcerations. Haydon lamented that despite the risks, some soldiers did not pursue the enemy "as eagerly as they pursue the whores."

The Union army recorded roughly 200,000 cases of venereal disease, which worked out to 8 percent of all men being infected. How many undiagnosed victims returned to their families with a murderous spirochete in their bloodstream is unknown. In his book *The Story the Soldiers Wouldn't Tell: Sex in the Civil War*, physician and historian Thomas P. Lowry cited the study of another expert, Robert W. Waitt, who estimated that as many as one-third of all the men who died in veterans facilities like the Michigan Soldiers Home were in the terminal stages of venereal disease. The havoc didn't end with a victim's burial, Lowry added. "No one knows how many…wives and widows went to their graves, rotted and ravaged by the pox that their men brought home, or how many veterans' children were blinded by gonorrhea or stunted by syphilis. Like ripples in some Stygian pond, the wounds of war spread long after the shooting died away."

Happily, it appears that far more soldiers returned home faithful and disease-free than did not. As might be expected, the promise of a truly romantic coupling usually was a big part of the happy homecoming. "I have no objections to make if you lay until noon," Melissa Wells wrote her husband, Ben, as he neared the end of his enlistment in the 11th Michigan Infantry, "but I will not promise you how much you may sleep."

A frightful view of a Union soldier in the terminal stage of syphilis. During the war the only known treatment was salts of mercury, leading to the familiar saying: "An evening with Venus, a lifetime with Mercury."

For those who stayed home, a world severely depopulated of adult males called for adaptability and increased self-reliance. Mary Austin Wallace, a farm wife in Calhoun County, demonstrated an admirable survivability during this difficult period.

Mary was 24, with a two-year-old son and an infant daughter, when her husband Robert Bruce Wallace tramped off to war with the 19th Michigan Infantry in August 1862. She was left alone with the responsibility of managing their 160-acre farm as well as supervising the construction of a new house. In the diary she kept while Bruce was away, Mary wrote simply and matter-of-factly about her daily grind, keeping any thoughts of loneliness or frustration out of her entries. Some excerpts:

Sept 17 [1862]
I gathered wood boiled soap pulled weeds hoed turnips and baggas and got Mr. Harrisons pigs out of the corn two or three times

Sept 19
I lathed some went and borrowed Mr. Rowe's shovel emptied the leach put a barrel of new ashes back in the leach carried the shovel home borrowed his cutter cut corn drove Harrisons pigs out of the corn cut 10 stouts of corn drove the pigs out again drove them home told them they troubled me carried the corn cutter home

Sept 24
I cut corn most all day I sewed some

Oct 28
I dug the early June potatoes buried them for winter....I put a door in the corn crib I husked some corn

Oct 29
I hitched up the horses on the wagon went in the north corn field husked a load of corn drawed it to the crib unloaded it drawed a load of pumpkins

Nov 14
I pulled some turnips helped load some pumpkins

Nov 15
I lathed some I finished my dress skirt mended my dress picked some skoke berries

Nov 21
I chopped some wood wound up my yarn set me a knitting work Bruce a pair of socks I dug some potatoes picked them up

Farm wife Mary Austin Wallace and her two children, circa 1863.

Opposite: Hartman Sharp Felt, a 25-year-old from Bunker Hill, enlisted in the 7th Michigan Infantry in the summer of 1861. He survived gunshot wounds to the head and the leg at the Battle of Fair Oaks, Virginia and left a Philadelphia hospital to rejoin his regiment. Between stints as a recruiter, Felt survived scarlet fever and the battles of Fredericksburg, Chancellorsville and Gettysburg. Felt was a "ranker," promoted up through the ranks from corporal to second lieutenant. He was wounded in the left arm and chest at Deep Bottom, Virginia, dying at a Washington hospital on August 24, 1864. He was originally buried at the grounds that became Arlington National Cemetery, but his parents had him removed to a small cemetery in Grass Lake, where he rests to this day.

And so it went, until Bruce—shot through the shoulders at the Battle of Thompson's Station in Tennessee—was discharged and came home the following spring.

Every army on the move was trailed by a mixed bag of patriots and opportunists broadly known as "camp followers." Their number included private servants, contract laborers, sutlers, contrabands, barbers, bakers, and even personal physicians. Many women accompanied their husbands, sons and brothers as they left Michigan for the front, bringing their much appreciated domestic expertise and matronly qualities with them. They mended clothes, washed laundry, prepared meals, and basically pitched in wherever they were needed in camp. Women unofficially attached to a regiment were known as "vivandieres." In the tradition of their European counterparts, they sometimes wore stylized uniforms to help distinguish them from some of the less desirable categories of camp followers, such as prostitutes, card sharks and moonshine merchants.

Bridget Divers—"Michigan Bridget"—was a notable vivandiere. The stout, robust Irish immigrant followed her husband's regiment, the 1st Michigan Cavalry, to war, attracting considerable attention as a caretaker and as a combatant. Although Divers usually worked behind the lines, helping to bring in and nurse the wounded, she was known to occasionally pick up a fallen soldier's weapon and join in the fighting. According to a postwar account by noted U. S. Sanitary Commission leader Mary Livermore, Divers—who was nicknamed "Irish Biddy" by admiring soldiers—twice rallied faltering troops, helping to stave off defeat each time. Another contemporary recalled how active Divers was around Petersburg and Richmond in the last stage of the war:

One of the more enigmatic female figures of the war was Pauline Cushman, the self-described "Spy of the Cumberland." Born Harriet Wood and raised in New York and Michigan, she took the stagename "Pauline Cushman" in the 1850s. While performing with a theatrical troupe in Louisville, Kentucky in 1863, Cushman did some minor spying for the Union army. She reportedly was caught in Nashville and sentenced to hang, but managed to escape when the Confederates were hurriedly forced to retreat. While the true extent of Cushman's activities may never be known, she was able to capitalize on her little slice of fame through lectures, a book, and appearances at P. T. Barnum's New York museum. In her later years she was desperate and destitute, finally winding up in a San Francisco boardinghouse. She was found dead of an overdose on the morning of December 1, 1898 and buried with considerable pomp at the national cemetery, where her headstone identifies her as "Union Spy."

In one of Sheridan's grand raids, during the latter days of the Rebellion, she as usual rode with the troops night and day, wearing out several horses until they dropped from exhaustion. In a severe cavalry engagement, in which her regiment took a prominent part, her colonel was wounded, and her captain killed. She accompanied the former to the rear, where she ministered to his needs; and, when placed in the cars bound to City Point Hospital, she remained with him, giving all the relief in her power, on that fatiguing journey, although herself almost exhausted, having been without sleep four days and nights. After seeing her colonel safely and comfortably lodged in the hospital, she took one night's rest, and returned to the front. Finding that her captain's body had not been recovered, it being hazardous to make the attempt, she resolved to rescue it, as "it never should be left on rebel soil."

So, with her orderly for sole companion, she rode 15 miles to the scene of the late conflict, found the body she sought, strapped it upon her horse, rode back seven miles to an embalmer's, where she waited whilst the body was embalmed; then, again strapping it on her horse, she rode several miles farther to the cars, in which with her precious burden she proceeded to City Point, there obtained a rough coffin, and forwarded the whole to Michigan. Without any delay, Bridget returned to her regiment, and told some officers that wounded men had been left on the field from which she had rescued her captain's body. They did not credit her tale, so she said, "Furnish me some ambulances, and I will bring them in." The conveyances were given her, she retraced her steps to the deserted battlefield, and soon had some eight or ten poor sufferers in the wagons on their way to camp.

"At this place the soldiers of the 15th Michigan Volunteer Infantry had laid out a nice graveyard, and at every grave a board was erected, bearing the soldier's name and regiment. Near this spot we had found a young man who must have been one of the outside pickets at the battle of Pittsburg Landing, and been captured and tied to a tree. We had him taken down and buried, but never learned his name or command. He was one of the 'missing.'"

Army nurse M. V. Harkin, describing the aftermath of the Battle of Shiloh (Pittsburg Landing)

The roads were rough, and their moans and cries gave evidence of intense agony. While still some miles from their destination, Bridget saw several rebels approaching. She ordered the drivers to quicken their pace, and endeavored to urge her horse forward; but he balked, and refused to move. The drivers, becoming alarmed, deserted their charge, and fled to the woods, while the wounded men begged that they might not be left to the mercy of the enemy, and to suffer in Southern prisons. The rebels soon came up. Bridget plead with them to leave the sufferers unmolested; but they laughed at her, took the horses from the ambulances, and such articles of value as the men possessed, and then dashed off the way they came. Poor Bridget was almost desperate, darkness coming on, and with no one to help her, the wounded men beseeching her not to leave them. Fortunately, an officer of our army rode up to see what the matter was, and soon sent horses and assistance to the party.

When the war ended, Divers accompanied the 1st Michigan Cavalry when it was assigned to Texas as part of the army of occupation. She then returned to Michigan. After a spell she headed west, rejoining the regular army as a laundress during the Indian Wars. Nobody knows what happened to this remarkable woman after that.

Female nurses were a phenomenon of the war. Prior to that, invalided enlisted men had always taken care of the needs of their sick and wounded comrades. But the sheer magnitude of the suffering, coupled with the manpower shortage, made women essential. Union nurses were

"The City Was In a Wild State of Excitement"

Resentment over the draft boiled over into violence in several Northern cities, and blacks took the brunt of the rage. The bloodiest riot occurred in July 1863 in New York, where Federal troops—including men from the 7th Michigan Infantry Regiment, fresh off the killing fields of Gettysburg—were needed to put down a three-day rampage that saw hundreds die. While it was not nearly as deadly, Detroit had already experienced its own race riot four months earlier. City historian Clarence M. Burton, then a 10-year-old boy, later recalled the particulars of that tumultuous and shameful event.

In 1863 the effects of the war began to tell upon the country. The demand for men was greater than the supply and drafts became necessary, but Michigan kept up her quota until near the close of the war. When the draft began, some of the rebel sympathizers and the "peace-at-any-price" men were drawn in with the rest, and they were bitter in their denunciation of what they termed "the nigger war." This feeling culminated in bloody riots in New York and other cities during the dark days of 1863, and Detroit had its riot with the others, only a little earlier than most of the cities.

A mulatto named William Faulkner, who lived in Detroit, was charged with making felonious assaults upon two little girls: Mary Brown, white, and Ellen Hoover, colored. He was tried on the charge March 5, 1863, and before Judge Witherell. J. Logan Chipman and A. W. Hessler conducted the defense, and James Knox Govin was prosecuting attorney. When the time came for the noon recess a great mob of hoodlums awaited the appearance of Faulkner at the door of the courthouse, which was at the corner of Congress and Griswold Streets. They intended to lynch him while he was being conducted to jail. The prisoner was kept in the courtroom during the noon hour to avoid the fury of the mob.

In the afternoon Faulkner was convicted and sentenced to Jackson prison. At that time the provost marshal had a strong guard to keep the drafted men in custody, and 75 of the guards were called to the courtroom to guard the prisoner on his way to jail. The sheriff then started with Faulkner. The mob gathered in great force and the provost guards were saluted by a volley of paving stones while crossing the Campus Martius. The guards, after warning the mob back, fired upon the crowd, wounding several persons, and one inoffensive citizen named Christopher Lang, was killed by a stray bullet. Faulkner was landed safely in jail and then the cry was raised: "Drive the niggers out; they're the cause of all our troubles."

It was just after nightfall, and the mob divided into two sections to attack the Negro residents. Wherever a colored person was seen on the street the hoodlums attacked him, and neither age nor sex was spared. Ephraim Clark, the aged sexton of the colored Episcopal church, was knocked down and kicked into insensibility. Louis Pierce, who kept a little clothing store at 69 Lafayette (now Champlain Street), was seen standing in front of his door; the crowd pursued him inside his shop, where he was brutally pounded with clubs. Then his shop was fired and utterly destroyed, while the owner and his family, who lived upstairs, narrowly escaped with their lives. A young colored woman, who carried an infant in her arms, was knocked down on the street and the baby was thrown from hand to hand in the crowd until it was nearly dead.

In the vicinity of East Fort, Brush and East Congress Streets was a large colony of colored people, extending from Randolph to Beaubien Streets. In that district the mob burned 32 buildings,

26 of which were tenements, and left 200 people shelterless, besides destroying all their household effects and pounding the victims with clubs.

Solomon Huston and his brother kept a cooper shop near the corner of East Fort and Beaubien Streets. They were regarded by the people as champions of their race, and the panic-stricken Africans fled from their blazing tenements to take shelter in the cooper shop. The mob followed and set the building on fire in a dozen places, and as fast as the inmates attempted to escape they were knocked down and thrown back until their lives were in imminent danger. Edward Crosby, a Michigan Central fireman, was shot by some person in the crowd during the scene at the cooper shop, and 33 shots were picked out of his back and neck.

The mob tried to burn the colored Episcopal church, but Constable Sullivan, of the Seventh Ward, took his stand on the steps, pistol in hand, and threatened to kill the first man in the crowd who showed a light, and the mob gave way before him. He was afterward presented with a gold watch by several public spirited residents. Fire engine No. 2 was working at the fire when the mob made a rush and tried to disable it, but several brave citizens came to the rescue of the firemen, and the streams of water were turned upon the hoodlums with good effect.

Even the women of the city did what they could in sheltering the victims of the mob. Mrs. Isaac W. Ingersoll saw a Windsor Negro running along the alley in rear of her house pursued by a blood-thirsty mob. She ran out and cried: "Stop, you shall not touch him, you devils." She took him into the yard of her husband's sash factory on Fort Street and at night lodged him in her house in safety.

The city was in a wild state of excitement. In response to the call for military force to restore order, the following companies turned out: the Light Guard, under Captain Mathews; the Lyon Guard, under Captain Stanton; the 19th U. S. Infantry from Fort Wayne, and five companies of the 27th Infantry from Ypsilanti. The mob scattered before the military arrived, and next day 16 of the ringleaders were arrested.

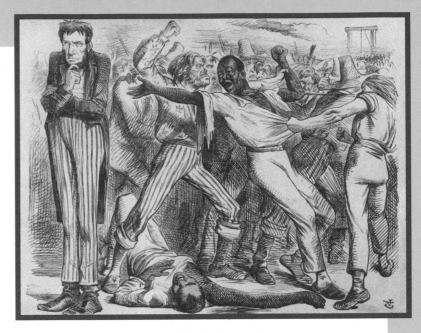

Above: The English magazine Punch *published this cartoon in its April 8, 1863 issue, a month after the draft riot in Detroit. While a Negro pleads for help as he is hauled away by ruffians, Lincoln can do nothing but ponder the consequences of an unfair draft law that exempts anybody who can afford to pay $300 to the U. S. Treasury.*

Opposite: Five companies of the 27th Michigan Infantry were sent to Detroit in March 1863 to help secure the peace in the wake of a draft riot that singled out Negroes as scapegoats. Arno Jaking belonged to the regiment.

The active portion of the mob was composed of excitable boys and young men, some being the sons of prominent citizens. While they were setting fire to the shanties and rookeries and making bonfires of the household goods in the middle of the street, older persons stood by encouraging their acts of lawlessness, and a disturbance which might have been quelled in a few moments by two or three determined men assumed the proportions of a riot, and many citizens passed the night in fear of a general conflagration that might destroy the town.

In the course of time it became evident that Faulkner had been wrongfully convicted and after serving six years he was pardoned. To make some amends for the injustice done him, some charitable citizens set him up in business in a stall of the Central Market, where he was for many years a well known character.

Orrin D. Curtis was 25 years old when he enlisted in the 5th Michigan Cavalry on August 18, 1862. The Butler native fought at Gettysburg and other battles involving the Michigan Cavalry Brigade, his wounds finally resulting in his transfer to the Veteran Reserve Corps in December 1864. The Veteran Reserve Corps was an important component of the Union army. Under its auspices disabled soldiers saw duty as clerks, nurses and garrison troops, freeing able-bodied men for frontline service. After the war Curtis resided in Quincy.

formally organized under the stern leadership of Dorothea Dix, who favored plain-looking women to work the wards of government hospitals so as not to invite unwanted fraternization between nurse and patient.

In hospitals nurses comforted the sick and the wounded, brought them food, changed their bandages, and read and wrote letters. In a predominantly male environment, any act of matronly compassion was well received by soldiers homesick for the touch of a wife, mother or girlfriend. Janette Maxwell Morrill, commissioned a nurse by the colonel of the 6th Michigan Infantry in 1861, left Lawton for a Washington hospital. One day she was frantically trying to attend to the varied needs and requests of several dozen patients when the sound of soft sobbing caught her ear.

"I passed slowly along the ward," she recalled, "among the 50 or 60 beds, and finally reached a youth who looked as though his place were in the schoolroom rather than as a soldier. When he saw me watching him he broke down completely, and cried like a child. My own tears mingled with his as I tried to comfort him. I learned that he was not 16 when he left his widowed mother…and started for the front, and that night was the first time in 18 months that he heard a woman's voice."

One of the Union's most prominent caretakers was Julie S. Wheelock, who was dubbed "Michigan's Florence Nightingale." Like many nurses, Wheelock had a vested interest in going to the front. In September 1862 the 29-year-old schoolteacher left Ionia to look after her wounded older brother, who had been badly wounded at the Battle of Chantilly. She arrived in Washington only to be informed that Private Orville Wheelock, a member of the 8th Michigan Infantry, had died several days earlier.

Julia S. Wheelock, known as "Michigan's Florence Nightingale," emerged as the state's most famous nurse of the war. She is seen here in the doorway of a small hospital operated by the U. S. Sanitary Commission at City Point, Virginia, in 1864.

Grief-stricken, Julie returned to Michigan just long enough to resign her teaching position and be appointed a visiting agent of the Michigan Relief Association. This was just one of several "soldiers' relief" societies organized during the war. All did invaluable work, from scraping lint for bandages to shipping boxes of delicacies to the wounded. Under its auspices Wheelock and another woman, Elmina Brainard of Lapeer, ministered to the needs of state soldiers sprinkled among the many Washington-area hospitals and convalescent camps that sprang up after the war's first battle at Bull Run. They were indefatigable, with Wheelock often capping a hectic 12-hour day with a long evening of baking at her boardinghouse. She was known to bake as many as 40 pies, which she would then distribute to the wounded. Even after being laid low by typhoid fever in 1864 (the disease would hasten her death in 1900), Wheelock cut short her recuperative stay in Michigan. She staged benefit suppers and lectures throughout the North, "begging for the soldiers." For their work Wheelock and Brainard received $5 a week from the Christian Commission, the money provided by donations from Michigan citizens.

Annie Etheridge had just turned 17 when she joined the 2nd Michigan Infantry as a nurse when it set off for Washington in May 1861. Over the next four years, during which time she also served with two other state infantry regiments, the 3rd and the 5th, the gentle but gutsy Detroit girl became a minor folk heroine, with stories of her battleground escapades regularly appearing in print. It was said that her dress was riddled with bullet holes, but that she suffered only one wound, a bullet striking her left hand during the Battle of Chancellorsville. She is supposed to have rallied retreating troops at Spotsylvania.

George Peppet, a private in the 6th Michigan Infantry, shared space in this locket with his wife, Sarah. Mrs. Peppet was made a widow when George, a locomotive engineer after the war, died in a spectacular train wreck in Jackson in 1895.

"Her work was in the field hospitals and on the battlefields," recalled one of her fellow nurses, Mary Gardner Holland, "but it was in the latter service that she accomplished the greatest amount of good and displayed a heroism and devotion to her work that have not been excelled in the annals of the war. Often in the very thickest of the fight she never flinched for a moment in her self-appointed task. Seeking out the wounded who had been overlooked or not reached by the surgeons, she bound up their wounds with the skill and promptness of a practical surgeon. On one occasion the soldier whose wound she was dressing was struck by a shell and literally torn to pieces."

Dubbed "Michigan Annie," Etheridge usually rode a horse on the march, but at night "she wrapped herself in her blanket and slept upon the ground with all the hardihood of the common soldier." As a volunteer Etheridge received no pay, but after the war the heroine was rewarded by the government with a civil service job in Detroit. It wasn't until 1892 that army nurses were allowed to apply for pensions for their wartime service. When they were approved, recipients could look forward to a $12 check every month for the rest of their lives.

A handful of audacious women tried to enlist, and in at least two recorded cases were successful. The state fielded perhaps the most famous female soldier of the entire conflict, Sarah Emma Edmonds of Flint, who managed to keep her gender a secret during her two years with Annie Etheridge's original unit, the 2nd Michigan Infantry. Just before the war Edmonds, a Canadian by birth, had fled an arranged marriage and settled in Rhode Island. There she found a job selling Bibles and was soon transferred to Michigan. With the shelling of Fort Sumter, the confused 18-year-old pondered her role. "It was not my intention, or desire, to seek my own personal ease and comfort while so much sorrow and distress filled the land," she later wrote. "But the great question to be decided, was, what can I do? What part am I to act in this great drama?"

Lewis Fry strikes a confident pose. The young private from Burr Oak signed up with the 7th Michigan Infantry and was one of several hundred Union soldiers taken prisoner at the Battle of Reams Station, Virginia on August 25, 1864.

Rufus Snook followed his older brother into the ranks of the 22nd Michigan Infantry. Unfortunately, the 17-year-old private from Utica caught a fever while the regiment was encamped in Chattanooga, Tennessee. He died on May 10, 1864, causing his brother to scrawl a note across the top of a photograph of their camp: "Rufus A. Snook died in HdQr tent."

She enlisted as a male nurse with the 2nd Michigan, diligently carrying out her duties at Bull Run and subsequent battles under the alias "Franklin Thompson." Although there's evidence that a few of her comrades knew or suspected her real gender (one of whom she may have had an affair with), she was never "outed." Her postwar memoirs, which she admitted to embroidering in order to spur sales, had her occasionally serving as a spy after the regiment was reassigned to the western theater. She later downplayed this role with the observation, "So much mean deception is not pleasant to think about in times of peace." Afraid that her gentler deception would be uncovered by a doctor when she came down with malaria in April 1863, Edmonds deserted her regiment and joined the U. S. Christian Commission for the last half of the war. Following her wartime service, Edmonds returned to Michigan, married a Canadian carpenter, and eventually settled in Houston, Texas. She died there in 1898.

Several years before her death, Edmonds attended a reunion of her regiment in Flint. Colonel Orlando Poe and the rest of the men of the 2nd Michigan were chagrined when the

Sisters in Arms: "I Am Not What I Seem"

Nobody knows how many women were able to disguise themselves as men and join the Union army; estimates range from just a handful to as many as two or three hundred. What is certain is that only one of them, Sarah Emma Edmonds, who served at various times as a soldier, spy and mail carrier with the 2nd Michigan Infantry, was ever granted membership in the Grand Army of the Republic. In this passage from her 1865 memoir, *Nurse and Spy in the Union Army*, Edmonds describes finding a wounded Yankee on the battlefield of Antietam and discovering that, as Private "Franklin Thompson," she was not alone in her subterfuge.

In passing among the wounded after they had been carried from the field, my attention was attracted by the pale, sweet face of a youthful soldier who was severely wounded in the neck. The wound still bled profusely, and the boy was growing faint from loss of blood. I stooped down and asked him if there was anything he would like to have done for him. The soldier turned a pair of beautiful, clear, intelligent eyes upon me for a moment in an earnest gaze, and then, as if satisfied with the scrutiny, said faintly, "Yes, yes; there is something to be done, and that quickly, for I am dying."

Something in the tone and voice made me look more closely at the face of the speaker, and that look satisfied me that my suspicion was well founded. I went to one of the surgeons in attendance, and requested him to come and see my patient. He did so, and after a moment's examination of the wound told me that nothing could be done whatever to save him. He then left me, and I administered a little brandy and water to strengthen the wounded boy, for he evidently wished to tell me something that was on his mind before he died. The little trembling hand beckoned me closer, and I knelt down beside him and bent my head until it touched the golden locks on the pale brow before me; I listened with breathless attention to catch every sound which fell from those dying lips, the substance of which was as follows:

"I can trust you, and will tell you a secret. I am not what I seem, but am a female. I enlisted from the purest motives, and have remained undiscovered and unsuspected. I have neither father, mother nor sister. My only brother was killed today. I closed his eyes about an hour before I was wounded. I shall soon be with him. I am a Christian, and have maintained the Christian character ever since I entered the army. I have performed the duties of a soldier faithfully, and am willing to die for the cause of truth and freedom. My trust is in God, and I die in peace. I wish you to bury me with your own hands, that none may know after my death that I am other than my appearance indicates."

Then looking at me again in that earnest, scrutinizing manner, she said: "I know I can trust you—will you do as I have requested?"

I assured her that she might place implicit confidence in me, and that I would do as she had desired me. Then I sought out a chaplain, who came and prayed with her. She was calm and peaceful. I remained with her until she died, which was about an hour. Then making a grave for her under the shadow of a mulberry tree near the battlefield, apart from all others, with the assistance of two of the boys who were detailed to bury the dead, I carried her remains to that lonely spot and gave her a soldier's burial, without coffin or shroud, only a blanket for a winding-sheet. There she sleeps in that beautiful forest where the soft southern breezes sigh mournfully through the foliage, and the little birds sing sweetly above her grave.

Battlefield nurse "Michigan Annie" Etheridge. This picture was taken several years after the war.

Private Thompson" who had served as an orderly at Fredericksburg and carried mail in Kentucky arrived in women's clothes. After the initial shock wore off, they readily accepted her as one of their own. "I think I would have recognized her anywhere," stated Poe, who added that a "single glance at her in the proper character caused me to wonder how I ever could have mistaken her for a man, and I readily recall many things which ought to have betrayed her, except that no one thought of finding a woman in a soldier's dress."

Because physical exams were rudimentary and so many beardless young men were in uniform, women like Edmonds were able to sneak into the army more often than Colonel Poe ever suspected. Maintaining one's secret was difficult, however. One whose true sex was quickly discovered belonged to the 7th Michigan Cavalry. As the *Detroit Advertiser and Tribune* reported in its February 25, 1863 edition:

> A FEMALE SOLDIER This morning about 11 o'clock, a very pretty woman who gave her name as Mary Burns, was arrested by officer Ven for being attired in soldier's habiliments. It appears that about two weeks ago her lover enlisted in the Seventh Cavalry, and immediately was made a dashing sergeant. Mary, with a remarkable love for Union (of herself and Sergeant) donned soldier's garb, and also enlisted in the regiment, with the determination to follow him. She enrolled her name as John Burns. She had been in the regiment indicated for about ten days. She was taken to jail and will be arraigned at the Police Court.

The legendary vivandiere, "Michigan Bridget" Divers, is credited with twice rallying faltering troops in battle.

First Sergeant William Shakespeare: "Do not be alarmed, dear mother...."

Later that year the *New York Illustrated News* published a story detailing the exploits of Annie Lillybridge. Under the heading of "The Romance of Poor, Young Girl," the paper breathlessly told of Annie, madly in love with a lieutenant in the 21st Michigan Infantry, who "resolved to share his dangers and be near him." Thus she slipped into uniform, behaving with "marked gallantry" at the Battle of Pea Ridge, where she shot a Rebel who was drawing a bead on her lover. During the course of this subterfuge, Annie "managed to keep her secret from all—not even the object of her attachment, who met her every day, was aware of her presence so near him."

The sensational story turned out to be sheer fiction—in fact, it may even have been inspired by the Mary Burns incident—but if nothing else it did help illustrate the growing reputation of Michigan women during the war.

Homesick warriors wasted little time getting "reacquainted" with wives and lovers. When Captain George Burchell of the 24th Michigan Infantry returned to Detroit on leave in late November 1864, he wrote his commanding officer, "We have had four inches of snow here....been cold as thunder, but I feel all right at home." His infant son, George Jr., had been the result of an earlier leave, and Burchell slyly noted, "If I have not made another boy, I assure you it is no fault of mine."

Home fires fed on intermingled feelings of hope and dread. On farms and in towns across the state, those with loved ones at the front waited—and fretted. "We were surprised to hear that you had inlisted," Lydia Watkins wrote her 19-year-old son, Benton, after he had impulsively left their Cannon Township farm one spring day in 1863 and joined the 8th Michigan Cavalry.

I hope you considered what you were doing when you took that step you could not have done it ignorently and therefouer I would have you be a faithful soldier and bear with patience and fortitude the hardships a soldier has to bear. I hope you will never allow yourself to be tempted to do wrong such as drinking swearing gambling or any of the vices so prevalent in the army. Benton I have made it my rule to retire to that little back bedroom every evening and thier Pray to God to keep and preserve you from harm…and pray that this war may come to a speedy close. This is my only support now   there is not an hour in the day but what I think of you.

William Shakespeare's mother in Kalamazoo was another one of the thousands of noncombatants in Michigan whose daily thoughts were of a soldier who at any moment might fall dead or hideously disfigured on some broken ground hundreds of miles beyond one's reach. Her boy was 17 years old when he enlisted in the 2nd Michigan Infantry in the spring of 1861. Over the next two years the slightly built teenager displayed a commendable blend of grit and intelligence as his regiment participated in the two battles of Bull Run and the siege of Vicksburg, among other actions.

Michigan nurses tend to the wounded at Cold Harbor, Virginia in 1864.

On July 11, 1863, Shakespeare—by now a first sergeant—was shot through both legs near the hips during the 2nd Regiment's charge on enemy lines at Jackson, Mississippi. As he lay helpless and softly groaning on the battlefield with both thigh bones shattered, his pain-addled mind conjuring up visions of the gentler and more orderly life he had led back in Kalamazoo, he received several more gunshot wounds.

By the time Shakespeare was removed to a field hospital, he was so far gone that the regimental surgeons, after a conference, concluded his wounds were mortal and his case hopeless. One of them, Dr. Henry Cleland of Detroit, sat down and wrote a letter to Mrs. Shakespeare, informing her of her son's condition. Before sending it off, Dr. Cleland read it to the soldier.

"Doctor," Shakespeare responded feebly, "I want to add a few words to it."

"Why," the surprised doctor asked, "do you think you can write?"

"Why, yes, I think I can scrawl out a few words if you prop me up," said Shakespeare. With that he took pen to paper and in an unsteady hand wrote: "Do not be alarmed, dear mother; the doctor is mistaken. I am going to get well and come back to you."

Unlike his namesake, this William Shakespeare claimed no literary genius, but his postscript demonstrated a cast-iron spirit.

"Some time after that," recorded the regiment's postwar chronicler, "he was brought up to the general hospital at Cincinnati, Ohio, where he lay for nine long months on his back, in an agony of suffering, unable to stir from one side to the other, and during all that time the doctors were in doubt about his final recovery. But his obstinate determination not to die and to

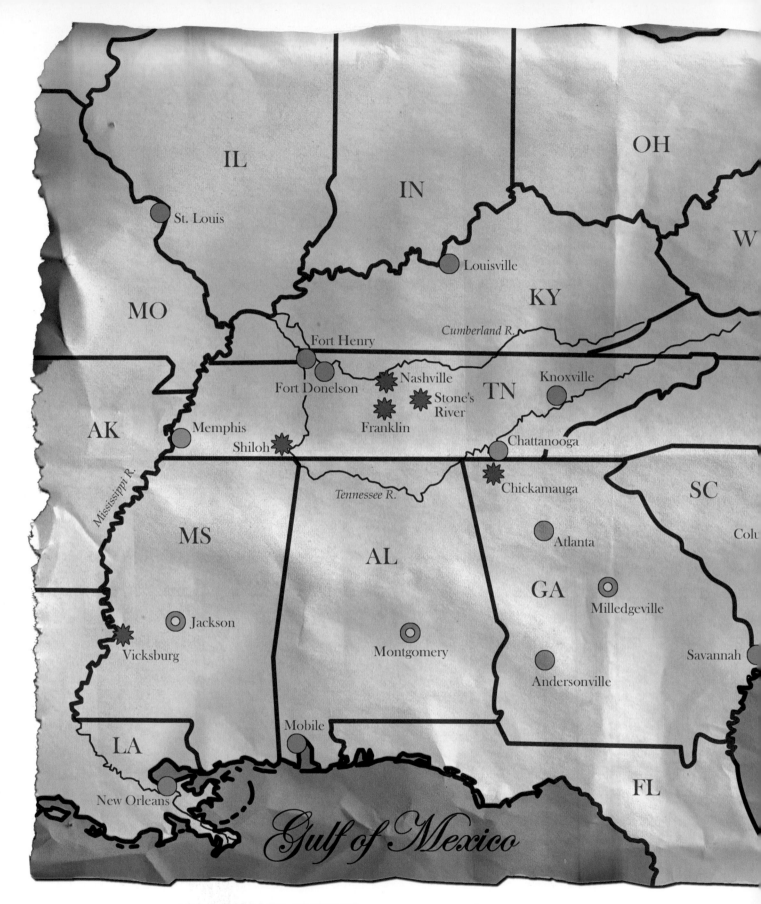

PA

Gettysburg

Philadelphia

MD

DE

VA

Appomattox

C

Raleigh

Wilmington

eston

Fort Sumter

Atlantic Ocean

N

100 Miles

PA

Gettysburg

MD

Antietam Cr.

Harper's Ferry

Antietam

Baltimore

Annapolis

Washington

Winchester

Potomac R.

Arlington

Bull Run

Chancellorsville

Bull Run

Wilderness

Fredericksburg

Cedar Mountain

Rappahannock R.

Spotsylvania

Cold Harbor

Chickahominy R.

Gaines' Mill

James R.

Malvern Hill

Richmond

York R.

Appomattox

Yorktown

VA

Petersburg

Norfolk

⬤ City or Town

◎ State Capital

National Capital

✴ Battle

53 Miles

Bruce Worden 2004

Like so many other young men in the war, Josiah Ketchum of the 6th Michigan Infantry was cut down in the prime of life. Before falling victim to disease at New Orleans in 1864, the veteran volunteer from Lenawee County posed for this photograph with an older member of the family, possibly his brother. Ketchum's family remembered him with a lock of his blond hair and the inscription, "this lock of hair I used to Ware But now trust it in your care Josiah Ketcun."

come back to that dear mother, pulled him through to final recovery." Shakespeare was discharged on June 1, 1864, his active career in the field terminated, but not his life. Twenty years later he was serving the state as its appointed quartermaster general.

As seen, the thoughts of loved ones back in Michigan often sustained and inspired men facing a dire fate. One August day in 1862, as the stage was being set for the Battle of Cedar Mountain in Virginia, Lieutenant William Duncan Wilkins of the 2nd Michigan Infantry took the daguerreotype of his wife Elizabeth out of his valise and tucked it into his pocket—"that if I died, it might be buried with me," he later explained.

Instead Wilkins was captured and moved to Libby Prison, a four-story tobacco warehouse converted into an airless, sweltering holding pen for thousands for captured Yankees. "The floor is an inch deep in thick black grease," the 35-year-old officer recorded in his diary. "An open privy is on one side of room for the common use of this crowd, exhaling the most dreadful smells. The walls are smeared from the floors above with the slops & excretions of the hundreds of men confined overhead."

Before volunteering, Wilkins had been a lawyer and president of the Detroit Board of Education. He had led a predictable and fulfilling life. Now he was reduced to the level of a beast, wallowing in filth and vermin, slowly starving, and gradually losing his mind as scores of men died around him. During these trying times, he confided in his diary, "thoughts of home & its treasures will sometimes fill my heart to overflowing….I have been indulging in a sweet fancy of how Home looks on this summer evening; the shady porch, the children playing round the steps; & the leafy chestnut whispering words of love to her whose heart must be so saddened. God grant her strength, & faith, & hope." Thanks in part to whatever sustenance he could derive from dreams of his home in Michigan, Wilkins survived Libby. He was paroled and discharged, returning to Detroit late in the summer of 1863.

Not every family enjoyed a happy homecoming. Lucius "Lute" Shattuck was one of 9,200 men from Wayne County to serve in Mr. Lincoln's army during the Civil War. Many of them, including the 26-year-old lieutenant from Plymouth, were surprisingly literate. Shattuck, a member of the 24th Michigan Infantry, routinely penned long letters home, describing camp conditions and enemy engagements as the regiment moved towards its destiny at a crossroads village in Pennsylvania in the summer of 1863. Many of the surviving letters are housed at the Plymouth Historical Museum, where they were donated by family members years ago.

"This has been a quiet Sabbath for camp," Shattuck wrote one Sunday from a campsite in Virginia. "It used to seem to me that Sunday never came to the Army, or if it did it brought with it extra duties. Since we have been in winter quarters, however, it seems to have been the aim throughout the regiment to respect the day in a civilized manner"—reading, playing cards, playing ball. The young volunteer did admit to bouts of homesickness. "I often think of the Plymouth Brass Band and wonder if they still sustain themselves and how they progress."

Shattuck and the rest of the 24th ran into a buzzsaw on July 1, 1863. Union and Confederate forces more or less stumbled across each other, leading to the costliest and most storied battle of the war. The Michigan regiment suffered a frightful number of casualties, one of whom was Shattuck. He was wounded twice but refused his captain's order to leave the battlefield. In the chaos that accompanied three days of intense fighting, Shattuck's friends lost track of him. Eventually the lieutenant's diary was found on a nearby ridge. A bullet hole was shot through it. Subsequent searches and interviews with comrades provided no solace for Shattuck's mother, whose letter to her own mother in Pontiac, dated July 26, 1863, confirmed everybody's worse fears.

"We know nothing more of poor Lute's last hours or of his resting place than at first," she wrote. "It may be some one in after years will turn up what could give some tidings of him [but] others think we shall never know any more of him than that he lost his life in the battle of Gettysburg." ●

"Ten Died Last Night": The Prison Diary of Henry Ladd

Andersonville, Georgia was the most infamous of the Confederate prison camps, as the "dead wagon" in the left foreground of this northern print suggests. By the last year of the war upwards of 32,000 Union enlisted men were packed into the 26-square-acre stockade. Due to the lack of food, medicine and sanitation, at least 12,912 of them perished and were buried there. Most historians believe the actual death count was much higher.

More than 200,000 Union soldiers were captured during the war, including several thousand from Michigan. Among their number was Henry Ladd. A Dearborn farmer before he joined the 24th Michigan, Ladd endured seven months of misery inside a succession of prisons in Virginia and South Carolina. It was Ladd's misfortune to fall into Rebel hands at a time when the parole system used earlier in the war had been suspended by General U. S. Grant, who saw no advantage in allowing exchanged Confederates to return to their severely depleted units. The North, which enjoyed a huge edge in manpower and thus could better afford to let their soldiers sit out the war, did not resume prisoner exchanges until February 1865. Despite the severe privations, Ladd considered himself lucky—by war's end, 22,600 Northerners, including several comrades from his regiment, died while prisoners of war. This is an abridged version of the diary Ladd kept in captivity.

August 19, 1864: I am a prisoner; marched to Petersburg and lodged in gaol.

August 20, 1864: Start for Richmond. Escorted to a tobacco warehouse near Libby Prison.

August 21, 1864: Feel rather rough after sleeping on the hard floor with wet clothes on. Move into Libby Prison. All are searched for the third time. Marched to Belle Isle.

August 22, 1864: Slept on the ground without a rag under or over me. No tents on the island. Had one meal to-day, half a cup of bean soup and corn bead. Rained all the afternoon and night. No tents nor blankets.

August 25, 1864: Up and ready for my corn dodger. Wish I was home to have a good meal. There are 4,500 prisoners on about two and one-half acres here. Bought a loaf of bread for $1.50.

August 28, 1864: Dreamed of home last night. How I wish that it was so. I would attend church in old Dearborn. Had a cup of bean soup and one-quarter pound corn dodger to-day.

September 1, 1864: Our Government refuses to parole us. The men think it hard.

September 11, 1864: Got half a loaf for this day's ration. Have an old bag for a bed.

September 13, 1864: Sold my haversack for two loaves and ate them for breakfast. Had a good prayer meeting with large attendance.

September 15, 1864: Sick with fever. Sold my ring for a loaf of bread.

October 4, 1864: This is a hard life to live and starve, but hope for better days. 1,000 men went south to North Carolina today from Belle Island.

October 6, 1864: Left Belle Island to-day and reached Danville at 5 p.m. Sixty men in one cattle car. Such a crowd and such a time! Sell my ink bottle for bread. Good-bye Belle Isle, may I never see it again. Have ate all of my bread. Still hungry.

October 7, 1864: No rations. Sell my eye-glass for two apples.

October 8, 1864: Slept in an open field. Arrived at Salisbury, North Carolina. No rations. Staid all night in an open field. Have not slept for four nights.

October 9, 1864: We are in an inclosure of twelve acres. Got two meals to-day. Am shivering with cold.

October 13, 1864: Got some soup and 5 hard tack to-day. Flour is $225 a barrel, Confederate money. Pies and cakes three dollars each.

October 16, 1864: Wish that I was home to go to church in Dearborn. Home, sweet home—will I ever see you again? Shall keep up the good cheer and trust in Providence. One of our officers was shot to-day while hanging his clothes on a tree.

October 18, 1864: How hard to be here starving and suffering cold when one has a home with plenty. Could I only have the crumbs of my table I would not complain.

October 20, 1864: No news yet from home. Eighty a week are dying here. Boys digging and making earth shanties. The hospital is overflowing. Diarrhea and black fever prevail, caused by starvation.

October 23, 1864: Up and ready for my half loaf. It can't be colder in Michigan.

October 24, 1864: Got a cup of flour and molasses to eat to-day. Got one tent for 100 men to-day.

October 25, 1864: Sold my hat band for a loaf of bread. Two loads of dead went out. They bury our men without coffins or straw.

October 26, 1864: Noon and no rations. Discouraged. Ten died last night. Oh, will our government leave us here to perish.

October 27, 1864: Cloudy and rainy, How our men suffer. Will get no provisions till to-morrow. Will not the Almighty punish men for such treatment of prisoners?

October 29, 1864: No food for 36 hours. Will get no bread to-day. Almost famished. The men are about to raise a mob and break out. Twelve died this morning and others dying every hour.

George W. Robertson left Mount Clemens in 1862 not knowing he was to spend half of his enlistment in a series of prison camps. On September 20, 1863, the 25-year-old lieutenant of Company F, 22nd Michigan Infantry was captured at the Battle of Chickamauga. Over the next 19 months he was confined at 12 different camps in four states; the peripatetic prisoner finally was freed on April 26, 1865 and discharged exactly two months later at Nashville. He came home a captain, having been promoted while in captivity.

October 31, 1864: Got half a loaf of bread to-day. Eighteen dead hauled out to-day.

November 1, 1864: Sold my hat for a loaf of bread and $500 Confederate money.

November 5, 1864: A few of our men are enlisting in the Confederate army hoping to escape death here. The men are forced to it by starvation. Language nor pen can describe the suffering we undergo. Men die every hour.

November 7, 1864: How I wish I was back to my old Wayne County home. God has kept me thus far, and I will rely on his mercy. Six hundred came from Richmond last night.

November 14, 1864: Hear that Lincoln is elected. Bourassas of Company F, Twenty-fourth Michigan is dead.

November 19, 1864: Lay abed all day to keep warm. Cold and Stormy. Got half a loaf of poor corn bread. Men are dying like sheep with the rot.

November 24, 1864: Thanksgiving day at home. We get only a quarter loaf of bread. Hardly enough to live on. Forty die daily.

November 25, 1864: I write with sad heart. Only got four ounces of bread today. Suffering with cold. Nearly naked. Covered with lice. Oh, what a fate! Must we die? Will not God deliver us from this hell?

November 26, 1864: Yesterday the mob secured the guard and rallied to get out. We lost in killed and wounded about ninety.

December 11, 1864: Men still dying over fifty a day. Hear that Sherman is twenty-five miles of Savannah. Hope something will turn up.

December 13, 1864: Slept none last night it was so cold.

December 15, 1864: On quarter rations. Hear that we are to go to South Carolina. Hope that we will get out of this accursed place. Shall I ever see home again?

December 17, 1864: Bought an onion for a dollar.

December 23, 1864: Nearly frozen. No fire. Only a piece of raw corn bread to eat. How long must we suffer so?

December 25, 1864: Had a loaf of bread and rice soup for Christmas dinner.

December 30, 1864: Half a loaf only. Getting discouraged. Men still dying like sheep. No relief. Our government has forsaken us! God forgive but we never can.

January 2, 1865: Living in bed to keep warm. Oh, how dreary is such a life. Will we ever get out of this place?

January 13, 1865: Hunted lice on my shirt all day. Oh what a life!

January 20, 1865: Been in bed six days to keep warm.

January 23, 1865: Men dying like sheep every hour. Oh, what a horrid place! Such a stench and lice. One can hardly live.

From Battle Creek, Wyman Dietzel enlisted in Company C of the 20th Michigan Infantry on August 9, 1862. He was captured at Peebles' Farm, Virginia on September 30, 1864 and spent the next six months in prison camps before being exchanged. He was discharged at Detroit on June 2, 1865.

January 26, 1865: Nearly frozen to death. No fire, no clothing, nor anything to keep warm. One can lie down and die of despair. Hope is all that is left.

January 30, 1865: Get less to eat every day. Am poor; will not weigh ninety pounds.

February 19, 1865: Parole papers are made out and we are to start for our lines. Thank God, the day of deliverance has come. One thousand left last night. There have died in this prison 5,019 prisoners since I came here last October.

February 22, 1865: Left Salisbury prison for the north at noon.

With that final entry, Ladd filled up his dairy and began the long trek home. He returned to Dearborn, dying there in 1910.

The 24th Michigan on the first day at Gettysburg, as depicted by artist Robert Thom.

Chapter 5

IRON
MEN

William Keagle, who hailed from Hudson, joined the 24th Michigan on March 15, 1865, by which time the storied regiment had fought its last battles. Prominently resting on the young recruit's knee is the famous black hat of the Iron Brigade.

On a warm, breezy Sunday in June 1989, with much of the rest of Michigan staying home to watch the Detroit Pistons battle the Los Angeles Lakers in the NBA finals, a group of middle-aged men in itchy wool uniforms and square-toed boots left their vans and cars and, as smartly as they could manage, marched with their wooden muskets a quarter-mile to the site of the statue located in the western part of McPherson's Woods at Gettysburg National Military Park. Salutes were exchanged, a prayer was said, and speeches were delivered. The governors of Michigan and Pennsylvania sent regrets, but two busloads of tourists did stop out of curiosity and watched the proceedings with interest from the road.

Thirty-minutes after it started, the ceremony was over, and the men of the reconstituted 24th Michigan Volunteer Infantry piled into their vans and cars and drove the nine hours back to Detroit, in time to go to work Monday morning.

It was more than Captain Malachi O'Donnell ever was able to do. The 25-year-old company commander, an Irish immigrant who had been a printer in Detroit before joining the 24th, was killed on July 1, 1863. He was shot through the back of the head, not all that far from where the marble statue commemorating his regiment's storied stand was erected in 1889. Lieutenant Michael Dempsey, himself a printer by trade, hastily tried to retrieve his fallen friend's sword, a treasured gift that the popular captain had vowed never to dishonor. But a Confederate advance forced the Michigan men off the field. After the battle a search was made for O'Donnell, but, reported the *Detroit Free Press*, "owing to the length of time which had elapsed, and also to the

115 IRON MEN

Willie Young, a 13-year-old Detroiter, served as a drummer in Company G of the 24th Michigan.

fact that the rebels had stripped every dead body wearing a good uniform, it was impossible to identify his remains." O'Donnell is presumed to have been buried in one of the many mass graves at Gettysburg.

Joe Toth is fascinated with any story involving the *real* 24th Michigan, and for good reason. As part of the fabled Iron Brigade, Captain O'Donnell and the rest of the regiment helped hold off an overwhelmingly larger force of Confederates on the first day at Gettysburg. It's been said that these men may have saved the Union. One could hardly ask for better role models. But the public memory of such heroics has faded past the point of apathy.

"The average person in the street doesn't know or care what the 24th Michigan did at Gettysburg," conceded Toth, who can tell you that on that distant afternoon, an appalling 80 percent of the Michigan volunteers were lost in several hours of point-blank musketry. It was a loss unmatched by any of the other 400 Union regiments that fought there. Such historical acumen comes naturally to Toth, who spearheaded the drive to refurbish the monument grateful Michigan citizens erected in 1889. He is a longtime member of the 24th Michigan Volunteer Infantry, an organization of Civil War buffs whose costumed members look like they've just stepped out of a Mathew Brady daguerreotype. Since his retirement, the former auto designer has worked fulltime crafting leather accoutrements for fellow 19th-century hobbyists.

Like many monuments at national battlefields, the one honoring the 24th Michigan had fallen into disrepair. Its marble was flecked, its plaque was discolored. The financially strapped National Park Service, responsible for the upkeep, had fallen way behind in its restoration efforts. In 1983, Toth decided he would have the monument refurbished in time for its centennial.

Colonel Henry A. Morrow was wounded and captured at Gettysburg, but escaped to fight on. The commander of the 24th Michigan was wounded a second time at the Battle of the Wilderness. At the time of his discharge he was a brevet brigadier general. He returned to his law practice in Detroit but found civilian life boring. Morrow joined the regular army in 1866, serving mostly in the West while rising to the rank of colonel. He died in Arkansas in 1891.

To make that happen, he called on fellow members of the 24th Michigan. Most were blue-collar workers, many were veterans, and all knew how to handle a rifled musket. Indeed, the very purpose of this group has always been participating in black-powder shooting competitions with similar units around the country. They're not really re-enactors nor "living history" types; they're basically just a bunch of guys who like to blow holes in paper targets with period weapons. But Toth understood that every once in a while something comes along and stirs the soul—something like restoring and rededicating a monument honoring one's namesake.

The National Park Service normally charges about $1,500 to clean a monument, payable in advance. It took a long time, but by the spring of 1989 a string of $10 and $20 contributions left the modern-day Iron Men only about $250 short. The Park Service, impressed with the sincerity of their fund-raising efforts, went ahead and cleaned the statue anyway. At the ceremony, said Toth, "the park ranger gave a speech on the achievements of the 24th Michigan, describing what they had done. But he also spoke about how monuments can bring you a little bit closer to history. He talked of the importance of rededicating monuments so that future generations won't forget the sacrifices they represent."

Michigan's most famous Civil War outfit resulted from one of the few smudges on the state's otherwise praiseworthy record, as in the summer of 1862 citizens found themselves searching for a way of erasing their collective shame over a debacle at a recruiting rally in Detroit.

With the war going badly for the North, President Lincoln had issued a call for 300,000 volunteers. Governor Austin Blair

First Sergeant Augustus Pomeroy (seated at right) with three unidentified non-commissioned officers. The Salem farmer fought in all the major actions of the 24th Michigan and was wounded at Gettysburg. Eighteen months later he was wounded again, this time at Dabney's Mill, Virginia, the decimated regiment's last battle.

responded with a pledge of six new regiments. In mid-July, Detroit Mayor William C. Duncan called for an inspirational rally at the intersection of Woodward and Michigan Avenues to recruit volunteers. But the crowd, incited by Confederate sympathizers from across the river in Canada, mistakenly thought a draft was being proposed and began rioting. The rally broke up.

Humiliated civic leaders decided to do the governor's pledge one better. They would raise an additional infantry regiment, to be called the 24th Michigan Volunteers. By August hundreds of recruits were drilling at the State Fairgrounds, renamed Camp Burns.

The average age of the volunteers was about 25. The oldest was 70-year-old James Nowlin, who dyed his beard and convinced a recruiter he was only 43. The Romulus farmer, who had been born when George Washington was president, would be among the regiment's first casualties, dying of disease. The youngest enlistee was 13-year-old Willie Young of Detroit, who served as a drummer boy. Eighteen-year-old Nelson Pooler, accompanied by his parents, enlisted in Company C. "A few of these boys I already knew," said the Canton farm boy, "but the great majority of them were strangers to me but they proved with few exceptions to be noble characters and who became friends tried and true."

The 24th's commander was Colonel Henry A. Morrow. Born in Virginia and educated in Washington, D.C., the 33-year-old Morrow had served in the Mexican War before opening a law practice in Detroit. At the time he enlisted he was dispensing justice as the first elected judge of Recorder's Court.

On August 29, 1862 the new regiment marched out of Camp Burns. Thousands of citizens packed balconies, sidewalks, rooftops and windows along Woodward and Jefferson

> **"The battle field of Gettysburg was one vast slaughter pen. Dead & wounded lay in all directions. A man that went through the carnage unhurt may call himself a lucky man....Tell father I would as soon throw my old musket down & take a turn at farming as not."**

Letter from Henry C. Matrau, a Michiganian serving with the 6th Wisconsin, to his parents, July 29, 1863

Captain William Speed commanded Company D of the 24th Michigan at Gettysburg. The 32-year-old attorney from Detroit was killed on July 1, just one of many regimental officers to fall that day.

Avenues to wave and cheer them on. It was a spectacular send-off, filled with fluttering handkerchiefs and slaps on knapsacks. "It was worth a life, that march!" said one soldier, unaware of the irony of his remark. One year later, less than 20 percent of the men who boarded two boats to begin the journey east, to the war, would answer roll call.

Near Washington, the regiment joined the Army of the Potomac, where it was assigned to the Iron Brigade. The severely depleted brigade was comprised of the 2nd, 6th and 7th Wisconsin and 19th Indiana regiments, making it the only all-western brigade in the eastern theater. Members of the Iron Brigade displayed a fierce pride that was evident in their choice of headgear. While other Union soldiers wore the standard-issue kepi, they sported wide-brimmed, bell-shaped hats, known as Hardee hats, with the left side turned up and a feather tucked into the crown. The western volunteers had already made a name for themselves at Bull Run, South Mountain and Antietam. The veterans, believing rumors that the Wolverines were "bounty men" who been paid to enlist, gave the newcomers a cool reception.

Admittedly, the Michigan men sometimes gave their comrades from Wisconsin and Indiana reason to wonder about them. On November 4, 1862, Wisconsin soldier Lyman C. Holford noted in his diary:

a little after dark I saw something which was a little the worst of any thing I have yet seen in the army. Some of the boys of the 24th Mich (a new Regt lately attached to our Brigade) found a cow which had been dead for several days and being a little meat hungry they went to work and cut meat from the cow and carried it to camp and ate it

The officers of the 24th worked hard to maintain discipline, drilling their men six hours a day, with an additional four and a half hours spent on "other evolutions of the school of the

Abel Peck was the first of several color bearers to be killed carrying the 24th Michigan's flag, which was shot to ribbons by enemy musketry.

soldier," recalled one soldier. By modern infantry standards, however, the 24th—like all Civil War regiments—spent a pitiful amount of time on their marksmanship. During the regiment's only known target practice during this period three soldiers were wounded and another man died of a heart attack, hardly the kind of performance to inspire awe in the rest of the brigade.

One sunny December day in 1862, the men of the 24th Michigan at last got a chance to prove their mettle. In a prelude to the battle of Fredericksburg, the regiment was called on to clear some woods of rebel horse artillery and snipers. The rest of the brigade, held back in reserve, looked on with interest as the untested Michiganians entered the woods.

A cannon ball immediately tore the head off 18-year-old Private Lewis Hattie, who ingloriously became the regiment's first death in action. Within short order another man went down with an arm wound, a second was decapitated by a cannon ball, and several others were struck by shellfire. Sensing panic, Colonel Morrow halted the advance and—as the rest of the brigade watched incredulously—put the 24th through the manual of arms. The drill had a calming effect on the men, who then went on to rid the woods of the enemy. The action cost the regiment several dozen men killed and wounded, but it won them the respect they had so long desired. One Wisconsin soldier changed his mind, calling the 24th the "most pugnacious and frightful array of Wolverines, all teeth and toenails."

The following May, the Michigan men were issued the brigade's trademark hats, the ultimate sign of acceptance. "No other troops wore them," said one thrilled Wolverine. "They made our appearance, like the name of our brigade, unique."

The 24th's Henry Randall, a 23-year-old farmer from Birmingham, had a finger blown off at Gettysburg. He is seen here in his hospital shirt.

Following page: In this Dale Gallon painting, Colonel Morrow, flag in hand, and the rest of the 24th Michigan hold |their ground as the regiment is hammered by overwhelming numbers of Confederates.

By the end of that June, Robert E. Lee's army had side-stepped the Union army defending Washington and invaded the North via Pennsylvania. In Lee's sights was the state capital of Harrisburg, from which assaults on Baltimore or Philadelphia could be attempted. On the morning of July 1, 1863, the men of the 24th Michigan ate a breakfast of pork, hardtack and coffee, after which suddenly came orders to march. A few miles north, in the crossroads town of Gettysburg, an advance force of rebels hoping to find a store of shoes to replace their own battered footwear had stumbled across a handful of Union cavalrymen. Shots were exchanged in the gray morning light and, quite unexpectedly, the titanic battle that would eventually involve more than 170,000 men (including 4,834 from Michigan) and cause 43,000 casualties was underway.

Lee had cautioned his advance troops to avoid a pitched battle until two sections of his army, each about 25 miles away, could be brought up. As the sun rose on a warm, clear day, however, overconfident Confederate field commanders threw more and more troops against the outnumbered Union cavalrymen. The Iron Brigade and other Union forces rushed into the fray, some loading their weapons on the run.

By 10 o'clock the Iron Brigade was at the crest of McPherson's Ridge. There, 40 yards away, stood the first of several Confederate brigades. The rebels had expected a soft touch, most probably a state militia, to defend the ridge. As the rebels furiously exchanged volleys with the Wisconsin regiments, the Michigan and Indiana men fixed bayonets and rushed through a ravine, quickly outflanking the startled Southerners. "That ain't no militia!" shouted one. "There's them damn black hats!"

Harrison H. Jeffords, colonel of the 4th Michigan Infantry, was killed by a bayonet thrust in the wheat field at Gettysburg. The "whirlwind in the wheat field" cost some 500 Confederates their lives (opposite). Later, Private John Houghton of the 4th examined the bodies as they were buried in a mass grave: "on the bank near the trench Lye a large Rebel Sargent one of our mineys balls had passed through His Head so quick that it dislocated all the Confedracy there was in it and it was gradualy oozing out onto the Ground for the flies to Diagnosis. It was said that He was the man that Stabed Colonel Jeffords."

The 24th chased the enemy across a stream. There followed ferocious hand-to-hand combat, with Lieutenant Colonel Mark Flanigan, who was Wayne County sheriff before the war, suffering a leg wound that would eventually require amputation. The Iron Brigade had little time to enjoy the rout, however, as Union troops on its right were overrun. The Iron Brigade beat back the attack, seizing more than 400 prisoners. In the span of an hour, the two leading brigades of Lee's army were destroyed before the Confederate commander-in-chief was fully ready to fight.

Nevertheless, rebels were pouring onto the battlefield faster than Union troops. By noon a Confederate force of 32,000 had formed an arc north and west of Gettysburg. This was more than double the size of the Union forces on the ridges facing them. The Iron Brigade was moved to the extreme left of the forward line, in a grove of trees known as McPherson's Woods, with the 24th Michigan occupying an awkward and exposed salient. Enemy cannon was positioned on a hill above it.

At 3 o'clock the Confederate assault began, signaled by a heavy artillery barrage. Thousands of gray-clad infantry in three long lines stepped forward into the July heat, unleashing the piercing rebel yell that one Michigan soldier remembered as sending "corkscrews down the spine."

Colonel Morrow's men held their fire for what seemed an eternity. Finally, as the rebels splashed across a shallow stream in front of the woods, the colonel gave the order to fire. Licks of flame spit simultaneously from hundreds of rifle barrels, mowing down the front rank of attackers. "No rebel crossed that stream and lived," a soldier later bragged. However, the long line of attackers extended a quarter-mile beyond the Iron

Brigade's position, enabling the rebels to swing around the brigade's left flank. The 24th Michigan was exposed to a murderous crossfire, with volleys crashing into them from their front and left. As rebels poured through the woods, the Michiganians found themselves up against the 26th North Carolina, one of the South's finest regiments. Firing from behind every available tree and log, the Michigan men kept the Tar Heels at a distance as the brigade fell back to the rear of the woods where it formed a second line of battle.

There a fresh brigade of rebels hit the Iron Brigade's right flank. At a distance of only 20 paces the two sides poured round after round into each other's ranks. The noise was deafening. Cannons roared, muskets barked, men cried out. The 24th formed a new line of battle behind a small ravine. By now almost three-quarters of the regiment was gone, its dead and wounded carpeting the woods and slopes. Although fresh Union troops were gathering near Cemetery Hill, south of the town, more time was needed to get them properly deployed.

Among the 4th Michigan's casualties at Gettysburg were Albert Boise (left), who was wounded, and Adelbert Day, who was captured. Today, a monument commemorating the regiment's valor during those three hot days in July 1863 stands close to the spot where Colonel Jeffords fell.

The Michiganians retreated to an open field. The corporal carrying the regimental flag fell, shot through the chest. Colonel Morrow seized the torn banner to rally the men. Private William Kelly intervened, saying, "The colonel of the 24th Michigan shall not carry the colors while I am alive." A second later Kelly was shot dead, and another private grabbed the flag before it reached the ground.

Men fought in a fog, as smoke boiled from the battlefield. A bullet struck Morrow in the head, leaving Captain Albert M. Edwards in command. As the desperate action reached its final stage, Edwards looked around for the regimental flag. He discovered the shredded banner fluttering upright in the breeze, its staff cradled in the crook of a dead soldier's arm. Finally, as the afternoon began to draw to a close, the brigade was ordered to quit the field. It withdrew as orderly as it could through the town, through a "tempest of death," said a correspondent for the *New York World*. The shell-shocked reporter was just a few feet away from an "old man, a private in a company belonging to the 24th Michigan," who was struck "by a cannon ball which tore through him, exhorting such an intense cry of mortal pain as I pray God I shall ever hear again."

The remaining members of the mauled regiment struggled up the slope of Cemetery Hill, where Captain Edwards planted the flag next to a cannon and then collapsed, utterly exhausted, on a tombstone.

On the afternoon of the second day at Gettysburg, the 16th Michigan Infantry was rushed to Little Round Top to help secure an unoccupied position on the Union army's left flank. After beating back two desperate enemy assaults, some of the Wolverines began to abandon their position– until Colonel Vincent Strong, commanding the brigade, rushed forward, riding crop in hand, and shouted, "Don't give an inch!" Seconds later Vincent was shot in the groin; he died five days later.

Of the 499 Michigan men who had started the day, only three officers and 96 enlisted men made it back to Cemetery Hill by the following morning. Many of the wounded had been captured and would remain prisoners for the duration of the war; dozens were destined to die in Southern prison camps. The shattered regiment would see limited action through the rest of the war. The brigade as a whole lost 1,212 of its 1,883 men, a casualty rate of 65 percent. In proportion to its numbers, the Iron Brigade sustained the heaviest loss of any brigade in the entire war. But in the opening hours of the greatest battle ever fought on the North American continent, it had inflicted devastating losses on some of the South's finest troops, possibly saving the Union in the process. For the black hatters in the 24th Michigan and its sister regiments had managed to buy time for the Army of the Potomac to concentrate its strength along a strategic piece of ground, Cemetery Ridge, upon which Lee would unleash a famous and ill-fated charge two days later.

Meanwhile, a private in the 24th summarized the first day's slaughter on the pages of his diary. "Gettysburg terrible," wrote Edward Raymor, who by his count had personally killed 14 Confederates. "Lieutenant [Buhl] rebuked me for drinking after. Said I would not be promoted. I do not care."

Colonel Norval E. Welch, an Ann Arbor attorney before the war, commanded the 16th Michigan Infantry at Gettysburg. The usually dependable officer was criticized for having "a bad day" for prematurely withdrawing some of his men from Little Round Top. Welch would redeem his reputation the following year, leading a charge on a strong Confederate position at Peebles' Farm, Virginia. Welch, his term of enlistment expired, was shot in the head and killed. "Had he survived the day's battle he would probably be home with his friends," observed a correspondent. "Such is war."

The 24th wasn't the only Michigan regiment heavily engaged at Gettysburg. Away from the bullet-scarred trees of McPherson's Woods, nearly a dozen other state units also saw action. On the second day of the battle, men of the 16th Michigan Infantry helped stave off a Confederate assault on Little Round Top, shooting, slugging, punching and at one point desperately rolling boulders downhill at their attackers. At the same time the 400 men of the 4th Michigan Infantry were part of a series of charges and counter-charges through a wheat field that produced some of the most vicious hand-to-hand fighting of the war.

Commanding the 4th was Colonel Harrison H. Jeffords, a 26-year-old attorney from Dexter. According to the recollections of one 4th Michigan soldier, Robert Campbell, the regiment's "beautiful flag was seized by a Confederate, who was triumphantly bearing it off [when] Colonel Jeffords rushed after him, slew him with his sword, and seized the flag." Moments later, another rebel thrust his bayonet through Jeffords. He died the following day, deliriously moaning "Mother, mother, mother…." His death became his distinction, as Jeffords is the only man absolutely known to have been killed by a bayonet at Gettysburg. Today, a monument to the 4th Michigan stands in the lower part of the wheat field where Jeffords was slain.

As Jeffords lay dying on July 3, the stage was being set for two almost impossibly dramatic actions. That afternoon Lee decided to roll the dice, sending 12,000 men under the command of General George Pickett in a frontal assault on the Union line, centered on Cemetery Ridge. Standing shoulder to shoulder in a line that seemed to stretch for eternity, the men advanced over a mile of ground under withering fire. Pickett's charge was grand, but doomed.

The men of Battery I of the
1st Light Artillery—also known
as the 9th Michigan Battery—
helped repulse Pickett's charge.
Lieutenant John P. Church, seated
at right, hailed from Hudson.
After the war he became a doctor
and settled in Washington,
D.C. He died in 1919 at age
79 and was buried at Arlington
National Cemetery.

Charles L. Rice, a lieutenant in the 16th Michigan, survived to tell friends back in Detroit about the fight amongst the boulders on Little Round Top.

William C. Way, chaplain of the 24th Michigan, helped bury the dead and care for some of the 21,000 Yankees and Confederates wounded at Gettysburg and left behind in the village after their armies marched off. "It is sad to look upon the decimated ranks of one of the bravest regiments that ever left the Wolverine State," the reverend wrote. "Gettysburg is one vast hospital. The Court House, College, Seminary, Churches, Schoolhouses, warehouses and private buildings are filled with wounded....I went upon the field with two of our regiment and buried several of our comrades and there witnessed a strange vandalism—our dead were robbed of everything, their bodies stripped of clothing and shoes!"

"The artillery duel before the charge was something terrific and awfully sublime," Private Campbell remembered. "It seemed like madness for men to press forward as they pressed forward, while our artillery and musketry was mowing them down." In less than an hour 8,000 Confederates—two-thirds of the attacking force—were swept away, with only a handful even reaching the mouths of the Yankee barrels. "Many rebs crawled on their hands and feet under the sheet of fire, and coming to our line, surrendered themselves as prisoners," reported Major Sylvanus Curtis of the 7th Michigan Infantry, which lost scores of men as it helped repulse the storybook charge.

At the same time, a climactic collision of cavalry took place three miles east of Gettysburg, where four brigades of Confederate horsemen led by General Jeb Stuart attempted to crash into the rear of the Union line. For several days before and during the battle Stuart had attempted to link up with Lee. But he had been dogged by the Michigan Cavalry Brigade, consisting of the 1st, 5th, 6th and 7th Michigan Cavalry regiments and commanded by newly promoted Brigadier General George Armstrong Custer. One of Custer's many admirers, Major James Kidd of the 6th Michigan, thought the boy general to be "the most picturesque figure" of the war, and he wasn't referring just to Custer's flowing locks and eye-grabbing garb.

In a key moment during the fight of July 3, Custer—his saber raised overhead and shouting "Come on, you Wolverines!"—led the 1st Michigan Cavalry in a storybook charge of his own against the head of Stuart's column. Thundering herds of opposing horsemen crashed into each other with a violent force that one participant described as "falling timber." Horses wereturned over, riders were crushed, and in the end, thanks to supporting cavalry and artillery, the rebels were driven back.

On June 12, 1889, 126 Michigan veterans returned to Gettysburg to dedicate a 21-foot-high monument in the western part of McPherson's Woods. Floral contributions came in from all over the state, most bearing notes such as: "Put this on my dear son's grave." One hundred years later, a group of Civil War buffs re-dedicated the statue honoring the 24th Michigan, wearing ribbons that replicated those worn on the original Michigan Day at Gettysburg.

"Again, for the third night, the army bivouacked the bloody field, and as the tired soldiers laid down to rest, they might well have sang, for a consoling lullaby; 'The soldiers weary from the fight, tho heeded not the rebels might, for Michigan's on guard tonight; Michigan, my Michigan....' "

Corporal James Henry Avery, 5th Michigan Cavalry, recalling the conclusion of three days of fighting at Gettysburg

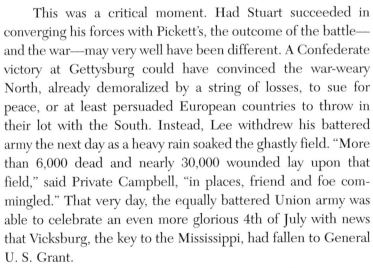

This was a critical moment. Had Stuart succeeded in converging his forces with Pickett's, the outcome of the battle—and the war—may very well have been different. A Confederate victory at Gettysburg could have convinced the war-weary North, already demoralized by a string of losses, to sue for peace, or at least persuaded European countries to throw in their lot with the South. Instead, Lee withdrew his battered army the next day as a heavy rain soaked the ghastly field. "More than 6,000 dead and nearly 30,000 wounded lay upon that field," said Private Campbell, "in places, friend and foe commingled." That very day, the equally battered Union army was able to celebrate an even more glorious 4th of July with news that Vicksburg, the key to the Mississippi, had fallen to General U. S. Grant.

"What a difference in our breathing!" exclaimed Campbell. "Even the wounded and the dying seemed to catch the spirit. They felt the high-water mark had been reached and that the victory was ours. Nevertheless we had Grant's overland campaign after that, the bloodiest campaign of the war. And we all realized that the downfall of the rebellion, the death of slavery and the 'Last Ditch' had a costly meaning." ●

The Boy General

Major James H. Kidd of the 6th Michigan Cavalry never forgot his first glimpse of George Armstrong Custer.

"An officer superbly mounted....," recalled Kidd. "Tall, lithe, active, muscular, straight as an Indian and as quick in his movements, he had the fair complexion of a school girl. He was clad in a suit of black velvet elaborately trimmed with gold lace, which ran down the outer seams of his trousers, and almost covered the sleeves of his cavalry jacket. The wide collar of a navy blue shirt was turned down over the collar of his velvet jacket, and a necktie of brilliant crimson was tied in a graceful knot at the throat, the long ends falling carelessly in front. The double rows of buttons on his breast were arranged in groups of twos,

One of Custer's troopers, Frederick Bush, astride his thousand-pound warhorse. In many ways Bush was the ideal cavalryman: young, single, slightly built and fearless. The 18-year-old farm boy enlisted in the 7th Michigan Cavalry in 1862 and was killed at Hawes Shop, Virginia two years later.

indicating the rank of brigadier general. A soft, black hat with wide brim adorned with a gilt cord, and rosette encircling a silver star, was worn turned down on one side giving him a rakish air. His golden hair fell in graceful luxuriance nearly or quite to his shoulders, and his upper lip was garnished with a blonde mustache. A sword and belt, gilt spurs and top boots completed his unique outfit."

Colorful, charismatic and courageous, Custer was the very embodiment of the medieval knight, a cavalier the equal of Jeb Stuart or Phil Sheridan or any other horse soldier in the war. Retired cavalrymen loved to tell the story of Custer at Tom's Brook in the Shenandoah Valley when, just prior to the start of the battle, he trotted out between the lines to doff his hat and give a sweeping bow to an old West Point classmate commanding the opposing force. "If there was any poetry or romance in war," General Sheridan said, "he could develop it." When Kidd saw Custer for the first time in June 1863, he had just taken command of the Michigan Cavalry Brigade. At 23 he was the youngest general in the war.

Custer was born in New Rumley, Ohio on December 5, 1839, and graduated from West Point in 1861, dead last in his class. He was commissioned a second lieutenant in the 2nd U. S. Cavalry and reported on the morning of the First Battle of Bull Run. He would spend the next four years almost continuously in the saddle, advancing from an aide to General George McClellan to major general of the 3rd Cavalry Division at war's end. Along the way he would distinguish himself time and again—capturing the first flag for the Army of the Potomac near Williamsburg one spring day in 1862, for example, or overwhelming an entrenched brigade at Winchester two years later, his men taking 700 prisoners in the process. Whether handing Stuart's "Invincibles" their first-ever defeat at Gettysburg or pacifying the Shenandoah Valley, he seemed to lead a charmed life, surviving charge after charge, campaign after campaign. He had nearly a dozen horses shot out from under him but was

"General Custer is our Briggade General he is a Michigan Man and his Briggade are all Michigan Men. Wolverines he calls them. He feels proud off his men and is always at the head of them. He has had nine horses shot from under him since this was commenced and he is still alive and after the rebs!"

David R. Trego, 6th Michigan Cavalry, in a letter to his brother, June 4, 1864

George Armstrong Custer in 1865, sporting the red necktie that was a fashion statement among members of the Michigan Cavalry Brigade. One national magazine called the trademark neckwear an "emblem of bravado and a challenge to combat."

wounded only once. He found battle to be intoxicating, once declaring to a friend, "Oh, could you but have seen some of the charges that were made! While thinking of them I cannot but exclaim 'Glorious War!'"

Custer was tireless in harassing Lee's retreating army in the closing days of the war. In appreciation Sheridan, who was at Appomattox, gave Custer's wife, Libbie, a priceless piece of furniture from the McLean home. "My Dear Madam," the attached note read, "I respectfully present to you the small writing table on which the conditions for the surrender of the Army of Northern Virginia were written by Lt. General Grant—and permit me to say, Madam, that there is scarcely an individual in our service who has contributed more to bring about this desirable result than your gallant husband."

Custer, a national hero, stayed in the regular army after the war, reverting to his permanent rank of captain. He headed west as commander of the 7th U. S. Cavalry, the public memory of his remarkable service to the Union destined to be obliterated by a single, spectacular failure of judgment in Montana. However, Little Big Horn didn't erase the high opinion of the Wolverines who had served under him. "So brave a man I never saw….," was Major Kidd's assessment. "Under him a man is ashamed to be Cowardly."

Chapter 6
YOUNG BLOOD

*Young Charlie Gardner
of Flint followed his father
into a soldier's grave.*

Children are, by nature, excitable beings, but the war made them especially anxious. The story is told of a little girl named Annie racing home from church one day, breathless with the news that the Confederates were invading Detroit. Why, they were practically marching up Woodward Avenue!

"Put the kettle on, Annie," was all her unimpressed grandmother said, "we need a cup of tea."

"Nothing could have been said that would bring back composure more quickly," Annie's friend, Florence Marsh, later recounted. "The tea was drunk, the family went to bed, and the enemy never came."

If Annie didn't get her gun on that occasion, a youngster known to history only as "Emily" reportedly did. A transplanted New Yorker living in Michigan when the war broke out, Emily managed to sneak into uniform and join the Army of the Cumberland as it moved south. Although the details of her abbreviated life are sketchy, she evidently was able to keep her gender a secret until she was mortally wounded at the Battle of Lookout Mountain in the fall of 1863.

While the thought of boys marching off to war is only slightly less distressful than that of little girls dying in combat, the record here is clearer. Dozens of boys, some as young as 12 or 13, served as drummers and fifers with Michigan units, experiencing the same mix of boredom, fatigue, camaraderie and terror as their older comrades. Several of them died—usually of measles, pneumonia or dysentery, but occasionally by bullets and shells. Many more adolescents

Each company in the Union army was authorized two musicians, who sounded calls in camp and battle and provided entertainment. Fifer William Seekel and his 12-year-old twin sons, Charles and James, joined the 11th Michigan Infantry together on August 24, 1861 and served as musicians in Company E. The family trio was broken up in October 1862 when William died of disease in Nashville, Tennessee. The boys were discharged by order of the War Department and sent home to Lenawee County four months later.

shouldered a rifle, filling a soldier's grave at Chickamauga Creek, Seminary Ridge or some other hill, stream, hamlet or woods that no Michigan schoolteacher before the war had ever felt the need to point out in geography lessons.

Boys like Charlie Gardner of Flint, who begged his mother to allow him to follow his favorite teacher, Samuel Guild, into the 8th Michigan Infantry. Unlike many musicians in uniform, Charlie actually knew how to handle a drum. Charlie's father, Charles, was already serving with the 2nd Michigan Infantry, so his mother was reluctant to see him go as well. She finally bowed to Charlie's insistence that he be allowed to "take the place of a man who can handle a musket." Charlie enlisted in Company A of the 8th Michigan, commanded by Captain Guild.

In early 1862, Charlie and his father had a brief reunion in Washington, D.C., as the 8th Michigan was on its way to Port Royal, South Carolina. The excitement and naivete with which the Flint schoolboy went to war quickly faded. By the end of 1862 both of Charlie's father figures would be dead—Captain Guild was killed at the Battle of James Island, and Charles Gardner died of typhoid fever in Alexandria, Virginia. Nonetheless, little Charlie soldiered on, shouldering the daily miseries of his older companions until he was wounded during the siege of Knoxville, Tennessee. The regiment was recalled to Detroit, but Mrs. Gardner and her two other children had a grim surprise waiting for them. Charlie, who was thought to be recovering nicely, died en route. He was 14 years old.

Nobody knows exactly how many Charlie Gardners fought in the war. According to historians' estimates, anywhere from 1 to 10 percent of the Union army was underage. Accepting the lowest guess would mean nearly a thousand Michigan troops were 17 or younger, a figure that, based on anecdotal evidence,

George Wheelock was only 12 years old when he went off to war with the 6th Michigan Infantry Regiment.

"So young and so ardent, so soon 'neath the sod, Beloved by those whom he knew; The goal that he sought was the throne of his God, Having done well what he had to do."

Lyrics from "The Drummer Boy of Vicksburg, Or, Let Him Sleep," a song published to commemorate Charlie Gardner of the 8th Michigan Infantry

probably is quite conservative. Given that the Wolverine State supplied some 90,000 soldiers to the cause, the number of Michigan boys mustered into service more likely approached a few thousand. This doesn't include any youngsters serving in the Navy, where their presence on ships as stewards and "powder monkeys" (carrying ammunition from the magazine to the gun crews) was not only considered unremarkable, it was traditional.

Government policy regarding the ages of soldiers varied. When the war began, the minimum age requirement of 18 could be waived with a parent's or guardian's permission (the same rule in effect in today's armed forces). In 1862 the War Department forebade minors completely. Regulations concerning drummer boys and musicians were more lax, with no minimum age set until March 3, 1864 when Congress, alarmed by the growing number of casualties among this group, issued an act prohibiting the enlistment of anybody under the age of 16.

It hardly mattered. Enterprising youths still found their way into uniform. Recordkeeping was nothing like it is today, so in lieu of a birth certificate or other documentation it was easy to have an accomplice vouch for an eager recruit's age. Those underage lads concerned with

Colonel William A. Fenton, the namesake of the town in eastern Genesee County and a future lieutenant governor, raised and commanded the 8th Michigan Infantry Regiment. He contracted a serious illness and was honorably discharged on March 15, 1863—much to the relief of his daughter, pictured here.

committing the un-Christian act of lying often placated their guilty conscience by placing a slip of paper, the number 18 written on it, in their shoe. Thus when the recruiting officer asked the boy his age, he could truthfully answer, "I'm 'over' 18."

Recruiters looking to fill their quotas didn't ask too many hard questions, especially as the pool of available recruits dried up. By 1863 one member of the 8th Michigan Cavalry, Albert Hathaway, was grousing that some companies, their ranks depleted by deaths and desertions, seemed to be composed largely of recruits 15 to 19 years old. According to another trooper, Quintas Foster of the 3rd Michigan Cavalry, the phenomenon wasn't peculiar to Michigan. Foster reported from the field in 1864 that some Indiana and Pennsylvania regiments had boys as young as 12 and 14 in the saddle. "Large numbers of them are not as long as the swords they wear. They are the dirtiest set of small thieves I ever saw."

Of course, "boy" is a relative term when speaking about Michigan in the middle of the 19th century, a time and place when adolescents were forced by the circumstances of frontier life to be responsible beyond their years. Rural youngsters lived in an environment of guns, knives, axes, horses, fires and epidemics. They grew up quickly, though, conversely, they were considered "children" until their 18th birthday. (The word "teenager" did not exist then.) Life expectancy in the 1860s was half of what it is today—39 years for men, 41 for women. The family plot often contained children who had died young of disease or calamity, and possibly a mother or father—or both. Life was a little different in the cities, where urban youths were already being criticized in editorials and sermons of the day as "lacking vigor." But all in all, the typical youth who joined Mr. Lincoln's army was made of stern stuff.

George Sidman received the Medal of Honor for his gallantry at Gaines Mill, Virginia.

Sixteen-year-old George Sidman of Owosso was the youngest and smallest member of his regiment when he enlisted in the 16th Michigan Infantry as a drummer in 1861. As a musician, Sidman made a good infantryman. Despite his inability to play the many calls required of him, he was kept on the rolls as a drummer "in order to let him grow to a soldier's stature," a colleague said.

Sidman attained that stature at Gaines Mill, Virginia in 1862. During the melee, Sidman was conspicuous in fighting off the enemy and encouraging his comrades until a minie ball ripped through his hip. Down but not out, Sidman continued to fight until he fainted. "Dragging himself to an open ditch in the rear, he clubbed his musket over a stump to destroy its usefulness to the enemy, and throwing his accoutrements in the ditch, he crawled on his hands and knees off the field of battle and through Chickahominy Swamp," reported an eyewitness. Captured and then exchanged, Sidman twice escaped from hospitals, eager to rejoin his friends in the 16th. Hobbling along on crutches, then grabbing a ride on an ambulance, Sidman worked his way back to his unit the best he could. He finally stumbled into camp riding a broken-down horse he had found by the wayside, his improvised bridle consisting of a number of knapsack straps tied together.

According to a colleague, "Sidman had developed a means to remain with his command and his officers and comrades were loud in their approval of his patriotism and faithfulness to duty." Although weak and in constant pain, Sidman went on to serve with distinction. He was given the honor of carrying the 3rd Brigade's new flag in the charge on Marye's Heights at Fredericksburg, where he was again wounded. Promoted to corporal, Sidman was shot through the foot at the Battle of

The Real Johnny Shiloh?

John Lincoln Clem. The little drummer added his middle name after becoming famous.

Opposite: Unlike some other Michigan drummer boys, William Gilby wasn't a household name, but he was young. The 16-year-old Detroit boy enlisted in the 17th Michigan Infantry and was wounded at the Battle of Antietam. Nine months later he was mustered out of service, possibly because he was underage at the time of his enlistment.

IN 1959, AS AMERICA was on the cusp of commemorating the centennial anniversary of the conflict, James A. Rhodes published *Johnny Shiloh: A Novel of the Civil War*. Four years later the book was made into a popular movie by Walt Disney, with Kevin Corcoran playing the title role of a runaway boy who tries to join the Blue Raiders of Ohio but is rejected as being too young. This doesn't stop the persistent and courageous Johnny, who in the end proves size and age aren't the only measures of a fighting heart.

Johnny Shiloh was a character based in part upon the most famous drummer boy of the Civil War, Johnny Clem of the 22nd Michigan Infantry, whose reported exploits sometimes were as fictional as those gracing movie screens in 1963. Newspaper readers throughout the North loved reading about the spunky lad who was photographed with a musket sawed down to accommodate his diminutive size.

Separating fact from myth is always hard when it comes to celebrity soldiers like Clem. He was born on August 13, 1851 in Newark, Ohio, and was just nine years old when he "ran off to join Mr. Lincoln's army" (as the song in the movie goes). He was reportedly rejected by the commander of the 3rd Ohio, who said he "wasn't enlisting infants," before finally managing to hook up with the 22nd Michigan Infantry in the late summer of 1862. The four-foot-tall youngster made himself indispensable around camp and the following spring was officially mustered into the regiment as a musician. Intelligent despite his limited education, Clem was given the important duty of regimental marker, carrying the guidon that a unit formed its line on.

A few months later, the 22nd and the rest of the Army of the Cumberland were heavily engaged at the Battle of Chickamauga. On September 20, 1863, in the midst of a retreat, Clem found himself face to face with a Rebel colonel on horseback. As the story goes, the officer yelled, "Stop, you little Yankee devil!" Clem refused to surrender. As he later described it, he picked up a discarded rifle, pointed it at the officer—and to both combatants' great surprise, shot him out of the saddle. As one typically overheated newspaper account of this remarkable incident put it, "the proud Colonel tumbled dead from his horse, his lips fresh stained with the syllable of vile reproach he had flung upon a mother's grave in the hearing of her child."

It evolved that the colonel wasn't killed, and that Clem had not shot him with a custom-fitted miniature musket, as widely reported. But he did evade capture by rolling himself in a blanket before finally making it back to his unit, which had been decimated. Of the 22nd Michigan's 455 men engaged at Chickamauga, only 66 avoided being killed, wounded, or captured. Word of the exploits of 12-year-old Johnny Clem spread quickly among the demoralized troops.

The youngster's admirers in the press and the army didn't quibble over all the details of his heroism. Before he knew it, "The Drummer Boy of Chickamauga" was a celebrity, written up in national publications, posing for studio photographs, and accepting the gift of a pony. According to some sources the popular song, "When Johnny Comes Marching Home Again," was based on Clem, who was promoted to sergeant and served out the rest of his time as a courier at the headquarters of the Army of the Cumberland. Countless youths were motivated by his example. One general, employing his best once-upon-a-time style, was moved to write his own young son:

What shall I write to you about? I will tell you a story of a little boy who once lived in Michigan. His name is John Clem….He was a good boy—always obeyed his Captain and always tried to do his duty like a man. Being a good boy everyone liked him, because good boys always have a great many friends—he had many. Last summer his drum was broken by some accident and poor Johnny often cried because he had no drum to beat, but he always kept up with his Company in either hot or cold weather and often he had to sleep on the cold damp ground without a blanket….Johnny will make a great man some of these days and so will any boy who is obedient and faithful in the performance of his duty.

Clem didn't quite approach "great man" status as he grew older, but he was able to seize advantage of the connections fame had brought him. After his scant education torpedoed his attempt to enter West Point, he prevailed upon President U. S. Grant to appoint him a second lieutenant in the Regular army. Clem served from 1871 to 1916, when he retired as a mildly competent but much beloved major general. He was the last Civil War veteran to leave active duty. He died at his San Antonio, Texas home on May 13, 1937, and was buried at Arlington National Cemetery.

Curiously, for all of his adult life Clem often was erroneously referred to as "The Drummer Boy of Shiloh." This was no fault of Clem's. Rather, it was the result of an 1871 newspaper article that mistakenly identified him as the brave (and possibly fictional) youngster who'd famously had his drum destroyed by a shell at the Battle of Shiloh in the spring of 1862. That incident inspired one of the most popular songs of the war, "The Drummer Boy of Shiloh," which in turn begat a play by the same name. Performances of this patriotic tear-jerker were a staple of school fundraisers and veterans' gatherings well into the 20th century and kept the name alive in the public mind.

The story was widely circulated as a pamphlet and found its way into Clem's service jacket. The appellation stuck, though a number of other young soldiers would always claim to be the real "Johnny Shiloh." Writers and historians used the 1871 article for more than a century without bothering to check its claims against Clem's official service records. As historian Dennis M. Keesee finally made clear in his meticulously researched book-length study of Union boy soldiers, Clem's participation at Shiloh would have been impossible. At the time the 22nd Michigan hadn't even been organized, and in any case Clem had yet to join the regiment.

Clem never really claimed to be Johnny Shiloh. He was satisfied being, as his gravestone at Arlington reads, "The Drummer Boy of Chickamauga."

On December 11, 1862, Michigan troops distinguished themselves at Fredericksburg, Virginia, crossing the Rappahannock River in pontoons boats under murderous fire to secure the opposite bank. It was during this action that Robert Hendershot became "The Drummer Boy of the Rappahannock," an identity he clung to as mightily as the side of the boat he claimed dragged him through the icy water.

Middleburg, Virginia, on June 21, 1863. At that point the thrice-wounded soldier was hospitalized for several months and, over his protestations, reassigned to the Invalid Corps until his discharge in November 1865. In recognition of his fidelity and courage, Sidman was later awarded the Medal of Honor—one of the youngest recipients of the Civil War and still the youngest Michigan soldier ever to receive the decoration.

Henry Matrau was another sturdy 16-year-old who was determined to go to war—if not with an outfit from his own state, then with that of any state that would have him. A round-faced boy who stood only five-foot-four, Matrau was the oldest

> **"I now take my pen in hand to inform you that I am well. I wish I could say so of Father but he is wounded and perhaps dieing at this hour."**

Letter from George Lutz, a 14-year-old drummer in the 22nd Michigan Infantry, describing the fate of his soldier-father at the Battle of Chickamauga

Robert H. Hendershot
Drummer
8th Mich Infty

of six children born into a farm family in Bainbridge Township in Berrien County. Immediately after the news of the shelling of Fort Sumter, Henry tried to enroll in a local regiment then forming, but was rebuffed. Undeterred, he traveled to Chicago, where he failed in two more attempts to enlist. In a sharp-tongued exchange he told a recruiter that he "didn't know his business," who responded by threatening him with arrest. Having been rejected in Michigan and Illinois, Matrau next journeyed to Beloit, Wisconsin, where he was accepted into the local militia group, the Beloit Star Rifles. The Star Rifles were mustered into federal service as one of the companies in the 6th Wisconsin Volunteer Regiment, which became part of the Iron Brigade. Passing the inspection of the mustering officer was a challenge that Henry, who had lied about his age, was able to meet. In order to satisfy the minimum height requirement, the nimble-minded recruit stuffed cardboard into his shoes and wore a high-peaked cap.

Henry wanted no part of being a musician; he favored the shock and excitement of being an infantryman. Known as "the Baby of Company G," Matrau showed his grit at many of the major engagements of the war, including Fredericksburg, Chancellorsville, Gettysburg, Spotsylvania and Cold Harbor. At Gettysburg, he reported in a letter to his parents, "The best hearted fellow in our company was killed right close to me so near that he nearly fell on me."

Sixteen-year-old Corporal John Death enlisted in the 27th Michigan's Company A in the summer of 1862 at Ontonagon for three years. He was wounded in action but still managed to outrun his namesake, at least during the war.

By the fall of 1864 the battle-hardened youngster had matured to the point that he had been promoted to second lieutenant. "I dont wish to be thought any egotistical in thus speaking of myself," he wrote from Virginia, "but there ain't many that know how hard it is for a private to rise, as I have, from the lowest rank in the army to that of a Commissioned officer, with no help but my own right hand." Henry, proud of his elevated station, asked his parents to send him thirty dollars so he could exchange his "seedy" clothes for a "respectable" officer's uniform, sword and belt. Responding to the news that his 15-year-old brother Frank had gone to Kalamazoo to enlist in the 28th Michigan Infantry (another brother, Morgan, had previously joined the 12th Michigan at the same age), Henry displayed the knowing air of the "weather beaten, tanned old veteran" he had become. "It may be the best thing for him that he could do," he reasoned, "for soldiering teaches one hard lessons, but they will last a man his life time." Henry would be a captain by the time his four years of wartime service ended. He and his brothers all returned safely to enjoy long and productive lives.

While Henry Matrau's climb up the ranks was steady but unspectacular, Robert Hendershot of the 8th Michigan Infantry became a national celebrity by dint of a single audacious act. According to an account that first appeared in the *Detroit Free Press* and then was reprinted in other papers and the popular magazine, *Youth's Companion*, the 12-year-old drummer from Cambridge had clung to the side of a boat as Michigan troops crossed the icy Rappahannock River at Fredericksburg on December 11, 1862. Once on the other bank, Hendershot's drum had been "blown to atoms," but he still managed to capture one of the enemy. Hendershot reportedly had earned the praise of a general at the scene, who declared, "Boy, I glory in your spunk."

Boys ran away to join the army right up through the end of the war. In the early spring of 1865, Charlie Warnica walked several hundred miles from his home in upper Ontario, Canada to Detroit to enlist in the 15th Michigan Infantry. Upon joining the regiment in Kentucky he contracted typhoid fever and died inside a Louisville hospital. The money the 16-year-old had received in bonuses was almost exactly what it cost his family to ship his body back to Canada for burial.

Hendershot, a fatherless hellion who found himself an object of admiration for the first time, spent the rest of the war—indeed, the rest of his life—capitalizing on his fame. He accepted an expensive and ornate drum from a New York newspaper, traveled to England to be showered with praise, appeared at P. T. Barnum's museum of curiosities, and visited the White House to meet the president. He posed for countless photographs, shamelessly promoting himself as "the most wonderful Drummer in the World." Several poems were written about him, including "The Hero of the Drum." Hendershot's presence at a recruiting rally in Michigan "created much enthusiasm," reported the *Free Press*. More than a few wide-eyed boys in attendance could see themselves standing on the platform, boasting of his exploits and soaking in the admiration and the applause, just like "The Drummer Boy of the Rappahannock."

Years later it would develop that Hendershot, by now a staple of the convention circuit, was a fraud, the tale he had weaved for newspapers wholly discounted by members of the Michigan regiments on the scene. The real story of his time in service revealed a litany of discharges, desertions and other unseemly behavior. "Worse than useless," was one veteran's appraisal of the boy who had demonstrated absolutely no ability to play an instrument or shoulder a weapon. If Hendershot was remembered for being at Fredericksburg at all it was for joining in the looting that took place there—"the Forager of the Rappahannock," said another Michigan vet. But in the early stages of the war the North was hungry for all the heroes it could get, authentic or manufactured. Hendershot, undaunted by the controversy, would keep on beating his own drum right up until his death in 1925.

Thanks in part to the well-publicized exploits of Hendershot and another nationally celebrated juvenile, Johnny

The exploits of drummer boys inspired an outpouring of songs, poems, plays, books and articles, such as this songsheet dedicated to Charlie Gardner of the 8th Michigan Infantry. Some were genuine tributes, but most were the product of simple commercial opportunism.

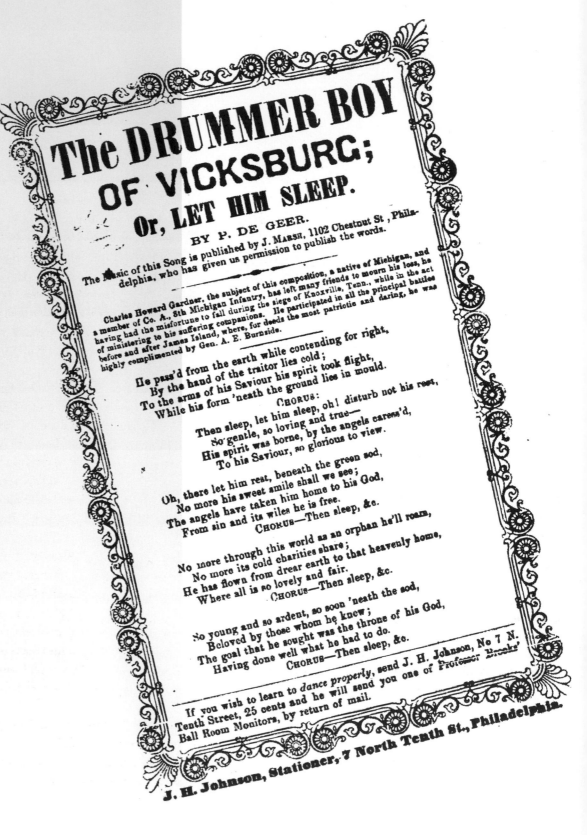

The DRUMMER BOY OF VICKSBURG; Or, LET HIM SLEEP.

BY P. DE GEER.

The Music of this Song is published by J. MARSH, 1102 Chestnut St., Philadelphia, who has given us permission to publish the words.

Charles Howard Gardner, the subject of this composition, a native of Michigan, and a member of Co. A., 8th Michigan Infantry, has left many friends to mourn his loss, he having had the misfortune to fall during the siege of Knoxville, Tenn., while in the act of ministering to his suffering companions. He participated in all the principal battles before and after James Island, where, for deeds the most patriotic and daring, he was highly complimented by Gen. A. E. Burnside.

He pass'd from the earth while contending for right,
By the hand of the traitor lies cold;
To the arms of his Saviour his spirit took flight,
While his form 'neath the ground lies in mould.

CHORUS:
Then sleep, let him sleep, oh! disturb not his rest,
So gentle, so loving and true—
His spirit was borne, by the angels caress'd,
To his Saviour, so glorious to view.

Oh, there let him rest, beneath the green sod,
No more his sweet smile shall we see;
The angels have taken him home to his God,
From sin and its wiles he is free.
CHORUS—Then sleep, &c.

No more through this world as an orphan he'll roam,
No more its cold charities share;
He has flown from drear earth to that heavenly home,
Where all is so lovely and fair.
CHORUS—Then sleep, &c.

So young and so ardent, so soon 'neath the sod,
Beloved by those whom he knew;
The goal that he sought was the throne of his God,
Having done well what he had to do.
CHORUS—Then sleep, &c.

If you wish to learn to *dance* properly, send J. H. Johnson, No 7 N. Tenth Street, 25 cents and he will send you one of *Professor Brooks'* Ball Room Monitors, by return of mail.

J. H. Johnson, Stationer, 7 North Tenth St., Philadelphia.

Charles Strewing was born in Detroit on August 18, 1845. He was orphaned at the age of eight by a cholera epidemic that swept the city, after which he was fostered out to a German family in Ecorse. When he was 15 he took a job with an outfit gathering horses for the army. This took him to New York, where he gave his age as 18 and enlisted in the 42nd New York. In October 1863 he was captured and confined at the notorious Libby and Andersonville prison camps, where his weight fell from 180 to 89 pounds. Strewing survived to return to Detroit after the war, working for the Union Pacific Railroad and then becoming a leader in Michigan's charcoal industry.

Clem of the 22nd Michigan ("The Drummer Boy of Chickamauga"), heroic boy soldiers—some toting a rifle, others banging a drum—became staples of songs, short stories, poetry and stage skits throughout the North. It's easy to imagine a bored farm boy in Cross Village or Farmington, for example, eagerly devouring the pages of the latest *Youth's Companion* one June day in 1863 and being inspired by "The Little Soldier":

> "O would I were a soldier,"
>   Cried little Bertie Lee;
> "If I were only older,
>   How very brave I'd be;
> I'd fear not any danger,
>   I'd flee not from the foe,
> But where the strife was fiercest
>   There I'd be sure to go.
>
> "I'd be the boldest picket,
>   Nor fear the darkest night;
> Could I but see a rebel,
>   How bravely I would fight.
> I'd nobly do my duty,
>   And soon promoted be, --
> O, would I were a soldier,"
>   Sighed little Bertie Lee.

Unlike little Bertie Lee, youngsters like Benjamin Force and Henry Loss didn't just sit back and daydream of going off to war. They actually went, and often proved themselves as good as or better than many grown men in the ranks.

Edmund Beadle was 16 when he enlisted in Company H of the 1st Michigan Sharpshooters at Adrian on September 15, 1863. Private Beadle saw his first and last action at the Battle of the Wilderness. On the back of his portrait is a terse footnote to a young man's life: "Died June 30, 1864 from a wound received May 6th. In the confidant hope of a better life."

James Henry Avery, a member of the 5th Michigan Cavalry, recalled the ridicule Private Benjamin Force endured when the 16-year-old joined the regiment in August 1864. The youngster "was very slow, and the boys used to laugh at him, on account of the strangeness of his manner and slowness," remembered Avery. Under fire, though, Private Force "sat on his horse and delivered his fire as cool and steady as the best of them, showing that he had force in this direction at least."

Henry Loss was born in Mecklenberg, Germany in 1845 and was 12 years old when he accompanied his father to Michigan. The family settled in Dundee. Soon afterward some sort of unrecorded family catastrophe forced young Henry to shift for himself. He worked on a farm during the summer and for his board in the winter, attending school when he could. Then came the call to arms in the spring of 1861. After being rebuffed by a recruiter for being too small and too young to carry a rifle, he entered the 6th Michigan Infantry Regiment as a drummer.

Soon Loss found himself in Louisiana, participating in the battles at Baton Rouge and Port Hudson. It was at Baton Rouge that he was struck in the temple by a minie ball; thankfully for Loss, the shot had been fired at a great distance so the bullet's velocity was only enough to knock him senseless, not kill him. Nonetheless, some of his comrades saw the boy's still body and reported him dead. "This report reached his friends in Michigan," a chronicler noted, "who to honor the soldier as was customary had his funeral sermon preached, an act that made him more popular when it was learned he was alive and well. This is a distinction few men can claim."

Loss recovered from his wound. However, he subsequently fell ill and spent several months in the hospital. Nearing the end of his three-year enlistment, he was discharged and sent home to recuperate. After a few months of civilian life, Loss

"I have been surprised at the large number of young, beardless boys who crowd the ranks and fill our hospitals....Yesterday I sat by the bedside of one of these; a little fellow.... his voice is gentle and boyish too, and listening you would wonder what there had ever been of the soldier about him, till you looked into his eyes. But look while he is speaking, and telling of the rapid marches, the surprise, the charge, the victory, and his eyes will betray the child nature yet strong within him...."

Lois Bryan Adams describing a hospital visit with Jacob Baker, a 17-year-old Michigan private wounded at Spotsylvania

discovered he missed the excitement and camaraderie of army life. He reenlisted in the 24th Michigan, staying with the regiment through the battles of Gaines Mill and Hatcher's Run. After several narrow escapes, he was discharged in June 1865, at which point he transferred his energy to peaceful pursuits. He operated a hardware store in Wayne for many years, homesteaded briefly in South Dakota, and was a fixture on a variety of charitable, political and veterans commissions in his community. In 1896 he was appointed postmaster of Nankin.

As they grew into old age, boy soldiers like Loss could look back with considerable satisfaction on their days of adolescent derring-do and credit the hardships endured and lessons learned in uniform as forming the foundation for a successful adult life. Thus, several decades after the war, a published compilation of Michigan's most accomplished citizens would note approvingly that the former Corporal Loss had become society's gain: "He is one of the most liberal of men; while he is small in body he is large in mind. He has proved himself a careful business man, a valuable neighbor, a warm friend to his old comrades in arms, a generous citizen, and in every walk in life the Christian gentleman." ●

"Life Became a Strenuous and Tragic Affair"

The Civil War could be a formative experience for children left to look out for their own welfare. In her autobiography, *The Story of a Pioneer*, Anna Howard Shaw traced her self-reliance and independence to the difficult adolescence she spent on the large, undeveloped farm that her father, an educated but impractical dreamer from Massachusetts, carved out of the wilderness near Big Rapids. Fourteen when the fighting broke out, Anna taught school to help support her mother and siblings while the men of the family cavalierly went off to war. Later, she graduated from Albion College and a medical school in Boston and eventually became a leading figure in the women's suffrage movement. She died in 1919, the year women finally were given the right to vote.

When the news came that Fort Sumter had been fired on, and that Lincoln had called for troops, our men were threshing. There was only one threshing machine in the region at that time, and it went from place to place, the farmers doing their threshing whenever they could get the machine. I remember seeing a man ride up on horseback, shouting out Lincoln's demand for troops and explaining that a regiment was being formed at Big Rapids. Before he had finished speaking the men on the machine had leaped to the ground and rushed off to enlist, my brother Jack, who had recently joined us, among them. In ten minutes not one man was left in the field. A few months later my brother Tom enlisted as a bugler—he was a mere boy at the time—and not long after that my father followed the example of his sons and served until the war was ended. He had entered on the twenty-ninth of August, 1862, as an army steward; he came back to us with the rank of lieutenant and assistant surgeon of field and staff.

Between those years I was the principal support of our family, and life became a strenuous and tragic affair. For months at a time we had no news from the front. The work in our community, if it was done at all, was done by despairing women whose hearts were with their men. When care had become our constant guest, Death entered our home as well. My sister Eleanor had married, and died in childbirth, leaving her baby to me; and the blackest hours of those black years were the hours that saw her passing. I can see her still, lying in a stupor from which she roused herself at intervals to ask about her child. She insisted that our brother Tom should name the baby, but Tom was fighting for his country, unless he had already preceded Eleanor through the wide portal that was opening before her. I could only tell her that I had written to him; but before the assurance was an hour old she would climb up from the gulf of unconsciousness with infinite effort to ask if we had received his reply. At last, to calm her, I told her it had come, and that Tom had chosen for her little son the name of Arthur. She smiled at this and drew a deep breath; then, still smiling, she passed away. Her baby slipped into her vacant place and almost filled our heavy hearts, but only for a short time; for within a few months after his mother's death his father married again and took him from me, and it seemed that with his going we had lost all that made life worth while.

The problem of living grew harder with every day. We eked out our little income in every way we could, taking as boarders the workers in the logging-camps, making quilts, which we sold, and losing no chance to earn a penny in any legitimate manner. Again my mother did such outside sewing as she could secure, yet with every month of our effort the gulf between our income and our expenses grew wider, and the price of the bare necessities of existence climbed up and up. The largest amount I could earn at teaching was six dollars a week, and our school year included only two terms of thirteen weeks each. It was an incessant struggle to keep our land, to pay our taxes, and to live.

A Michigan farm, circa 1860. The fields would soon become depopulated of males.

Calico was selling at fifty cents a yard. Coffee was one dollar a pound. There were no men left to grind our corn, to get in our crops, or to care for our live stock; and all around us we saw our struggle reflected in the lives of our neighbors.

At long intervals word came to us of battles in which my father's regiment—the Tenth Michigan Cavalry Volunteers—or those of my brothers were engaged, and then longer intervals followed in which we heard no news. After Eleanor's death my brother Tom was wounded, and for months we lived in terror of worse tidings, but he finally recovered. I was walking seven and eight miles a day, and doing extra work before and after school hours, and my health began to fail. Those were years I do not like to look back upon—years in which life had degenerated into a treadmill whose monotony was broken only by the grim messages from the front....

The end of the Civil War brought freedom to me, too. When the peace was declared my father and brothers returned to the claim in the wilderness which we women of the family had labored so desperately to hold while they were gone.

*Charles Depuy and his wife, circa 1900. Depuy is proudly wearing his
Medal of Honor, awarded in 1896 for heroic action three decades earlier
at the Battle of Spotsylvania, and the Grand Army of the Republic medal.
The Kalkaska native died of pneumonia on January 5, 1935, at age 92.*

Captain William H. Withington of Jackson earned his medal by staying on the battlefield at Bull Run to render assistance to Orlando B. Willcox, the fallen colonel of the 1st Michigan Infantry. Willcox also was awarded the Medal of Honor for his actions that day.

Chapter 7
DEEDS OF VALOR

In the summer of 1863, Charles M. Holton, a 25-year-old sergeant in the hard-charging Michigan Cavalry Brigade, distinguished himself at Falling Waters, Virginia. Years later, Holton described what happened that day along the Potomac River:

"On the morning of July 14, 1863, Custer's Michigan Brigade came face to face with four brigades of rebel infantry strongly entrenched and supported by artillery. This was a division of Lee's army which had failed to cross the Potomac. Although greatly inferior in numbers, the Michigan men formed up and attacked them with great fury. Our skirmish line was rapidly approaching the enemy's battery, where General Kilpatrick ordered a charge by the 1st Battalion of the 7th Michigan....The little battalion, which comprised only seventy sabers, formed in column of fours, and charged up a lane which was occupied by the right of the Confederate line. They dashed through the enemy and into the field beyond, where the rebel reserve was drawn up. Unheeding the storm of bullets that assailed them, the little troop dashed into the enemy's ranks and cut its way through.

"Seeing the color-sergeant of the 55th Virginia fall wounded, I sprang from my horse and seized the colors. As I remounted, I heard the wounded color-bearer say, 'You Yanks have been after that old flag for a long time, but you never got it before.' While we were forming up to charge them again from their rear, the Confederates threw down their arms, and we marched 400 prisoners from the field.

"General Kilpatrick examined the captured flag and found on it the names of all the great

Charles M. Holton of the 7th Michigan Cavalry distinguished himself at Falling Waters, Virginia.

battles of the Army of Northern Virginia. The guard ordered me to join his staff with it for the balance of the day, and in the evening Adjutant Briggs wrote an inscription on the margin of the flag, telling how it had been captured by me."

Holton's boldness earned him a promotion to second lieutenant and, in 1889, the Congressional Medal of Honor. It was one of 70 awarded to Michigan men for heroic actions during the war. That figure includes more than a dozen received by Wolverines serving in the units of other states, as well as the two presented to Tom Custer, a lieutenant with the 6th Michigan Cavalry. In the long history of the country's most prized military decoration, the younger brother of General George A. Custer remains one of the few men to receive more than one.

That history dates to December 21, 1861, when Congress first authorized the awarding of the medal to deserving enlisted members of the U. S. Navy and Marine Corps. By early 1863 a separate decoration had been created to include officers and enlisted men of the army. The medal did not have the cachet it enjoys today. In fact, at the time it was the only medal given by the U. S. government to its soldiers and sailors. It was poorly publicized and the language spelling out what acts qualified for the medal was vague. On one infamous occasion every man in a Maine regiment was given the medal for reenlisting!

Nearly all of the medals actually awarded during the war to Michigan men were for seizing enemy flags. Six Wolverines (including two serving with a New York regiment) earned their medals on the same day at Sayler's Creek, Virginia, each time for snatching regimental colors. Flags, of course, were powerful practical and psychological assets in 19th-century warfare. Amid the din, smoke and chaos of combat, soldiers looked to them to gauge the course of the battle or to boost morale. Which is how Second Lieutenant Thomas Ward Custer came to earn two medals within three days.

Colonel Frederick W. Swift with fellow officers of the 17th Michigan Infantry in Grass Lake in 1865. Swift (fourth from right in the second row) was issued his medal in 1897.

Tom, six years younger than the brother-general he always called "Armstrong," enlisted in a company of Ohio infantry when he was 16, serving three years in the Western theater of the war before joining the 6th Michigan Cavalry in the fall of 1864. Slim, blue-eyed, rough-hewn and highly competitive, Tom was an outstanding horse soldier, displaying the same kind of reckless abandon and keen battlefield judgment that had made his golden-haired sibling into a national hero. Although nepotism was a regular feature of the Civil War, Armstrong didn't cut Tom much slack, causing Tom to complain to his sister-in-law, Libbie Custer, about "that old galoot" who criticized him for "every little damned thing because I happen to be his brother."

Grumbling turned to high praise when the Michigan Cavalry Brigade was at full gallop. On April 3, 1865, in an action at Namozine Church, Virginia, Tom grabbed the flag of the 2nd North Carolina and personally took a dozen prisoners, despite having his horse shot out from under him. Three days later, in a much larger engagement at Sayler's Creek, he was in the forefront of a

Tom Custer wearing his two "baubles."

"Armstrong, the damned rebels have shot me, but I've got my flag!"

Lieutenant Tom Custer to his brother at Sayler's Creek, where he earned his second medal in three days

charge to dislodge the Confederate line. General Custer described what happened in a letter to Libbie's father in Monroe:

> Tom led the assault upon the enemy's breastworks, mounted, was first to leap his horse over the works on top of the enemy while they were pouring a volley of musketry into our ranks. Tom seized the rebel colors and demanded their surrender. The color-bearer shot him through the face and neck….So close the muzzle Tom's face was spotted with burnt powder. He retained the colors with one hand, while with the other he drew his revolver and shot the rebel dead….I am as proud of him as can be, as soldier, as brother.

While recuperating in a hospital, Tom was recommended for a medal in each action. Within six weeks he had received both of them—quite a haul for the dashing 20-year-old, who made history by being the only Civil War soldier to be twice so honored. Eleven years later, he would make history of another sort, dying just yards from his brother at the Little Big Horn. To his credit, Tom always downplayed his Medals of Honor, often allowing his girlfriend of the moment to pin them to her gown. The vainglorious "boy general" also professed to pay scant attention to them, though he was known to privately refer to them as "Tom's baubles."

The Haight brothers, Sidney (left) and James, returned to their Hillsdale farm after meritorious service with the 1st Michigan Sharpshooters. Sidney, the younger of the two, was issued the Medal of Honor in 1896 for gallantry at Petersburg; he died in 1918. James, his arm permanently crippled by a bullet at Spotsylvania, passed away the following year.

The majority of "baubles" were dispensed in the decades following the war, as government review boards passed judgment on thousands of applications. These typically were sent in by a superior officer recommending someone in his command who, in his opinion, had performed an especially brave deed. A detailed report and corroborating eyewitness testimony, when possible, were required before a decision was made. The process often took years. Again, the criteria for qualification was liberally interpreted, with the result that many men continued to be given the medal for actions that fell far short of truly heroic standards. In 1916 a board of five retired generals was empowered to review the 1,519 medals issued by the army in the war and wound up rescinding 911 of them. This didn't necessarily end all of the controversy. One of the 608 soldiers allowed to keep his medal was Corporal Benjamin Youngs of the 1st Michigan Sharpshooters, who had never been too keen about accepting it in the first place.

And for good reason. On December 1, 1864, Congress had authorized that a medal be issued Youngs for capturing the flag of the 35th North Carolina the previous June at Petersburg. But Youngs, who at the time was sitting out the war in Canada, understandably had little interest in picking it up. It was bad enough that the officially sanctioned hero was classified a deserter by his unit, but there was an excellent chance that Youngs was not even a hero at all. According to his company commander, Captain George Murdoch, Youngs was a shirker and "a coward [who] kept up the rear from Wilderness to Petersburg."

*Captain Edward Hill,
16th Michigan Infantry.*

The face of Medal of Honor recipient Edward Hill graced the badge of the 16th Michigan's 1904 reunion in Flint.

Murdoch claimed the Canadian had deserted a New York regiment prior to enlisting in the Sharpshooters. At Spotsylvania, Youngs had to be forced to join in the attack by the point of Murdoch's revolver. Not long after again being cajoled into action at Petersburg, Youngs was captured, paroled, and went home on a 30-day furlough. He never returned, staying in Canada before moving to New York after the war. He eventually settled in California.

According to the application for the medal filed soon after the battle, though, Youngs claimed to have captured the flag at Petersburg himself. Murdoch, who had observed the incident from just a few feet away, was incensed. He insisted that a young private named Theodore Nash had actually done the dirty work, taking it at bayonet point from a rebel. While Nash bravely fought on (he would be killed a few weeks later), Youngs had carried the flag back to headquarters only after being ordered to do so, and even then (claimed Murdoch) only after realizing that this would conveniently excuse him from the battlefield. In recognition of his "valorous" conduct, Youngs was quickly promoted to sergeant by the brigade commander.

Murdoch, incensed by Youngs' duplicity, quickly busted him back to corporal. After the war he vigorously fought against the merit of Youngs' medal, filing a protest with the state adjutant general's office that went nowhere. Youngs, for his part, was in no hurry to receive his dubious decoration—an attitude formed as much by a guilty conscience, perhaps, as by his demonstrated insouciance. In any event, he finally picked up his medal in 1913, a half-century after his alleged heroics at Petersburg—and nine years after Murdoch's death. "It is a beauty," the old man said, "and I am proud of it."●

Michigan's Bravest

Sergeant Cornelius Hadley and his wife, Minerva. The cavalryman from Albion was issued his medal in 1898, four years before his death. Minerva lived another 30 years. Both are buried at Mount Hope Cemetery in Litchfield.

Here is a listing of all Michigan men awarded the Medal of Honor during the Civil War, including those who fought in other states' units. The recipients are chronologically arranged by the date of the medal's issue—which, as Corporal Youngs' story illustrates, was not always the same as the date of actual acceptance.

Seaman James Stoddard, U. S. Navy. Issued: April 16, 1864. Action: On March 5, 1864, the Detroit seaman embarked from the *USS Marmora* off Yazoo City, Mississippi with a 12-pound howitzer on a field carriage and, standing by his gun, contributed to the defeat of the enemy.

Corporal Gabriel Cole, 5th Michigan Cavalry. Issued: September 27, 1864. Action: The Allegan native was wounded while capturing a flag at Winchester, Virginia on September 19, 1864.

Sergeant Henry M. Fox, 5th Michigan Cavalry. Issued: September 27, 1864. Action: The sergeant from Coldwater also was honored for capturing an enemy flag at Winchester on September 19, 1864.

Private Ulric L. Crocker, 6th Michigan Cavalry. Issued: October 24, 1864. Action: Crocker, from Vergennes, captured the flag of the 18th Georgia at Cedar Creek, Virginia on October 19, 1864.

First Sergeant Joseph Kemp, 5th Michigan Infantry. Issued: December 1, 1864. Action: Kemp, from Sault Ste. Marie, captured the flag of the 31st North Carolina at the Battle of the Wilderness on May 6, 1864.

Sergeant Alonzo Smith, 7th Michigan Infantry. Issued: December 1, 1864. Action: On October 27, 1864 the Jonesville soldier captured the flag of the 26th North Carolina at Hatcher's Run, Virginia.

Corporal Benjamin F. Youngs, 1st Michigan Sharpshooters. Issued: December 1, 1864. Action: Youngs, a Canadian, was recognized for seizing the flag of the 35th North Carolina at Petersburg, Virginia on June 17, 1864.

Private James H. Robinson, 3rd Michigan Cavalry. Issued: April 4, 1865. Action: The Corunna cavalryman fought off seven guerrillas at Brownsville, Arkansas on January 27, 1865.

First Sergeant Joseph Kemp was the first infantryman from Michigan to be awarded the Medal of Honor. He received it for capturing the flag of the 31st North Carolina at the Battle of the Wilderness on May 6, 1864.

Second Lieutenant Thomas W. Custer, 6th Michigan Cavalry. Issued: April 24, 1865. Action: Custer, who Monroe claims as its own (although he didn't live in Michigan until after the war, and then only briefly), earned his first of two medals on April 3, 1865 at Namozine Church, Virginia, where he captured a North Carolina flag and 12 prisoners.

Captain Edwin F. Savacool, 1st New York (Lincoln) Cavalry. Issued: April 24, 1865. Action: Savacool, from Marshall, was wounded while capturing a flag at Sayler's Creek, Virginia on April 6, 1865. Note: Savacool died several days before his medal was issued. Because the Medal of Honor originally was intended to be conspicuously worn by its recipient, this was a rare case of the decoration being awarded posthumously during the Civil War.

Second Lieutenant Elliott M. Norton, 6th Michigan Cavalry. Issued: May 3, 1865. Action: Norton, from Wayland, captured the flag of the 44th Tennessee at Sayler's Creek on April 6, 1865.

Second Lieutenant John R. Norton, 1st New York (Lincoln) Cavalry. Issued: May 3, 1865. Action: The officer from Grand Rapids received his medal for capturing a flag at Sayler's Creek on April 6, 1865.

Sergeant John W. Menter, 5th Michigan Infantry. Issued: May 10, 1865. Action: Menter, from Ontonagon, was cited for a capturing a flag at Sayler's Creek on April 6, 1865.

Corporal Walter L. Mundell, 5th Michigan Infantry. Issued: May 10, 1865. Action: On April 6, 1865 the soldier from Marshall seized an enemy flag at Sayler's Creek.

Second Lieutenant Thomas W. Custer, 6th Michigan Cavalry (second award). Issued: May 22, 1865. Action: At Sayler's Creek on April 6, 1865, Custer managed to seize two stands of colors despite being shot in the face.

Private Morgan D. Lane, 5th Corps, Signal Corps, Army of the Potomac. Issued: March 16, 1866. Action: On April 6, 1865 the Allegan private captured the flag of the gunboat *Nausemond* near Jetersville, Virginia.

Chief Quartermaster Cornelius Cronin, U. S. Navy. Issued: July 3, 1866. Action: The Detroit sailor received his medal for "cool and vigilant" service while aboard the *USS Richmond* during action on the Mississippi below New Orleans in 1864.

Private Julius D. Rhodes, 5th New York Cavalry. Issued: March 9, 1887. Action: The Monroe trooper was honored for his gallantry at Thoroughfare Gap, Virginia on August 28, 1862 and two days later at Second Bull Run, where he was wounded.

First Lieutenant Orson W. Bennett, 102nd U. S. Colored Infantry. Issued: March 9, 1887. Action: At Honey Hill, South Carolina on November 30, 1864, Bennett—from Union City— led a small force 100 yards in advance of the Union lines and brought back three guns, preventing their capture.

First Sergeant Charles M. Holton, 7th Michigan Cavalry. Issued: March 21, 1889. Action: On July 14, 1863, the Battle Creek trooper dismounted to capture the flag of the 55th Virginia at Falling Waters, Virginia.

Private Benjamin Morse, 3rd Michigan Infantry. Issued: February 24, 1891. Action: Morse, from Grand Rapids, captured the flag of the 4th Georgia Battery at Spotsylvania, Virginia on May 12, 1864.

First Lieutenant Charles L. Barrell, 102nd U. S. Colored Infantry. Issued: May 14, 1891. Action: Barrell, from Leighton, was recognized for hazardous service in marching his troops through enemy country near Camden, South Carolina, in April 1865.

Major Byron M. Cutcheon, 20th Michigan Infantry. Issued: June 29, 1891. Action: The officer from Grand Rapids was recognized for gallantry for leading his regiment in a charge at Horseshoe Bend, Kentucky on May 10, 1863.

Captain Frank D. Baldwin, 19th Michigan Infantry. Issued: December 3, 1891. Action: Under "a galling fire" on July 12, 1864, the captain from Manchester led his company in a countercharge at Peach Tree Creek, Georgia, capturing two officers in the process. Note: Baldwin, who continued his career in the regular army, was simultaneously awarded a second medal, this time in recognition of his having rescued two women captured by Indians in 1874.

Private George Sidman, 16th Michigan Infantry. Issued: April 6, 1892. Action: According to his citation, on June 27, 1862 at Gaines Mill, Virginia, the 17-year-old drummer boy from Owosso "Rallied his comrades to charge a vastly superior force until wounded in hip."

Private Charles F. Sancrainte, 15th Michigan Infantry. Issued: July 25, 1892. Action: On July 22, 1864 the Monroe native captured the flag of the 5th Texas at Atlanta, Georgia.

First Lieutenant James I. Christiancy, 9th Michigan Cavalry. Issued: October 10, 1892. Action: The Monroe native, an aide-de-camp on General George Custer's staff, was twice wounded while leading a charge at Hawes Shop, Virginia on May 28, 1864.

Captain Edward Hill, 16th Michigan Infantry. Issued: December 4, 1893. Action: On June 1, 1864 at Cold Harbor, Virginia, the Detroiter was wounded while leading "a desperate charge" on enemy batteries.

The Battle of Chickamauga (right), where Sergeant William G. Whitney of the 11th Michigan Infantry earned the Medal of Honor.

Captain William H. Ward, 47th Ohio Infantry. Issued: January 2, 1895. Action: On August 3, 1863, Ward voluntarily commanded a nighttime expedition to run barges filled with foodstuffs past the Confederate batteries below Vicksburg. Ward, from Adrian, was the first of eight Michigan men serving with the 47th Ohio to receive the medal for this particular action and the only officer.

Captain William H. Withington, 1st Michigan Infantry. Issued: January 7, 1895. Action: At the Battle of Bull Run on July 21, 1861, the Jackson native remained on the field to assist his wounded superior officer.

Sergeant Moses A. Luce, 4th Michigan Infantry. Issued: February 7, 1895. Action: The soldier from Adrian saved a comrade's life at Laurel Hill, Virginia on May 10, 1864.

Colonel Orlando B. Willcox, 1st Michigan Infantry. Issued: March 2, 1895. Action: The indomitable Detroiter led repeated charges at Bull Run on July 21, 1861 until he was wounded and taken prisoner.

First Lieutenant William R. Shafter, 7th Michigan Infantry. Issued: June 12, 1895. Action: On May 31, 1862 at Fair Oaks, Virginia, the officer from Galesburg concealed his wounds in order to remain on the field and continue fighting.

Corporal Alexander A. Forman, 7th Michigan Infantry. Issued: August 17, 1895. Action: At Fair Oaks on May 31, 1862, the Jonesville native continued fighting until he passed out from his wounds and had to be carried off the field.

Private G. K. Ayers, 8th Missouri Infantry. Issued: August 31, 1895. Action: Ayers, who hailed from Washtenaw County, displayed conspicuous gallantry during the charge of a "volunteer storming party" at Vicksburg on May 22, 1863.

Sergeant William G. Whitney, 11th Michigan Infantry. Issued: October 21, 1895. Action: The noncom from Quincy received his medal for gallantry at Chickamauga, Georgia on September 20, 1863. According to the citation, just prior to another enemy charge Whitney bolted out in front of his lines to cut off and remove the cartridge boxes of fallen men, "the ammunition being used with great effect in again repulsing the attack."

Private Samuel S. French, 7th Michigan Infantry. Issued: October 24, 1895. Action: The enlisted man from Gifford became the third man from his regiment to be recognized for his gallantry at Fair Oaks on May 31, 1862.

Sergeant Alonzo Woodruff, 1st U. S. Sharpshooters. Issued: January 29, 1896. Action: Woodruff, of Farmington, saved a wounded comrade at Hatcher's Run, Virginia on October 27, 1864.

Corporal Henry E. Plant, 14th Michigan Infantry. Issued: April 27, 1896. Action: Plant, from Crockery, rescued the company colors at Bentonville, North Carolina on March 19, 1865.

First Sergeant Patrick Irwin, 14th Michigan Infantry. Issued: April 28, 1896. Action: On September 1, 1864, the Ann Arbor sergeant captured a Confederate general and his command at Jonesboro, Georgia.

Sergeant James W. Toban, 9th Michigan Cavalry. Issued: July 9, 1896. Action: On February 11, 1865, the Northfield trooper rescued his captain, William C. Stevens, near Aiken, South Carolina.

Private Robert F. Dodd, 27th Michigan Infantry. Issued: July 27, 1896. Action: At the Battle of the Crater outside Petersburg on July 30, 1864, the plucky Canadian repeatedly carried off wounded comrades while exposed to heavy fire.

Corporal John A. Falconer, 17th Michigan Infantry. Issued: July 27, 1896. Action: Falconer, from Washtenaw County, conducted the party that burned out a house of enemy sharpshooters at Knoxville, Tennessee on November 20, 1863.

Sergeant Daniel McFall, 17th Michigan Infantry. Issued: July 27, 1896. Action: On May 12, 1864 at Spotsylvania, the Ypsilanti soldier rescued Lieutenant George Herman of his regiment and also captured a Confederate colonel.

Sergeant Charles A. Thompson, 17th Michigan Infantry. Issued: July 27, 1896. Action: The Kalamazoo native was cited for gallantry at Spotsylvania on May 12, 1864, when he "fought single-handed for the colors."

Sergeant Conrad Noll, 20th Michigan Infantry. Issued: July 28, 1896. Action: The Ann Arbor sergeant saved the colors during the fighting at Spotsylvania on May 12, 1864.

Private Frederick Alber, 17th Michigan Infantry. Issued: July 30, 1896. Action: On May 12, 1864 at Spotsylvania, the Manchester native rescued Lieutenant Charles Todd while also taking two of his captors as prisoners.

First Sergeant Charles H. Depuy, 1st Michigan Sharpshooters. Issued: July 30, 1896. Action: Depuy, from Sherman, was cited for coolly working the guns at a dismantled fort in Petersburg, Virginia on July 30, 1864.

Corporal Sidney Haight, 1st Michigan Sharpshooters. Issued: July 31, 1896. Action: The 18-year-old from Goodland was recognized for his gallantry at Petersburg on July 30, 1864.

Private Charles M. Thatcher, 1st Michigan Sharpshooters. Issued: July 31, 1896. Action: Thatcher, from Eastmanville, was honored for his bravery at Petersburg on July 30, 1864.

Nineteen-year-old Smith Hastings strikes a confident pose. The Coldwater native was awarded the Medal of Honor for his valorous conduct during a skirmish at Newby's Cross Roads, Virginia, on July 24, 1863. By war's end he was the colonel of the 5th Michigan Cavalry Regiment.

Lieutenant Colonel Frederick W. Swift, 17th Michigan Infantry. Issued: February 15, 1897. Action: Swift, a Detroiter, rallied his men at Lenoir Station, Tennessee on November 16, 1863.

Private Joseph E. Brandle, 17th Michigan Infantry. Issued: July 20, 1897. Action: On November 16, 1863, Brandle made his friends and family back in Burr Oak proud by manfully bearing the regimental colors during the fighting at Lenoir Station despite being wounded twice.

Captain Smith H. Hastings, 5th Michigan Cavalry. Issued: August 2, 1897. Action: Disregarding orders, the Coldwater captain repelled an attack at Newby's Cross Roads, Virginia on July 24, 1863, saving an artillery detachment.

Corporal Irwin Shepherd, 17th Michigan Infantry. Issued: August 3, 1897. Action: On November 20, 1863, the Chelsea native led a burning party at Knoxville.

Corporal Andrew Traynor, 1st Michigan Cavalry. Issued: September 28, 1897. Action: On March 16, 1864, the trooper from Ovid helped overcome a detachment of guerillas at Mason's Hill, Virginia.

Quartermaster Sergeant Stephen E. Chandler, 24th New York Cavalry. Issued: April 4, 1898. Action: On April 4, 1865, the Calhoun County resident went between the lines at Amelia Springs, Virginia, to rescue a fallen comrade.

Sergeant Cornelius Hadley, 9th Michigan Cavalry. Issued: April 5, 1898. Action: On November 20, 1863 during the siege of Knoxville, the Adrian trooper successfully carried dispatches through enemy lines.

"Right where Pappy said I'd get it!"

Medal of Honor recipient William Shafter, shot in the buttocks during the Battle of Fair Oaks

Corporal George W. Clute, 14th Michigan Infantry. Issued: August 26, 1898. Action: Clute, from Marathon, wrestled the flag away from an officer of the 40th North Carolina at Bentonville, North Carolina on March 19, 1865.

Sergeant Charles S. Fall, 26th Michigan Infantry. Issued: May 13, 1899. Action: Fall, of Hamburg, received his medal for gallantry at the Battle of Spotsylvania on May 12, 1864.

Sergeant Joseph S. Keen, 13th Michigan Infantry. Issued: August 4, 1899. Action: On October 1, 1864, the Detroit sergeant—an escaped prisoner of war—carried vital information on the enemy to Union forces near the Chattahoochee River, Georgia.

Corporal Alexander U. McHale, 26th Michigan Infantry. Issued: January 11, 1900. Action: The Muskegon native was recognized for seizing a flag at Spotsylvania on May 12, 1864.

Private Andrew J. Kelley, 17th Michigan Infantry. Issued: April 17, 1900. Action: The private from Adrian volunteered to destroy a building sheltering sharpshooters in Knoxville on November 20, 1863.

Assistant Surgeon George E. Ranney, 2nd Michigan Cavalry. Issued: April 24, 1901. Action: The surgeon from Grand Rapids received his medal for rescuing a wounded soldier at Resaca, Georgia on May 14, 1864.

Private John Hack, 47th Ohio Infantry. Issued: January 3, 1907. Action: Hack, from Adrian, participated in the attempt to run the Confederate blockade at Vicksburg on May 3, 1863. He wound up spending three weeks in captivity.

Private Addison J. Hodges, 47th Ohio Infantry. Issued: December 13, 1907. Action: On May 3, 1863, the private from Hillsdale was part of a group that attempted to run food through the Confederate blockade at Vicksburg.

Private Frederick Ballen, 47th Ohio Infantry. Issued: November 6, 1908. Action: Ballen, of Albion, was the third enlisted man to be honored for his actions in attempting to run food through the enemy blockade at Vicksburg on May 3, 1863.

Corporal Henry Nash, 47th Ohio Infantry. Issued: February 15, 1909. Action: The corporal from Adrian received his medal for his participation in the blockade-running attempt at Vicksburg on May 3, 1863.

Private Peter Sype, 47th Ohio Infantry. Issued: September 13, 1911. Action: Sype, from Monroe, was cited for his actions in attempting to run food through the rebel blockade at Vicksburg on May 3, 1863.

Private Henry C. Peters, 47th Ohio Infantry. Issued: April 5, 1917. Action: The Adrian private was recognized for his participation in the blockade-running attempt at Vicksburg on May 3, 1863.

Corporal Henry Lewis, 47th Ohio Infantry. Issued: April 17, 1917. Action: Lewis, of Adrian, became the last soldier to be issued the Medal of Honor for actions during the Civil War. It came 54 years after he had assisted in the blockade-running action at Vicksburg, and 11 days after America had officially entered World War I.

Harvesting the remains of soldiers killed at Cold Harbor, Virginia in the spring of 1865. The previous June, 7,000 Union soldiers had fallen in less than 30 minutes in a suicidal assault at Cold Harbor. This included 14 men in a Michigan regiment reportedly killed by a single blast of grapeshot.

Chapter 8
WAR WITHOUT END

Alphonso Crane of Vicksburg, Michigan, killed July 11, 1863 in Mississippi.

The Union victories at Gettysburg and Vicksburg were the turning point of the war, though at the time that was not apparent. Many soldiers in both armies still clung to the belief that there would be one climactic battle, an American armageddon in the recent tradition of Waterloo that would settle matters once and for all. But the rapidly improving technology of warfare had squashed the romantic notion of a winner-take-all showdown between opposing massed formations of men. The conflict was settling into an implacable, sausage-grinding war of attrition, with engineers, giant mortars and trenches its essential, if non-heroic, elements.

The Vicksburg campaign, in which seven Michigan regiments participated, was a demonstration of how history's first "modern" war was being waged. The heavily fortified city of 4,000 was located on high bluffs overlooking the Mississippi, halfway between New Orleans and Memphis, Tennessee. Both of those cities fell to Union forces in 1862, leaving Vicksburg the last Confederate stronghold on the river. After two direct assaults on Vicksburg in the spring of 1863 failed, General U. S. Grant laid down a siege, intending to starve the Rebels and townspeople out. Every day for six weeks, gunboats and field artillery pounded the encircled city. The besieged huddled in caves to escape the shells constantly raining down on them and ate dogs to fend off starvation. No American city up to that time had ever undergone such a merciless, prolonged mauling, and in the end Grant was able to force it to capitulate. The Confederacy was now divided, east from west.

The siege of Vicksburg.

In July 1863, as the rest of the citizens of Vicksburg, Michigan were still digesting the happy news of the fall of the Mississippi stronghold of the same name, the father of Private Alphonso Crane received a four-page letter from Sergeant Lorrison J. Taylor of the 2nd Michigan Infantry. Taylor had written from a hospital near Jackson, Mississippi, and his first sentence acted like a shot through the elder Crane's heart. "Friend Crane," it began. "It becomes my painful duty to inform you of the death of your brave and noble boy Alphonso."

He was my tent mate and chum in the camp and we were comrades in battle and in his death. I have lost a brother dear and true. Our Regiment was ordered to charge the Rebel works on Saturday the 11th and poor Phons was killed on the enemies works. He was the first man to mount the hill and cheer on the other boys, but a ball struck him in the head and he fell without a single murmur. I feel confident that Phons is now in heaven where are neither wars nor rumors of wars. I never heard Phons swear or use any profane or vulgar language. He was indeed a model soldier. Brave almost to recklessness, never fault-finding however hard the duty. I have often talked with him on

Sergeant Beloni LaChance enlisted in the 7th Michigan Infantry Regiment at Portage Lake in the summer of 1861. He was promoted to sergeant major in 1863 and discharged a year later.

Isaac Lawrence of Oakland County was 19 when he joined Battery A of the 1st Michigan Light Artillery, otherwise known as Loomis' Battery. He was wounded at the Battle of Perryville, Kentucky on October 8, 1862 but served through the end of the war.

the subject of religion and I can assure you he had not forgotten the principles that his father taught him. We were obliged to fall back from the place where he fell so I could not get any thing he had about him. We have learned from the rebels that they buried him and Gilespie of our company together where they fell. As we are going to lay siege to Jackson it will not be possible to find the spot till some future day. He had about ($30.00) thirty dollars about him which the rebs took from him probably. His watch is in his knapsack and when they come to us, I will send it by mail to you. I hope you will excuse this hasty note (and the looks of the paper as it is the best I have). As my head is aching from the wound I received which has delayed my writing before. Our loved country has lost one more of its noblest defenders in the death of your dear son and we a noble comrade. But our loss is his gain and there is one more bright jewel among the crowned and blest. You have lost a beloved brave and noble boy. But you have a reason to thank God that he died in a good cause where the true soldier preferred to fall. If you wish any further information about Alphonso direct to me. May God bless you and sustain you in your affliction shall ever be the prayer of your friend.

After Vicksburg, attention was focused on the city of Chattanooga, a major Confederate railway center located in southeastern Tennessee. In September of 1863, the Army of the Cumberland under General William S. Rosecrans lost a two-day brawl at Chickamauga Creek, a few miles east of Chattanooga. Ten Michigan regiments were involved, including several batteries of the 1st Michigan Light Artillery.

Charles W. Newberry of Three Rivers enlisted in the 11th Michigan Infantry when it was raised at White Pigeon in 1861. In the fall of 1863 the 34-year-old lieutenant of Company E was killed at Chickamauga.

First Sergeant Edgar G. Spalding of Port Huron was 19 when he enlisted in the 22nd Michigan Infantry on August 12, 1861. He was wounded in action and taken prisoner at Chickamauga on September 20, 1863 and not paroled until March 1, 1865. After two months of recuperation, Spalding returned to his regiment. He mustered out as a first lieutenant at Nashville on June 26, 1865.

In command of Battery A was Lieutenant George W. Van Pelt, who in the opening hours of the Battle of Chickamauga stubbornly kept the unit's six guns firing in the face of a sledge-hammer blow on the Union left flank. Known as Loomis' Battery because it had been raised in Coldwater in May 1861 by Captain Cyrus O. Loomis, it had already distinguished itself at Perryville, Kentucky in October 1862. There the battery had stood firm while repulsing five enemy attacks, leaving rows of dead Rebels stacked in front of its muzzles.

On this day at Chickamauga, however, the Confederates succeeded in overwhelming Battery A. Nearly half of the command and most of the horses were lost in murderous salvoes of minie balls and canister. Drawing his sword, Van Pelt incongruously shouted, "Don't dare touch those guns!" as the attackers swarmed over the position. Moments later the 27-year-old officer from Detroit was dead, one of 1,657 Yankees to lose their lives at Chickamauga.

The defeated Union forces retreated into Chattanooga, where this time the Rebels kept them pinned down with guns on nearby Lookout Mountain and Missionary Ridge. Grant, given command of the entire western theater, took over the campaign and soon had his men on the offensive. Eight Michigan regiments participated in the bloody engagements around Chattanooga in November 1863.

The climax to the Chattanooga campaign was the successful storming of the daunting Confederate position atop Missionary Ridge, which was a stirring example of how individual resolve could still conquer powder and projectile. On the afternoon of November 25, 1863, the 11th Michigan Infantry Regiment was part of a large-scale assault on Missionary Ridge. After driving the Southerners from their entrenched rifle pits at

The storming of Missionary Ridge on November 25, 1863. Men of the 11th Michigan, clinging to shrubs and trees as they fought their way up the slope, were among the first to reach the summit.

A group of Michigan soldiers at a very popular spot on Lookout Mountain, shortly after Chattanooga fell into Union hands. An enterprising photographer had set up a small but thriving business near the rocky outcroppings overlooking the city.

the base of the hill, some of the attacking Yankees braved a withering fire and resumed their charge up the treacherous slope without waiting for orders. The rebels poured musketry and grapeshot into the advancing troops, killing Colonel William L. Stoughton of the 11th Michigan and shooting down two color-bearers. Captain Patrick H. Keegan kept the regiment racing toward the summit, where they broke the seemingly invincible line and drove the enemy down the opposite slope. An infantryman in a fellow Michigan regiment described this spectacular climb to the summit as "one grand rush without orders, sweeping the confederates from the crest like chaff. I have never witnessed a more inspiring sight than the advance of the army up Missionary ridge on that occasion, and can never forget the appearance of the line mounting up, up, on and on, until the gleaming bayonets of our men swarming over the confederate line on its top, could be seen."

A resident of Jamestown, Charles Peel enrolled as an artificer in Company H of the 1st Michigan Engineers & Mechanics at Grand Rapids on September 2, 1862. The 1st Michigan E & M was arguably the best of all Union construction regiments, building bridges and "corduroy" (log) roads and laying railroad track to keep vital supply and communication lines open. The men were equally adept at destroying enemy buildings and fortifications.

Accompanying Sherman on his march through Georgia was the 1st Michigan Engineers & Mechanics, commanded by Colonel William Power Innes, a civil engineer before and after the war. When they weren't cutting and hammering, members of this engineering regiment proved pretty handy with a musket. During one memorable encounter in Tennessee, they improvised breastworks out of wagons and beat back several enemy cavalry attacks. At one point the Confederate commander sent in a man under a flag of truce to demand the Wolverines' surrender. "We don't surrender much," was Colonel Innes' laconic reply.

This fortified battery emplacement was an example of the kind of construction projects the 1st Michigan Engineers & Mechanics excelled at.

Alpheus S. Williams, born in Connecticut in 1810, burned through a $75,000 inheritance before becoming a frontier lawyer in Detroit in 1836. As a volunteer he was the lieutenant colonel of the only Michigan regiment in the Mexican War. Although Williams was a Democrat, he was Governor Blair's choice to recruit and train the state's volunteers in 1861. Afterwards Williams proved himself an excellent division and corps commander, but higher rank and command eluded him because of his advanced age and his lack of West Point credentials and political connections. After a failed gubernatorial bid in 1870, Williams was elected to two terms in Congress. He died in 1878 and was buried in Detroit's Elmwood Cemetery. An equestrian statue honoring him was erected on nearby Belle Isle in 1921.

As both sides spent the winter of 1863-64 marshaling its resources for a new spring of campaigning, the Confederacy found itself in an almost hopeless situation. The South simply couldn't keep up with the North in terms of replacing lost men and equipment, and hopes of gaining recognition—and assistance—from foreign powers had faded. After suffering defeats at Gettysburg, Vicksburg and Chattanooga, the fight had moved from the Confederacy's front lawn to its front porch. Soon the Yankees would be in the kitchen—literally. But the North was hurting, as well. There seemed to be no end in sight to the fighting, no let-up in the dreadful casualties being reported in papers from Wyandotte to Owosso. "I am forced to see enough of human misery," David Lane of the 17th Michigan Infantry lamented in his journal that winter. "Would God I might never see more. Oh, this cruel, murderous war! Will it never end? Perhaps, when political intrigue can keep it going no longer."

The three-year regiments formed in 1861 were approaching the end of their commitment, and the push was on to entice as many of these valuable veterans as possible into reenlisting. Large bonuses and a 30-day furlough were some of the enticements offered, but Sam Hodgman, for one, decided not to tempt fate by signing up for another hitch. He had survived typhoid fever and leg wounds during his campaigning with the 7th Michigan Infantry, helped to repel Pickett's charge and quell draft riots in New York, and now he just wanted to go home. "I am pretty well worn in the service," he admitted. "All tell me I look 10 years older than I did when I joined the regiment."

Thousands of Michigan men did reenlist, however, determined to see the war through to the end. What remained of the 8th Michigan Infantry, for instance, re-enlisted as a "veteran regiment," a designation that appealed to a unit's pride.

Michigan's "war governor," Austin Blair, came into office a few weeks before the Confederacy was formed and left it just prior to its fall. Blair, a Jackson attorney who helped found the Republican Party, tirelessly supported the war effort in every way, to the ultimate detriment of his own law practice. His once promising political career went into decline along with his finances, as Blair served one term as a congressman but failed in his bid for a U. S. Senate seat. Not long before his death in 1894, friends presented him with a Christmas present of $4,000, asking that he accept it "not as charity, but as a token of affection."

Members of the 8th returned to Michigan for furlough and to recruit new men to replenish its ranks, which had been torn apart at Second Bull Run, Antietam and Fredericksburg. Then the "Wandering Regiment"—so called because it served in virtually every theater of the war—was ordered to the East, where it would leave even more of its men behind at such places as the Wilderness, Spotsylvania, Cold Harbor and Petersburg.

In February 1864 Lincoln called for an additional 500,000 men, producing a new round of criticism about the draft and the direction of the war. The quality of troops was falling considerably, much to the disgust of men like Theodore H. Crane, serving with the 18th Michigan Infantry. Crane abhorred the enlistment bounties being paid to "old grayheaded men and little puny boys" who quickly become "a burden to the Govt. and die or be discharged." Morale was sinking, with the ability of both officers and the administration to lead becoming a bigger question as the war dragged on. "The more I see of this business," stated Sgt. Newton T. Kirk of the 26th Michigan, "the more I am convinced that the best place for one half of the officers in the service would be in the ranks."

One officer who dressed as if he belonged in the ranks was U. S. Grant, who wore an ordinary soldier's sack coat despite the fact that in March 1864 he had been named commander-in-chief of all the Union armies. Lincoln, impressed by Grant's fighting ability, revived the three-star rank of lieutenant general—previously held only by George Washington—to honor his unassuming but relentless warrior. Grant reorganized the armies, coordinating a multi-theater strategy while assuming direct command of the Union forces facing Robert E. Lee's Army of Northern Virginia in the east. Lee's Virginians and General Joe Johnston's Army of the Tennessee were the two major remaining obstacles to defeating the Confederacy.

Mr. Lincoln's armies marched on their stomachs, which made foraging—a polite word for plundering—an essential if usually unsanctioned element of campaigning. "Peck has a hen tied by the leg to his bunk that supplies him with a fresh egg everyday," a member of the 2nd Michigan Cavalry wrote of an enterprising comrade looking to vary his diet of hardtack and beef. Most commanding officers took a dim view of pilferage and regularly punished offenders. On those occasions when the practice was authorized, official foraging parties were required to issue receipts, to be presented to a Union quartermaster for reimbursement for any food or livestock taken. But lower-grade officers not only usually looked the other way when their men "skirmished" with turkeys or chickens, they frequently shared in the spoils. Nothing quite put the spring in a tired man's step like a canteen filled with honey or a haversack stuffed with apples and mutton. "We are living fat on sweet potatoes, fresh meat of all kinds, dried fruit," reported a soldier in the 25th Michigan, on the move in Alabama, "and so it goes in the army, some days have plenty to eat and sometimes nearly starve to death."

Francis McElroy, a native of Bayfield, Wisconsin, came to Detroit to volunteer with the 5th Michigan Infantry. Sergeant McElroy was wounded at Petersburg on June 17, 1864 and discharged two months later.

A rare studio photograph of a color bearer holding his regimental flag, in this case Samuel S. Church of Company A, 18th Michigan Infantry. The life expectancy for those men who carried the flag into battle often could be measured in minutes, as they were principal targets for enemy soldiers looking to wreak havoc or hoping to literally grab some glory for themselves. Church, of Hudson, and the flag both managed to survive the war.

Corps badges were used to identify a combat soldier's unit and were originally no more than distinctively shaped pieces of colored cloth sewn onto the uniform. By the middle of the war they had become more elaborate, especially among officers. This badge was worn by Lieutenant Melancthon Millerd of the 4th Michigan Infantry, which belonged to the 5th Corps.

Colonel George W. Lumbard of Hillsdale was wounded at the Wilderness on May 5, 1864 and died the following day. Lumbard was the last of three regimental commanders the 4th Michigan Infantry lost during the war. Less than seven weeks after his death, the regiment mustered out of service, having lost 12 officers and 177 enlisted men killed or mortally wounded, with another 108 men fallen to disease. A new 4th Michigan was soon organized at Adrian and Hudson and by the fall had departed the state for the western theater of operations.

In the massive Virginia campaigns of 1864, Grant would suffer 100,000 casualties—a tremendous cost, but one that Grant and Lincoln knew Lee's dwindling army could not match. That May, in a heavily forested area near Fredericksburg called the Wilderness, Grant and Lee engaged in the equivalent of a knife fight inside a dark closet. The Battle of the Wilderness is known as "a soldier's battle"—that is, it was an engagement fought and ultimately settled by the actions of small knots of determined men shooting, stabbing, punching and wrestling each other beyond the control of their clueless commanders. At times the thickly tangled woods exploded into flame, roasting those wounded men who could not be carried out on makeshift stretchers. The 8th Michigan Infantry alone lost almost 100 men, including its commander, in a smoky, confusing, hellish encounter that produced 15,000 Union casualties. But instead of retreating, Grant moved grimly on, south toward Richmond.

A few days later at Spotsylvania, a hamlet southeast of the Wilderness, several Michigan regiments were part of a horrific two-week-long struggle that produced 12,000 Union and Confederate casualties in just one square mile of terrain. No less than seven Michigan men earned Medals of Honor at Spotsylvania, including Charles Fall of the 26th Michigan. The 22-year-old sergeant from Hamburg distinguished himself in the May 12 assault that produced a partial breach in Lee's fortified lines. According to the citation on his medal, Fall "was one of the first to mount the Confederate works, where he bayoneted two of the enemy and captured a Confederate flag, but threw it away to continue the pursuit of the enemy." The breakthrough created a hotly contested salient known as the "Bloody Angle." For 20 hours in a driving rainstorm, Johnny Rebs and Billy

The Battle of the Wilderness.

Yanks relentlessly shot and shelled each other to pieces. At times the lines were no more than a few yards apart, the thick fog and smoke transforming one-time farm boys and store clerks on both sides into spectral executioners. "During this engagement a green oak tree 22 inches in diameter was shot down by minie balls," recalled a member of the 26th Michigan, which was one of the first units to reach the salient.

Captain George W. Burchell of the 24th Michigan was wounded at the Bloody Angle. The following day he wrote, "I have fought eight battles in eight days, terrible engagements of musketry. Indeed that is the most horrible fight the world ever saw. This is the 9th day and they are fighting yet. God knows when it will end but it cannot last much longer I think. We shall whip them but I believe it is tough." About this time a Southern lady told a Michigan cavalryman, "I don't believe the war will end in 20 years because the South will never give up."

Above: On May 11, 1864, thousands of cavalrymen clashed at Yellow Tavern, six miles outside Richmond. As always, Custer's horse soldiers were in the thick of the fighting. Towards the end of the engagement, a dismounted trooper from the 5th Michigan Cavalry—Private John Huff, a Canadian who'd won several prizes for his expert marksmanship—leveled his revolver at Jeb Stuart and shot him in the side. The following day the "Cavalier of Dixie" was dead, costing Lee his most valuable cavalryman. Huff was shot in the head three weeks later and died shortly after being returned home to Michigan.

Left: The swallow's tail shape of the 6th Michigan Cavalry's regimental flag made it easier to handle on horseback. The 6th Michigan Cavalry, mustered into service in October 1862, was one of the four regiments of Wolverines that comprised the Michigan Cavalry Brigade. Based on the percentage of population, Michigan provided the most cavalrymen of any northern state.

This unidentified Wolverine poses with the 20-plus pounds of weaponry Union cavalrymen typically carried into battle: two fully loaded revolvers (one holstered and the other tucked into his belt), an ammunition pouch, a sword, and most significantly, a Spencer repeating rifle. Because of their $50 price tag, the seven-shot Spencers were not issued by the frugal War Department until 1863, but they gave Union troopers a tremendous advantage in firepower. Cavalrymen also wore shorter "shell" jackets for greater freedom of movement.

Members of the 6th Michigan Cavalry in camp. A horse soldier was responsible for his mount's feed and care before his own, and in the process became somewhat of an amateur veterinarian and all-around stable hand. Life in the saddle was more onerous than it appeared to ordinary foot soldiers, who frequently sneered, "Whoever saw a dead cavalryman?" Actually, Michigan units recorded some of the highest casualty rates of any cavalry regiment, Union or Confederate.

Captain George Murdock, a government clerk before and after his service with the 1st Michigan Sharpshooters, was a Republican from Berrien Springs. He was one of 9,402 Michigan soldiers to vote for Lincoln in the 1864 election, as opposed to just 2,942 for McClellan. All told, only four Michigan regiments went Democratic—the 1st, 14th, 15th and 16th Infantry—and even those majorities were attributed by veterans to the influx of draftees and substitutes understandably desirous of seeing the North negotiate a peace.

It was a chilling prophecy, one that gained credence with every hammer blow that produced a fresh wave of widows and orphans in Spring Lake, Gaylord, Alpena and other communities throughout Michigan. At Spotsylvania the 17th Michigan lost 194 of 225 men. Casualties for other state units were just as frightful: 144 men in the 20th Michigan, for instance, 139 in the 26th Michigan, and 195 more in the 27th Michigan. As always, death showed no respect for age. At Spotsylvania the 1st Michigan Sharpshooters took 162 casualties, ranging from 16-year-old Private Clark Fox, Jr. to 57-year-old First Sergeant Henry Graveraet, both of whom were killed. While their families grieved, Grant kept up the relentless and costly assaults. Although the attacks forced the tenacious Confederates to take casualties they couldn't afford, at the same time Grant was denied the knockout punch he hoped to deliver.

The ever-lengthening casualty lists made a second term for Lincoln anything but certain. Democratic presidential candidate George McClellan was running on a "Peace Platform" and accusing Lincoln of prolonging the war. Also working against the incumbent was the lingering distaste among many for his support of Negro emancipation and the growing presence of black troops in the army. John Slover, serving with the 17th Michigan, wrote that men were losing faith in Lincoln because he "wants the nigger on a level with the whites."

On the other hand, McClellan was "a disgrace to the service" in the opinion of one 18th Michigan soldier, who went on to tell his father that the regiment was solidly supporting Ol' Abe in the upcoming election. Actually, McClellan still was popular with many soldiers. If nothing else, they were grateful for his past timidity—his reluctance to throw more troops into

> **"A member of the 24th [Michigan] Regiment deserted to the enemy last night. He was a German & came from Canada to Detroit where he enlisted as a 'substitute.' As a general rule substitutes are not good soldiers. An army of substitutes would not stand an hour against the Rebel Army under Lee."**

Diary entry of Colonel Henry Morrow,
November 23, 1864

Charles S. Miller of Rockland was one of many who left the copper mines of the Upper Peninsula to join the 27th Michigan Infantry in the summer of 1862. Miller was promoted to second lieutenant on March 1, 1864. Three months later he was killed in a costly charge at Cold Harbor, Virginia. Unlike countless other soldiers who were buried as "unknowns," Miller's body was identified and buried in the national cemetery there.

combat on the Peninsula and at Antietam had probably extended their own lives. But his timorous nature also suggested that, as president, McClellan would seek a negotiated peace that would stop short of total victory. The men in the ranks could tolerate a lot, but not a dawdling defeatist in the White House.

Fortuitously for the president's chances, in early September the vital rail and munitions center of Atlanta fell to General William T. Sherman, who Grant had put in charge of the Union's western forces. With Grant's blessings, Sherman would soon embark on his daring march to the Atlantic Ocean, his army of "bummers" (which included six Michigan regiments) destroying railroads, bridges, factories and public buildings along a 250-mile route through Georgia. Atlanta's fall, coupled with General Phil Sheridan's successful Shenandoah Valley campaign that ravaged the breadbasket of Lee's army, suggested to the war-weary North that a final victory, if not exactly imminent, was at least now in sight.

Men of the 1st Michigan Sharpshooters. As the inscriptions on these photographs from one surviving soldier's album reveal, few emerged from the war unscathed.

Lieutenant Thomas Fowler of Jonesville was seriously wounded.

Captain Thomas H. Gaffney of Niles was killed.

Captain George C. Knight of Battle Creek was killed.

Major John Piper of Battle Creek was killed.

Lieutenant Garrett A. Graveraet of Little Traverse was killed.

Captain William H. Randall of Pittsfield spent eight months in a prison camp.

Lieutenant Robert Hill of Kalamazoo was discharged as disabled.

First Sergeant Edwin Conklin of Ypsilanti died in a prison camp.

A Union soldier on picket duty during the winter of 1863-64. Both armies used the winter months to gear up for spring campaigning, though monotony, overcrowding and foul weather caused many men to become irritable and quarrelsome and to drink heavily. Men were far more likely to be granted furlough during this period than at any other time of the year, but few enlisted men could afford the transportation home and thus endured several winters in camp. Union privates and corporals were paid $13 a month. At 43 cents a day, this was less than half of what a common laborer typically earned for a 10- or 12-hour day. Enlisted men's pay topped out at $21 a month for sergeant majors. Meanwhile, the monthly stipend for officers ranged from $105.50 for lieutenants to $212 for colonels, not including additional cash allowances for rations and fuel. Generals, of course, made far more money.

On November 8, 1864, citizens and soldiers went to the polls. "I had written home to my friends to vote for Lincoln if they wanted to see the war ended, for if he was defeated, we would not give up with our work only half done," recalled one Michigan cavalryman in Virginia. "We proposed to fight for peace, not to crawl and beg for it."

Michigan men in uniform voted overwhelmingly for Lincoln, with one Republican in the 19th Michigan boasting in a letter home that only six of the 506 votes cast in his regiment went to McClellan. At home, roughly three in five Michiganians voted Republican, handing the state's eight electoral votes to the incumbent. The story was the same throughout the North, as McClellan could carry only three states. Lincoln easily won re-election and with it, a fresh mandate to see the war through to its conclusion.

Sherman's march through Georgia ended on December 22, 1864, when the general delivered Savannah as a Christmas present to the newly re-elected president. After that Sherman turned north, up through the Carolinas.

By the end of 1864 Sherman had concluded his march to Savannah, Georgia, leaving a 50-mile-wide swath of desolation behind, and was preparing to swing his troops up through the Carolinas. As he had with Atlanta, Sherman would occupy Columbia, the capital of South Carolina, and then burn it. At the same time Grant, his move on Richmond stalled outside Petersburg, settled into a protracted siege of the impenetrable city. Torching cities and waiting out the enemy in trenches for months on end were a far cry from the gentlemanly war the volunteers of '61 had envisioned when they signed on to fight. But the strategy was effective. The tattered, starving, demoralized Confederacy, so depleted of fighting men that it was considering opening the ranks to slaves, was on its last legs.

The government-issued "dog tags" of future American wars were never as ornate as the identification badges some Civil War soldiers, worried over the prospect of being buried as an "unknown" on a foreign field, privately purchased or hand-crafted. Mason Safford, a private in Battery C of the 1st Michigan Light Artillery, wore this badge bearing the etching of a cannon. Although wounded in 1864 at the Battle of Kennesaw Mountain, Georgia, Private Safford returned safely to Detroit.

In the February 4, 1865 issue of the *Portage Lake Mining Gazette*, a member of the 27th Michigan Infantry—a regular contributor who signed his letters "Hardtack"—filled in Upper Peninsula readers with the "great changes [that] have taken place in the old 27th" since the unit had been formed.

We left the State about two years ago 800 strong, as well drilled, as well equipped, and as well officered as any regiment from Michigan. Our spirits were buoyant, the prospect of active service pleased us, and with confidence in ourselves, our leaders, and the speedy success of our cause, all looked bright before us. But now what a change; not one eighth of our original numbers are here, officers and men. And where are the others? Some lie in pleasant places in the churchyards of Kentucky; others in the lonely canebrakes bordering the Mississippi; others again sleep in the beautiful valleys of Tennessee or at Knoxville; while by far the most of them lie scattered over the ground from the Wilderness to Petersburg, and some without friendly sod to cover their

Peter Dibean (left) and his son Alexander. Peter died after being released from Andersonville prison. Alexander, who was 20 when he joined the 5th Michigan Infantry on August 9, 1861, was wounded at Williamsburg and Fredericksburg.

bleaching bones. But what of that? On our march from the Wilderness to Spotsylvania we halted to rest on the old battlefield of Chancellorsville and there I saw the unburied bones of over 200 of our brave men. They slept well; why should not the men of the 27th? However these reflections are saddening, thank God this sacrifice of life and limbs is bringing this infernal rebellion to a close.

That same day in Pontiac, Mary Till Dibean died, an indirect casualty of the "infernal rebellion" that had already claimed her husband and would rip their family apart. Peter Dibean had been 48 years old when he enlisted in the 5th Michigan Infantry in the summer of 1861, serving a little more than a year before being discharged for disability. Despite his age and having a family to support, he soon enlisted in the 8th Michigan Cavalry, and was captured in Georgia. He spent several months inside the hell of Andersonville prison before being released in December, 1864. At the time he weighed only 68 pounds and was so weak from disease he had to be carried from the train station.

The emaciated soldier returned to his Pontiac home on New Year's Day, 1865, but died there two weeks later. That proved time enough for several family members to contract the same diseases that had claimed him. Within a month Dibean's wife followed him in death, and shortly thereafter a daughter, Julia, also passed away. With both parents gone, surviving family members were placed with relatives and other families in the community. History, concerned with bigger doings, took no note of this particular calamity. They were just several more unheralded civilian victims of a war that would end soon, but not soon enough to save the Dibeans and many more like them.

Captains James S. DeLand (left) and Charles G. Conn of the 1st Michigan Sharpshooters. The Sharpshooters had the honor of being the first Union regiment in Petersburg after its fall, and the first to unfurl a U. S. flag over the city, but neither officer shared in the moment. Deland was recovering from a gunshot wound suffered in the final attack that left one arm four inches shorter than the other, while Conn had been taken prisoner in an earlier action. After the war DeLand returned to Jackson and tried farming and journalism. He died a helpless invalid in his daughter's Detroit home in 1926. Conn returned to his native Elkhart, Indiana and founded the famous musical instrument company bearing his name. After amassing a fortune and serving as mayor and congressman, he died penniless in Los Angeles in 1931.

Major Levant C. Rhines of the 1st Michigan Sharpshooters was killed on June 17, 1864 during a futile assault on the Confederate defenses at Petersburg. "Boys," the Battle Creek lawyer had said just before the attack, "this will be the last charge to some of us but let's do it bravely."

Corporal Alonzo Campbell was killed in the same assault as Major Levant Rhines. To the heartbreak of loved ones back in Superior, his body was not recovered and was assumed to have been buried somewhere between the lines.

Charles G. Day of Hudson served as quartermaster sergeant of Battery I of the 1st Michigan Light Artillery until he was commissioned in the summer of 1864. The battery, which served in the western and eastern theaters of war, mustered out at Detroit on July 14, 1865.

A group portrait of the band of the 4th Michigan Infantry (reorganized in 1864) taken near San Antonio, Texas, in the spring of 1865. Regimental bands were abolished in the summer of 1862, but many continued in service as privately funded units. Musicians often were used to carry off the wounded during and after a battle.

By war's end much of the Confederacy lay in ruins. This is Charleston, South Carolina, particularly despised by Union soldiers as "the cradle of secession."

On March 4, 1865, Lincoln was sworn in for a second term. His inauguration speech spoke to the hope of reconciliation, not the promise of retribution. "With malice toward none," he concluded, "with charity for all; with firmness in the right, as God gives us to see the right, let us strive on to finish the work we are in; to bind up the nation's wounds; to care for him who shall have borne the battle, and for his widow, and his orphan— to do all which may achieve and cherish a just, and a lasting peace, among ourselves, and with all nations."

Lincoln delivered those famous words on a raw, wet Saturday in Washington. Just as the president kissed the Bible, a shaft of sunlight split the overcast and spilled its warmth on the damp crowd. The symbolism was inescapable.

Meanwhile, the noose tightened around the Confederacy. Lee launched two failed attacks near Petersburg before the city fell. He evacuated Richmond on April 2 and headed west, hoping to join up with Johnston's forces in North Carolina and continue the fight. But Lee found himself boxed in. Four days

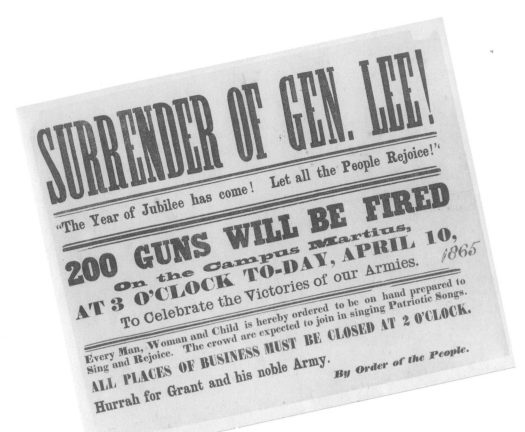

SURRENDER OF GEN. LEE!

"The Year of Jubilee has come! Let all the People Rejoice!"

200 GUNS WILL BE FIRED

On the Campus Martius, AT 3 O'CLOCK TO-DAY, APRIL 10, 1865

To Celebrate the Victories of our Armies.

Every Man, Woman and Child is hereby ordered to be on hand prepared to Sing and Rejoice. The crowd are expected to join in singing Patriotic Songs.

ALL PLACES OF BUSINESS MUST BE CLOSED AT 2 O'CLOCK.

Hurrah for Grant and his noble Army. By Order of the People.

Broadsides like this one announced the end of war and the coming of peace.

later, at Sayler's Creek, Virginia, some 8,000 Confederates, including six generals, were captured in a desperate engagement that saw a half-dozen Michigan men earn Medals of Honor. "My God!" moaned Lee, who lost one-quarter of the Army of Northern Virginia. "Has the army dissolved?"

And then finally it was over. On the morning of April 9, 1865, Palm Sunday, Webster Cole and the rest of the 26th Michigan halted in a pine thicket not far from the village of Appomattox, Virginia. They settled in, waiting for Lee's next move. "We could see the rebs on the side in rifle pits, but they did not fire on us," Cole later wrote.

We corrected our line and lay down in the shade, as we knew a flag of truce was out and nothing doing until that came in. All at once the men on the left of us jumped up, threw their hats and canteens in the air and began to scuffle like a lot of schoolboys. We saw them and wondered what was the matter. Just then an officer on horse back passed by and about every two rods called out "Lee has surrendered," and we played the fool as badly as the other fellows had.

Officers of the 4th Michigan Cavalry, the regiment responsible for capturing Jefferson Davis, who had fled Richmond and for weeks was the most wanted man in the country. The president of the Confederacy was nabbed in the early morning hours of May 10, 1865 near Irwinville, Georgia. Although Davis and his small group of followers were apprehended without bloodshed, an accidental exchange with Wisconsin cavalrymen also tracking Davis left two Michigan troopers dead. Colonel Benjamin D. Pritchard (seated third from left), a graduate of the University of Michigan law school, commanded the regiment.

Lee, saying "There is nothing left for me to do but to go and see General Grant, and I would rather die a thousand deaths," had met with Grant inside a house on the edge of Appomattox and agreed on the terms of surrender. It was another three days before the actual surrender took place, but by then people back home were delirious and soldiers on both sides were trying to digest the ramifications of all that they had all endured. "Everyone is wild with joy," observed one Michigan private. "As for myself, I cannot write! I cannot talk; only my glad heart cries 'Hosanna! Hosanna! in the Highest, the Highest!'"

Henry Henshaw was hospital steward of the 2nd Michigan Cavalry from September 1861 until being discharged for disability on January 5, 1865. This portrait was taken inside the Grand Rapids studio of O. W. Horton.

The discharge paper of a Michigan soldier. "A citizen again," exclaimed one Wolverine at war's end. "Four of the best years of my life were spent in the service of the best government on earth....I have no regrets."

"There is no use in trying to multiply words expressing the joy of the people over the great event of the week—LEE'S SURRENDER," Lois Bryan Adams, a Detroiter working as a clerk in Washington, wrote rapturously in one of her regular reports to the *Detroit Advertiser and Tribune*. "The tumult of excitements so intense, so rapidly succeeding each other during the past ten days, has almost bewildered our senses."

Adams described "the roar of cannon, the ringing of bells" and the "flash and glow of starry banners floating, streaming, wreathing everywhere." Like many others, she saw in the ripening springtime buds a symbolic new beginning after four years of total war. "The trees, shrubs, and flowers, which for days past have been on tip-toe for a 'burst,' could hold in no longer, but shook out their colors and filled the air with fragrance and spicy odors. The rains have opened the leaf and blossom buds, as the good tidings of great joy have opened the hearts of the people, and beauty and incense, rejoicing and thanksgiving fill the land."

Then, just as suddenly, a pall fell over the victorious North. On the evening of April 14—Good Friday—one of the country's leading actors, John Wilkes Booth, stole into the president's box at Ford's Theater in Washington and, while Lincoln and his wife were enjoying a performance of *Our American Cousin*, fired his derringer at the left side of Lincoln's head. The lead ball tunneled its way across the brain and lodged behind his right eye; by the following morning the president, his long bare feet dangling ingloriously off the end of an undersized bed, was dead. Newspapers trimmed their borders in black. There was bold and angry talk of reprisal and revenge.

On April 25, 1865, an estimated 30,000 Detroiters turned out to mourn President Lincoln's death. A catafalque and two-mile-long procession were part of the solemn memorial services. "Everywhere stores and residences were draped in black," wrote Silas Farmer, "and loving, tender, and patriotic mottoes, displayed in many forms, relieved and enforced the somber hangings."

The grief was palpable. "I had just put the second mess of egg on to cook and then took the paper and began to read," Lydia Watkins of Cannon Township wrote her son Benton, now stationed at Camp Douglas, Illinois. Immediately "the eggs were forgotten and no one wanted any more and I think I never spent so long and lonesome day in my life." "Every tongue is dumb and every pen paralyzed with the great woe that has so suddenly come upon the nation," wrote Lois Bryan Adams. "The city is like a widow in the first desolation of her grief today. The revulsion is so sudden from the delirium of joy which had made the past two weeks one gala-day of delight, that men scarcely know how to act or what to do. They meet upon the streets, wring each other's hands, and in broken sentences try to express their horror of the awful tragedy last night enacted in

The 24th Michigan Infantry served as honor guard when the slain president was returned to Springfield, Illinois for burial. Members of the regiment marched immediately behind his hearse and, as seen here, guarded his burial vault.

Colonel John G. Parkhurst of the 9th Michigan Infantry was an attorney in Coldwater before and after the war, dying there in 1906. A capable commander, Parkhurst was promoted to brigadier general in May 1865, one of at least 74 Michiganians to hold the rank of general during the war. Most, like Parkhurst's, were brevet (honorary) ranks awarded in the final months of the conflict.

our midst. Old and young are weeping, and the whole city is shrouded in mourning. All places of business are closed, public buildings and private dwellings are alike draped in black, and the mourners literally go about the streets. All the church bells are tolling solemnly….so sudden has been the shock, we cannot realize that the man to whom the nation has looked up to with such faith and trust, is gone from us past recall."

The assassin was soon hunted down and killed, and eight of his co-conspirators quickly were brought to justice. (Four were hanged and the others imprisoned.) Vice President Andrew Johnson assumed the presidency and by executive order enacted a Reconstruction program for the defeated South that was opposed by Zachariah Chandler and other radical Republicans in Congress. Over Johnson's objections, they were able to legislate a more punitive policy that included the installation of Federal military governments. Home rule would not return to the former Confederate states until 1877. During that period Reconstruction politicians would push through Constitutional amendments that extended civil rights protection to all citizens, regardless of color, and granted suffrage to Negroes. However, through the use of lynchings, convoluted poll taxes and other measures, Southern whites would frustrate these guarantees for the next century.

Lincoln's death and Reconstruction's failure could diminish, but not deny, the principal result of the four-year struggle. "The mad dream of a Southern Confederacy is over," the *Jackson Citizen Patriot* trumpeted in its April 29, 1865 edition. "The old flag will soon wave in triumph over every foot of American soil….The fruits of this contest, and death struggle, are seen in a restored Nationality, a stronger Union, a more vitalized national life, a government based on the idea of universal Freedom. We praise God who hath given us victory."

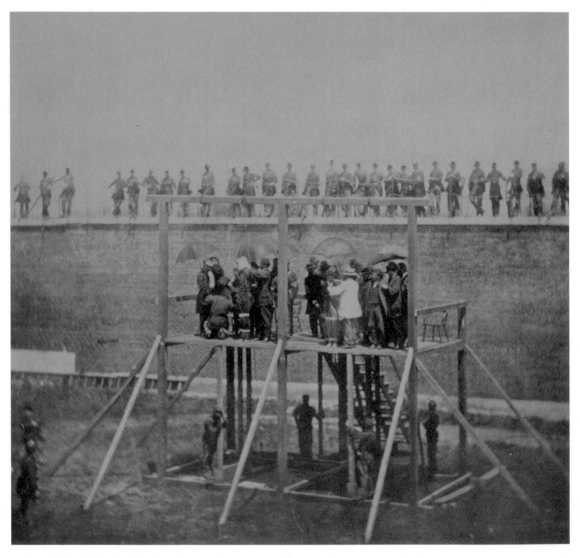

Christian Rath, conspicuous in his white coat, supervises the hanging of the four Lincoln conspirators at a Washington prison on July 7, 1865. Rath personally sewed hoods out of shelter halves for the condemned. At 1:21 p.m., he clapped his hands three times—and on the third clap the traps fell and the prisoners dropped five feet. "They bounded up like a ball attached to a rubber band," he said, "then they settled down." It took 25 minutes before the last of the conspirators was certified dead by doctors. Rath, who returned to Michigan after the war, was haunted by the executions for the rest of his life, especially the controversial hanging of Mary Ann Surratt, who many thought innocent. Convinced he was doomed to hell, Rath became a Christian Scientist.

A prewar portrait of Christian Rath, who served as hangman for the four conspirators sentenced to death for their part in Lincoln's assassination. Rath, from Jackson, enlisted at age 30 in the 17th Michigan Infantry, was wounded at Antietam, and spent time as a prisoner of war. By 1865 he was a captain assigned to the staff of division commander Orlando B. Willcox. Rath was made a brevet major on April 12, 1865, two days before Lincoln was shot at Ford's Theater.

Band of brothers. One autumn day in 1865, the men of Company C of the 10th Michigan Cavalry gathered for a final portrait before mustering out and going their separate ways. "I have been a soldier, have tried to do my duty," one Wolverine said at war's end. "Although broken in health, I am not sorry. I would not sell my experiences for large sums of money."

Meanwhile, there were odds and ends to take care of. Johnston's army, the last Confederate force in the field, finally capitulated in May, and Jefferson Davis was captured—an escapade involving Michigan cavalrymen. At the same time, the many pieces of the triumphant Union military machine reassembled in Washington for one final tour de force. The 26th Michigan arrived on May 13 to participate in the Grand Review of the Armies, a two-day event meant to showcase the 145,000 veterans of the eastern and western armies before

Lieutenant Philip D. Miller and the rest of the
25th Michigan Infantry participated in the
Grand Review of the Armies. During the march,
the regimental flag was snagged in the overhanging
branches of some trees lining the parade route.
After the festivities had ended, Miller returned
to rescue the flag fragments from the branches and
preserved them among his memories of the war.

After Appomattox, the Michigan Cavalry Brigade was sent west to suppress Indian uprisings. More than 100 truculent troopers in the 7th Michigan Cavalry alone deserted as men and horses made their way via trains and steamships to their new assignment, but Captain James B. Loomis dutifully remained with his regiment. The officer from Battle Creek described a massacre of settlers in the Dakota Territory: "The womans legs were cut off at the knees and the thighs, her heart and bowels had been cut out, her throat cut and scalped. The bodies of the men were treated in much the same manner." The veteran cavalrymen were mustered out in the spring of 1866 and Loomis eventually settled in Alaska.

As in all wars, soldiers often died in less than chivalrous ways—drownings, heatstroke, heart attacks, friendly fire. After four years of service in the 7th Michigan Cavalry, including several months of duty on the western frontier, Lieutenant Franklin B. Clark of Pontiac was killed by an accidental discharge of his own pistol while en route to Fort Leavenworth, Kansas for mustering out.

demobilization. "Everything and everybody was going to Washington," Webster Cole recalled some 60 years later. "The roads were lined like a river out of its banks. When we got to Arlington Heights we camped and then the fault-finding began. Troops were pouring in from every direction. The cry was 'Send us old boys home!'"

The Grand Review was held on May 23 and 24. One member of the 2nd Michigan Infantry wrote his parents, telling them of how he and his comrades put candles in the barrels of their rifles for the parade, and describing the buzz from the crowd over the 26 battles listed on the regimental flag. Major General George Custer, flaunting regulations, wore buckskin breeches and a crimson necktie. When an adoring lady stepped out of the crowd and threw a bouquet of flowers at the general, his horse bolted. Custer, his hat blown off and his long golden hair billowing behind him, went flying past the reviewing stand in front of the White House. Whether it was an accident or showmanship, Custer's impromptu charge was one of the highlights of the big parade.

"Then a new howl went up," Cole said of his bored and homesick comrades. "Two more months of idleness. At last we left for Michigan, got our pay and some citizens clothes and we were happy." ●

Detroit's Elmwood Cemetery, where many Civil War veterans rest.

Chapter 9

SLEEP, COMRADES, SLEEP

The butcher's bill was staggering. Some 650,000 Americans had died on both sides, an additional indeterminate number were physically maimed or psychiatric casualties, and much of the South had been burned and plundered. Hundreds of thousands of men, women and children were displaced. It would take the South a quarter-century just to replace the livestock it had lost, even longer for the enmity and bitterness between the two sections of the country to simmer down to a smoldering disrelish. Congress made Decoration Day a national holiday in 1874, but states in the former Confederacy refused to observe it, preferring their own dates for honoring their war dead. Many generations later, the tradition still continues. This contrariness extended to the naming of the conflict; to Southerners it would always be known as "The War Between the States" or, more romantically, as "The Lost Cause." When Ty Cobb played for the Detroit Tigers a half-century after the war ended, his remarkably nasty behavior often was dismissed with the explanation that, as someone whose ancestors had fought for the Confederacy, the "Georgia Peach" was naturally predisposed to be hostile to any Northerners, especially blacks. "He came up from the South, you know," one of his teammates recalled, "and he was still fighting the Civil War. As far as he was concerned, we were all damn Yankees before he even met us."

Cobb's virulent racism was far from extraordinary for the times, especially in the South. There, the failure of Washington's postwar Reconstruction policies negated the gains of free blacks and resulted in a society built around the doctrine of "separate but equal." Not that Northern whites were appreciably more enlightened. In 1867, Michigan voters failed to ratify a

SOLDIERS MONUMENT, PORT HURON, MICH.

The Soldiers Monument in Port Huron was just of one of more
than 400 memorials honoring Michigan's Civil War veterans
to be erected after the war.

new state constitution because it included a provision allowing black men to vote. When the state legislature later ratified the 15th Amendment to the U. S. Constitution, which formally prohibited racial discrimination at the polls, Michiganians just narrowly approved a similar amendment to the state constitution. During this same period the Detroit Board of Education stubbornly fought the School Integration Act. When it finally capitulated to the law, the school system spent its last dime replacing double-seated desks with single desks to prevent black and white students from sitting next to each other. For all that, the South remained the true bastion of bigotry. A century after Appomattox, Southern states were still defiantly flying the stars and bars over capitol buildings, still denying basic civil rights to black citizens. The climate would change, fitfully and forcefully, but by then the Michigan men who had helped squash the secession and guarantee emancipation would be long gone.

As near as can be determined, Michigan contributed 90,747 soldiers and sailors to the Union cause (though this number, and those that follow, are open to constant revision and debate). A total of 358 officers died—262 of whom were killed or died of wounds and another 96 of disease. Among enlisted men 3,945 were killed or mortally wounded and another 10,040 succumbed to disease. (The "died from disease" was a catch-all category, its total also reflecting men who had died in prison camps or from a variety of miscellaneous causes, including accidents, heat stroke, drownings, heart attacks, etc.) In all, at least 14,343 Michiganians died. Rounding off the numbers reveals one of every six Michigan combatants never lived to see the Union restored.

Those who did return home to Calumet and Grand Rapids and Fowlerville were considered worldly and important, men to

The Michigan Soldiers' Home in Grand Rapids was erected in 1886 to ensure that the state's disabled and destitute veterans "should not be treated as public paupers but as honored and respected wards of the state." At least 13 members of a single state regiment, the 1st Michigan Sharpshooters, died there.

be respected. In an era where the majority of people spent their entire life within a short radius of where they grew up, a man who had seen the bayous of Louisiana or brought home a Confederate revolver from a battlefield in South Carolina was regarded as the local version of Marco Polo. These adventurers returned to a state that, on the surface, seemed to have not changed much at all.

In stark contrast to ruined states like Virginia (where 60 percent of the fighting had taken place) and Georgia, Michigan was fortunate in that no battles were fought within her borders. In fact, it can be said that the war barely touched a sizable share of the citizenry. Half of all draft-age males in Michigan never served a minute in uniform. Thanks to government contracts, farmers had prospered, providing the war effort with wool, wheat, and livestock. The Union army had gone through 650,000 horses, for example, and a large percentage of them came from Michigan. The manpower shortage had caused inflation—farm laborers saw their wages double during the war to $2.50 a day at harvest time—but it had the positive effect of accelerating the move to labor-saving machinery. New industries, such as the cultivation of tobacco and the brewing of hops, flourished because of shortages caused by the war.

A Mother's Flowery Farewell

Sergeant Emile Mettetal.

Emile Mettetal was a fair-skinned, blue-eyed farm boy from Redford who went off to war with the 24th Michigan in the summer of 1862 and never came back. Sergeant Mettetal fought from Fredericksburg to the Wilderness before being captured. After spending several months at a stockade in South Carolina, he was paroled in early 1865 and loaded onto the General Lyon for the journey north. The ship never made it. An explosion caused the vessel to burn and sink in a storm off the Carolina coast. Nearly 500 men, most of them prisoners of war, including Mettetal and several others from Michigan, either burned to death or drowned in the catastrophe. Twenty-five years later Mettetal's mother still mourned his loss. In 1890, Angelique Martine Mettetal wrote "Fate of Sergeant E. Mettetal" as a way of assuaging her anguish. Although considered hopelessly sentimental by modern standards, this maternal lament remains an excellent example of Victorian memorial poetry.

A prisoner lies in the Florence cell
With languid thoughts of home
Of parents dear, of friends beloved
From whom he sought to roam.
He heard his country's wild alarms
At traitrous hands upraised
To rend the banner, that our sires
With blood and sufferings raised.

The patriotic fires that glowed
Within his manly breast
Roused stern ambitions voice for fame
Sought in the fair lands oppressed.
Decked in a suit of deepest blue
And soldier's knapsack bound
He bade his home and friends adieu
For deeds of glory crowned.

At Fredericksburg the rebel hosts
Were met in strong attire
There many of our brave boys fell
Neath Secession's galling fire.
At Fitz Hugh's landing we will find
Our bravest boys in blue
At Gettysburg they fought, they bled
Still to their country true.

On many a battle field they fought
On fair Virginia's plains
And many of our twenty fourth
Were numbered with the slain.
At the battle of the Wilderness
The fate of one is told
The 'dashing sergeant' here was missed
Yet dear the prize was sold.

To southern dungeons he's reduced
To pine away in grief
While friends at home who know his fate
Can send him no relief.
For long—long months he's thus confined
With naught his heart to cheer
Though far away, are parents dear
From whom he longs to hear.

At length a message from the north
Proclaimed the captive free
Proclaimed him free to seek the home
And friends he longed to see.
Alas! poor Emile! tragic fate
Which we must call thine own
Has taken from thy parents dear
A worthy, noble son.

On board the 'General Lyon' bound
To fair Potomac's shore
He little thought that he should see
His native land no more.
Yes! there upon the burning deck
Me thinks I see him stand
With features turned to catch a glimpse
Of his dear native land.

Alas! the billows madly toss
Hope dies within his breast
Now conscious that he soon must lie
Beneath the ocean's crest.
The angry waves roll o'er the wreck
At midnight's awful gloom
And he's left struggling with the tide
Against a frightful doom.

But all in vain, exhausted now
He sinks beneath the wave
That rolls above that sinking form
To shroud the soldier's grave.
Still do I hear those accents mild
Oh father! mother! hear thy child
He sinks! he dies!
He's gone.

No little mound of earth is left
On which to strew my flowers
No marble slab by which to kneel
Mid Elmwood's shady bowers.
There's but one solitary rock
On Carolina's shore
Cape Hatteras on the Atlantic side
Mid billows' deafening roar.

Yes! there he sleeps our darling boy
Who fought our flag to save
But why these tears since now he fills
A martyred patriots grave.
A father's locks are turning gray
A mother's voice is dumb
The sisters smiles have flown away
While I bedeck his tomb.

O! brave defender of our rights
Renew affections chain
The memory of one blighted flower
Can make it strong again.
O! Emile we can never forget
The laurels thou hast won
Has made thee follower of our
Brave Gallant Washington.

Angelique Mettetal: "O! Emile we can never forget…."

More than a few Michigan veterans had a hard time adjusting. Henry V. Hinckley of Lansing, who served with the 20th Michigan Infantry and the 1st Michigan Sharpshooters, was mentally unhinged by a shellburst and frequently complained of its effects. On the evening of March 31, 1868, Hinckley went inside the room he kept at his sister's house and put a bullet through his head.

"United We Stand Divided We Fall." Frank M. Howe of the 20th Michigan Infantry (left) and Velorous W. Bruce of the 17th Michigan Infantry both lost legs in the conflict, but evidently not their sense of humor.

At some point after the war, Alpheus Hill, who served with the 1st Michigan Engineers and Mechanics, posed for this portrait with family members.

Protected from the early August sun by umbrellas and a canopy of elm trees, Detroiters turned out to watch Union veterans march smartly by in the 1891 parade. GAR members wore dark blue sack coats with brass buttons and wide-brimmed black hats.

By the time the GAR convention was held again in Detroit in 1914, some veterans were in their seventies and eighties and chose to ride in automobiles. As a point of pride, many veterans always walked at least a portion of the parade route, no matter how old they got. By 1933 there were only 33 Civil War veterans left in Detroit; in less than a decade all of them would be gone.

A sense of the ferocity with which the Battle of Chickamauga was fought can be gleaned from this 20-foot-long section of red oak tree, which Detroit resident C. A. Lorman brought back from a trip to Chattanooga in 1893. Embedded in the wood are several whole cannon balls, as well as numerous shell fragments and bullets. During the 30 years this tree stood on the battlefield the bark grew around the missiles until they were partially encysted. Lorman turned down several would-be buyers and presented this unusual war relic to the Detroit Post of the Grand Army of the Republic.

"Travelers commented on the obvious well-being of rural Michigan, noting that farm houses and outbuildings were in good repair and well painted, orchards carefully groomed, and roads and fences in excellent order," Richard H. Sewell wrote in one of the pamphlets published by the state during the war's centennial. "Spanking new machinery, shining carriages, cutters and bobsleighs all evidenced the fortunate condition of the land. Smokehouses for curing meats and impressive red barns sprang up over the countryside. Most striking of all were the large white houses, giving mute testimony to the affluence of their occupants. Saltpork, hams, potatoes, beans, and other foods filled the farmer's larder; company was always welcome." Due in large part to the 1862 homestead act that attracted a steady flow of immigrants, Michigan's population swelled by 60 percent between the beginning of the war and the end of the decade, from 750,000 to 1.2 million people. The state, already in the process of exploding into prominence because of its rich natural resources and spirited entrepreneurship, became a postwar powerhouse in lumbering, mining and other industries.

If Michigan's timeline is viewed as a seismograph, then the conflict registered as more hiccup than upheaval, its afterquake more social than economic. "The Civil War," historian George S. May decided, "brought no sharp break in the continuity of Michigan history, but it was such a momentous episode in the lives of the people of the time that afterward they tended to regard it as the dividing point in all their experiences."

On the faces of these Union veterans from Kalkaska can be seen the same kind of determination that must have made them formidable members of Mr. Lincoln's army.

Gone but not forgotten. This watch fob belonging to a veteran of the 2nd Michigan Infantry featured the face of the regiment's fallen commander, Colonel Israel Richardson.

Helping to keep Michigan a citadel of Republicanism was the Grand Army of the Republic, easily the largest and most powerful of the various veterans' groups to emerge from the war. The GAR was founded by two former Union generals in Springfield, Illinois in 1866. At its peak, in 1890, this fraternity of Federal veterans boasted a national membership of 427,981 men. (Seven years later it would accept its only female member, Sarah Emma Edmonds of the 2nd Michigan Infantry Regiment.) Members were organized into hundreds of posts, or "camps," which in turn were administered by state chapters called "departments." Michigan's chapter opened in 1867, was formally established in 1878, and by 1893 had more than 21,000 members. It operated out of the State Capitol building in Lansing until 1956, when its books were closed and its records transferred to the state archives.

John Pattee, a fiddle-playing private in the 24th Michigan Infantry, did his part to reunite North and South. A vigorous self-promoter in every sense of the word, the Huron farmer unilaterally assigned himself the postwar rank of colonel, hired a pair of musically inclined veterans from both armies, and billed the ensemble as Colonel Pattee's Original Old Soldier Fiddlers. "Vaudeville's Greatest Novelty Act" played Elks conventions, GAR reunions, and radio barn dances until December 1924, when Pattee (second from left) died at age 80.

ONE COUNTRY AND ONE FLAG

Members of the Grand Army of the Republic were entitled to wear this medal.

For years the GAR's National Encampment featured the country's largest parade. In 1891 Detroit became the first city in the state to host this monumental gathering of veterans and their families. Memorial arches were erected over all four major avenues along the parade route, and bunting and flags hung everywhere. Hotels, restaurants and saloons did a land-rush business (as did the downtown brothels discretely endorsed by local GAR members). Dignitaries included former President Rutherford B. Hayes, the secretary of war, and Clara Barton, founder of the Red Cross. Over the course of several days there were firework displays, a mock sea battle on the Detroit River, and a picnic on Belle Isle that drew an estimated 150,000 people—"a crush of humanity unequaled in Michigan," reported the *Detroit News*.

Russell Alger had a rag-to-riches life story as remarkable as any penned by the contemporary author, Horatio Alger Jr. (who was no relation). Orphaned at 12, the youngster started a lumber business in Grand Rapids, a venture interrupted by four years of notable war service as a Michigan cavalryman. He returned to make millions, building a magnificent mansion in Detroit where he often hosted presidents, generals, and other elite, and rising in Republican ranks to become governor, U. S. senator and secretary of war. Alger, whose private railroad car, named "Michigan," was a familiar sight in New York and Washington, died in 1907 while serving in the senate.

The GAR's activities were not all pyrotechnical or social in nature. They included pushing legislation through Congress to secure pensions for veterans, disabled and otherwise. This liberally interpreted and oft-criticized system of benefits wound up costing the U. S. Treasury $1 billion by the turn of the century. James Henry Avery, for example, had spent three years with the 5th Michigan Cavalry, during which time he was hospitalized with dysentery, a disease that killed tens of thousands of soldiers on both sides. Twenty-five years after mustering out of service and returning to his farm in Hopkins, Avery applied for a veteran's pension. On his application it was stated that the disease had "finally resulted in chronic diarrhea inducing hemorrhoids or piles from which he has never recovered." The twenty-five dollars a month he was granted did nothing to alleviate the discomfort and inconvenience of his condition, and Avery ultimately died from complications of the disease in 1902, when he was 65. As was the case with all widows who outlived their pensioned soldier-husbands, Avery's wife continued receiving the monthly stipend until her own death several years later.

Then, as now, being a veteran was a boost to political and professional ambitions. Cavalry commander Russell A. Alger, who grew wealthy in the lumber business after the war, used his GAR connections to successively become governor, secretary of war, and U. S. senator. "Waving the bloody flag" came to be associated with the Republican party, which would dominate state politics until the Great Depression of the 1930s caused it to be virtually swept out of office. However, even Democratic candidates benefited from the cachet of having served.

A flag-waving veteran from the Ralph Ely GAR Post in Shepherd, and his wife.

Charles G. Hampton, a former New York cavalryman who made his fortune in Michigan, was made commander of the Detroit Post in 1902, inspiring this unusual composite tracing his days from childhood through genteel respectability. The Detroit Post, one of five GAR posts in the city, was known as "the silk stocking post" because of its exclusivity. Its membership was limited to 150 veterans, most of whom were politicians, judges, publishers, and millionaire captains of industry and commerce. Its ranks included Mayor Hazen S. Pingree and ginger ale tycoon James Vernor.

In 1891 veterans petitioned the City of Detroit for a meeting hall. The result was a six-story complex that still stands at the corner of Cass and Grand River Avenues. The GAR Building, which cost $44,000 to build, served its purpose for a half-century before becoming part of the city's parks and recreation department. It has been boarded up and closed since 1973, its heavy stone walls and turreted towers causing passersby to refer to the forbidding looking property as "the castle."

Alonzo Dickerson of Ovid was 43 years old when he enlisted as a private in the 19th Michigan Infantry in 1862. He was discharged for wounds two years later and died in 1898, just as the Spanish-American War was beginning.

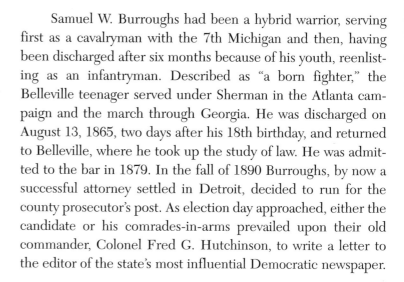

Samuel W. Burroughs had been a hybrid warrior, serving first as a cavalryman with the 7th Michigan and then, having been discharged after six months because of his youth, reenlisting as an infantryman. Described as "a born fighter," the Belleville teenager served under Sherman in the Atlanta campaign and the march through Georgia. He was discharged on August 13, 1865, two days after his 18th birthday, and returned to Belleville, where he took up the study of law. He was admitted to the bar in 1879. In the fall of 1890 Burroughs, by now a successful attorney settled in Detroit, decided to run for the county prosecutor's post. As election day approached, either the candidate or his comrades-in-arms prevailed upon their old commander, Colonel Fred G. Hutchinson, to write a letter to the editor of the state's most influential Democratic newspaper.

To the Editor of the Detroit Free Press: I see that Samuel W. Burroughs has been nominated and is a candidate for the Democratic ticket for the office of prosecuting attorney for Wayne county. It was my fortune to be a member of the 15th Michigan Infantry during its term of service in the late war, about two years of which I had the honor of commanding it. Mr. Burroughs was a member of the regiment and was one of if not the youngest member of his company. The record of Mr. Burroughs as a soldier is exceptionally good. He was never absent from duty without authority; never under arrest, or subject to complaint or reprimand during his service. He was present with his command and did his full duty in every battle in which he was engaged; was, in short, a meritorious, brave and faithful soldier in every respect. I earnestly hope his old comrades who live in Wayne county will not only vote for Sergeant Sam, but will do their best to secure his election.

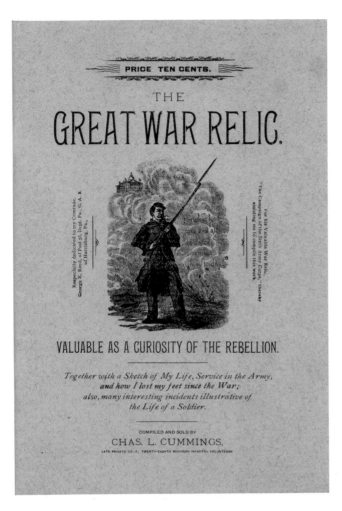

Charles Cummings sold copies of "The Great War Relic" to help make ends meet after he lost both feet in a postwar train accident.

As intended, the colonel's endorsement served nicely as an unpaid political advertisement. "Sergeant Sam" won handily and went on to enjoy a noteworthy legal and political career.

As with any large group, it's difficult to make any sweeping generalizations about Michigan's Civil War veterans. Some, like Alger and the man he succeeded as commander of the Michigan Cavalry Brigade, George Custer, became prominent figures on the national stage. Others, like those buried in the small prison cemeteries for unclaimed inmates, obviously had a hard time adjusting. As the years passed and memories of the great national calamity took on a certain nostalgic afterglow, scores of Michigan veterans felt the need to share their experiences with readers. A steady stream of magazine articles, regimental histories and memoirs of varying quality made it into print, including a modest offering by Charles L. Cummings, who'd been a member of 28th Michigan Infantry. The title of Cummings' quirky self-published pamphlet was nearly as long as the text: *The Great War Relic. Valuable as a curiosity of the rebellion. Together with a sketch of my life, service in the Army, and how I lost my feet since the war; also, many interesting incidents illustrative of the life of a soldier.* If the public didn't rush out to buy Cummings' little work, it nonetheless eagerly anticipated the memoirs of such household names as Custer. Unfortunately for everyone, the boy general discovered that the impetuosity that had made him a hero fighting the Confederacy didn't translate well when battling the Sioux. He and his command were wiped out at the Little Big Horn in Montana in 1876 and his Civil War memoirs were never completed.

The proudly assembled members of the Sedgewich GAR Post in Evart,
several years after the war.

For the most part, Michigan's veterans simply returned to the shops, farms and villages they had left behind, content to store their uniforms, letters and pocket diaries in closets, attics and barns. They were proud of their service, but more eager to resettle into the comforting rhythms of everyday life. Thousands felt no need to talk about, much less publish, their war experiences, unless it was with others who shared the same inwardness. Rigorously organized fraternal associations were not for everyone. As ubiquitous and influential as the GAR was, it's a fact that only about one in four Michigan veterans ever belonged to it. If there was one common denominator linking all these men, it was that they had once worn the uniform with varying degrees of distinction—and that usually was enough to keep friendships with comrades open and ever-lasting, but on an informal basis.

> **"Please accept my best wishes for all the good things of life...a peaceful death and a glorious resurrection in that distant land where so many of our old comrades have gone and are waiting for us."**

Letter written by John Anderson to Ira Evans, a fellow veteran of the 1st Michigan Sharpshooters

For years after the war the members of the 24th Michigan Infantry Regiment got together one day each summer for a river cruise and picnic, officers drawing laughs by dancing with enlisted men. The annual get-togethers eventually ended. By 1913, the golden anniversary of the Battle of Gettysburg, the dwindling number of survivors were scattered all over the map, from a soldiers' home in California to a military hospital in Kansas. Other members of the regiment had retired to Florida and New Hampshire. One old soldier, Corporal Menzo M. Benster, settled in Meade, South Dakota. For some unexplained reason the town's name was changed to Gettysburg—an irony not lost on Benster's comrades, who remembered that he had missed the battle that decimated the regiment because he was sent home to Michigan to regain his health. The last we hear of Corporal Benster is in a 1915 piece extolling local citizens, where he is described as being in his seventies, in poor health, but still active. Mention is made of his patented inventions, including a replaceable window ("the window without a fault") and an interesting mechanical contrivance described as a "flying machine with a reversible motor."

Were that Corporal Benster's contraption could fly back in time, or his faultless window provide a portal to the past. But lacking some sort of fanciful "way-back" gizmo to climb into, the veterans of Fredericksburg and Gettysburg could only keep marching forward as the passing years continued to put distance

Cover Them Over With Beautiful Flowers

A memorial service at Forest Lawn Cemetery in Dexter in 1875.

The exact beginnings of Decoration Day are murky, but its original purpose—to commemorate fallen Civil War soldiers by decorating their graves with flowers—is not. Although anecdotal evidence suggests the custom had begun more or less simultaneously in several communities during the war, in 1966 Congress recognized Waterloo, New York, as the "birthplace" of what we now know as Memorial Day. Despite that official endorsement, more than a score of towns across the country continue to argue that they were first. What is certain is that the practice quickly gained in popularity in the years immediately following the Civil War.

The first organized observances of Decoration Day in Michigan were the result of a general order issued by General John A. Logan, commander in chief of the Grand Army of the Republic. On May 5, 1868, he instructed: "The 30th of May, 1868, is designated for the purpose of strewing with flowers, or

> "John Hekhuis, of Holland City, aged 38, who served through the war in the 13th Michigan Infantry, and was wounded in the battle of Stone's River, the bullet entering the right breast, which could not be found at the time, died recently, the bullet having sunk down into his lungs. He was buried the next day. He leaves a wife and two children."

Obituary in a Fowlerville newspaper, June 7, 1878

otherwise decorating the graves of comrades who died in defense of their country during the late rebellion, and whose bodies now lie in almost every city, village, and hamlet church-yard in the land. In this observance no form of ceremony is pre-scribed, but posts and comrades will in their own way arrange such fitting services and testimonials of respect as circumstances may permit."

That spring observances were hastily organized across the state, with Detroit's service being typical. It was held in Elmwood Cemetery, the resting place for many soldiers (including a large number of Negro troops), abolitionists and Civil War-era politi-cians. Theodore Romeyn, a local attorney reputed to be the best orator in the city, addressed the crowd while standing in front of a backdrop that included several flags and a stuffed eagle. A band from Fort Wayne played the national anthem. Meanwhile, in Washington, General James Garfield spoke at the first nation-al observance at Arlington National Cemetery.

By 1890 Decoration Day was legally recognized in Mich-igan and every other Northern state and, thanks to the G. A. R.'s urging, was now regularly referred to as Memorial Day. Services typically featured patriotic speeches and sentimental songs, such as E. F. Stewart's popular *Cover Them Over with Beautiful Flowers*:

Cover them over with beautiful flow'rs,
Deck them with garlands, those brothers of ours,
Lying so silently night and day,
Sleeping the years of their manhood away.
Give them the meed they have won in the past,
Give them the honors their future forecast,
Give them the chaplets they won in the strife,
Give them the laurels they lost with their life.

Cover them over, yes, cover them over,
Parent, and husband, brother and lover;
Crown in your hearts those dead heroes of ours,
Cover them over with beautiful flow'rs.

To Bruce Catton, growing up in Benzonia at the turn of the 20th century, Memorial Day was "one of the pleasantest holi-days of the year," an observance that had as its signature smell the fragrance of the ubiquitous lilac. The gray-bearded Civil War vets "were men set apart," pillars of the community with an "unassuming natural dignity," Catton wrote.

"They gave an especial flavor to the life of the village. Years ago they had marched thousands of miles to legendary battlefields, and although they had lived half a century since then in our quiet backwater all anyone ever thought of was that they had once gone to the ends of the earth and seen beyond the farthest horizon....We looked at these men in blue, existing in pensioned security, honored and respected by all, moving past the mounded graves with their little flags and their heaps of lilacs, and we were in awe of them. Those terrible names out of the history books—Gettysburg, Shiloh, Stone's River, Cold

These five Detroit veterans helped to commemorate Memorial Day in 1916. From left: C. A. Bartlett, L. J. Culver, S. B. Dixon, H. S. Dean, and Alexander S. McWilliams.

Harbor—came alive through these men. They had been there…and now they stood by the G. A. R. monument in the cemetery and listened to the orations and the prayers and the patriotic songs, and to watch them was to be deeply moved."

As the years passed, Memorial Day grew to include the dead of subsequent wars, with the Arlington ceremony featuring the laying of a wreath at the Tomb of the Unknown Soldier. In 1971 the federal government moved its observance to the last Monday in May, completing the devolution of a national day of mourning into a three-day holiday weekend that by now signaled the unofficial start to summer.

Today the sense that Memorial Day's original purpose has been lost in a flurry of appliance and swimwear sales is perhaps felt more keenly in the North than in the South, where Virginia, Texas and seven other former Confederate states continue to observe a separate holiday—alternately called Confederate Heroes Day or Confederate Memorial Day—to honor the war dead of 1861-65.

The GAR held its 61st National Encampment in Grand Rapids in September 1927. At the time the veterans organization had nearly 39,000 members. When the GAR returned to Grand Rapids eight years later for its 69th National Encampment, its ranks had dwindled to just 6,244 members.

between them and the sensations of their youth. The GAR's National Encampment in 1914 was notably different from the one that had last been held in Detroit nearly a quarter-century earlier. The number of veterans had dropped by almost a quarter-million, and those who survived now were happy to get around in automobiles instead of on foot. The level of merry making also subsided, as old age continued to steal up on them. Several subsequent National Encampments were held in Grand Rapids, in part because of the proximity of the Michigan Soldiers' Home. The facility, which opened in 1886, had become a respected refuge for several hundred disabled and destitute Civil War veterans. Today 214 of them are buried in the home's cemetery.

As the 20th century rolled on, with all its horrors and fantastic changes, men who had survived grapeshot and dysentery now succumbed to clogged arteries and failed organs. They fell dead at picnics, they slumped over in rocking chairs, their hearts gave out in a thousand hospital beds. George Stone, an Albion orphan who had beat the drum for the 1st Michigan Sharpshooters during the regiment's toughest campaigning and lost his health because of it, remained feisty to the end. On November 11, 1921, the 72-year-old veteran traveled from Battle Creek to Lansing to participate in an Armistice Day parade. Physically drained after marching from the train depot to the local GAR hall, he dismissed suggestions that he sit out the second half of the parade. "I'm going to drum until I die," he declared. Stone was as good as his word. A short while later, in the midst of entertaining a group of disabled soldiers, he dropped dead of a heart attack.

Orlando LeValley as a young soldier.

The last Michigan veteran of the Civil War was Orlando LeValley. Born September 19, 1848 in Marathon Township in Lapeer County, LeValley had first tried to enlist when he was 13. He was sent home by the recruiter, who told him to come back when he was 16. LeValley did as he was told, enlisting in Company E of the 23rd Michigan Infantry in 1864. He guarded trains in Jackson and saw a little bit of the world—Tennessee, Georgia, and North Carolina—before returning home in December 1865.

On April 19, 1948, LeValley died at his farm five miles west of Caro, where he'd lived since 1876. The press reported that he'd already outlived his wife, Hannah, by 30 years, and one of their six children. He left behind 15 grandchildren—three of whom had served in World War II—and 29 great-grandchildren. LeValley, who'd enjoyed telling people that he had heard Lincoln's second inaugural address while on furlough in 1865, was just five months shy of his 100th birthday.

In September 1948, just about the time LeValley would have celebrated his milestone birthday, a 104-year-old gentleman by the name of Joseph Clovese moved without fanfare from his native Louisiana to Pontiac to live with some friends. Born a slave in St. Bernard Parish on January 30, 1844, Clovese had run away from his owner to join the Union army. He served as a drummer boy during the siege of Vicksburg, then joined the 63rd Colored Infantry Regiment. After the war he worked on Mississippi steamboats. The GAR, unlike the Masons and Odd Fellows and other fraternal groups, officially had no color bar, so Clovese was a longtime member of one of the New Orleans camps.

Many veterans fashioned unofficial unit badges, such as Livingston Hall, who served in Company A of the 22nd Michigan Infantry

A few weeks after moving to Michigan, Clovese called the local paper to casually inquire about the nearest GAR post. The next day readers were surprised to learn that Michigan had another "last man standing" in Civil War circles. In short order "Uncle Joe" Clovese became a minor celebrity, enjoying press coverage and large birthday celebrations. When the 83rd—and final—National Encampment was held in Indianapolis in September 1949, the GAR's roster had shrunk to a dozen members. Only six, including Clovese, were healthy enough to attend the reunion.

Clovese spent less than three years in Michigan. He was 107 years old and the last surviving black Civil War veteran when he died at the veterans' hospital in Dearborn on July 13, 1951. Clovese's passing left five former Union soldiers still alive. The last of them, former drummer boy Albert Woolson of

Minnesota, died on August 2, 1956. He was 109 years old. With that the Grand Army of the Republic passed out of existence, its legacy officially transferred to its Sons of Union Veterans auxiliary.

By then America was on the cusp of rediscovering the Civil War. Michigan, like all states, assembled a commission to coordinate the educational and celebratory aspects of the Civil War Centennial of 1961-1965. The hoopla coincided with the literary ascendance of Bruce Catton, a native Michiganian who emerged as one of the foremost chroniclers of the war. A former newspaperman and the founding editor of *American Heritage* magazine, Catton wrote a best-selling trilogy of the Army of the Potomac, whose ranks included many Michigan regiments. One of the books was awarded a Pulitzer Prize, cementing his reputation as an historian and brand-name author. Every few months Catton would meet with his agent to pick up another healthy royalty check. They would clink glasses inside a fashionable Manhattan restaurant, and the toast was always the same. "Thank God," Catton would declare, "for the Army of the Potomac."

Not that Catton dismissed the contributions of these men so cavalierly in his writing. Far from it. He was always properly reverential, his lyrical prose often betraying gentle bemusement over those citizen-soldiers he wrote about, his words glazed with a slight veneer of nostalgia. Pessimistic about the so-called progress of the 20th century, longing for something that had been lost, in time Catton came to agree with Mark Twain that man had become "one damned mess." If he was hopeful at all, it was because of the example set by the bearded old men he had admired as a youth in northern Michigan.

An elaborate Methodist funeral service for a South Haven veteran who has joined "the bivouac of the dead."

"In their final years the GAR men quietly faded away," Catton wrote in *Waiting for the Morning Train*, a memoir published not too long before his own death.

Their story had been told and retold, affectionate tolerance was beginning to take the place of respectful awe, and in Europe there was a new war that by its sheer incomprehensible magnitude seemed to dwarf that earlier war we knew so well. One by one the old men went up to that sun-swept hilltop to sleep beneath the lilacs, and as they departed we began to lose more than we knew we were losing. For these old soldiers, simply by existing, had unfailingly expressed the faith we lived by…a faith in the continuity of human experience, in the progress of the nation toward an ideal, in the ability of men to come triumphantly through any challenge.

"That faith lived, and we lived by it," Catton concluded. "Now it is under the lilacs." ●

For Further Reading

Because the literature on the Civil War is so vast and growing exponentially by the day, this recommended reading list is limited to selected books, pamphlets, articles and theses that might be of interest to the general reader seeking to find out more about a particular "Michigan angle" to the conflict.

Lois Bryan Adams. Ed. by Evelyn Leasher. *Letter from Washington, 1863-1865*. Detroit: Wayne State University Press, 1999. A compilation of Adams' newspaper columns written while she worked as a clerk in wartime Washington.

William M. Anderson. *They Died To Make Men Free: A History of the 19th Michigan Infantry in the Civil War*. Berrien Springs, Mich.: Hardscrabble Books, 1980.

Margaret T. Applegate. *"The Detroit Free Press* During the Civil War." M.A. thesis, Wayne State University, 1934.

Edward Bacon. *Among the Cotton Thieves*. Detroit: Free Press Steam Book and Job Printing House, 1867. Bacon relates his experiences as a member of the 6th Michigan Infantry Regiment.

Lorenzo A. Barker. *With the Western Sharpshooters: Michigan Boys of Company D, 66th Illinois*. Huntington, W. Va.: Blue Acorn Press, 1994.

Orvey S. Barrett. *Reminiscences, Incidents, Battles, Marches and Camp Life of the Old 4th Michigan Infantry in the War of Rebellion, 1861-1865*. Detroit: W. S. Ostler, 1888.

Robert Beasecker, ed. *"I Hope to Do My Country Service": The Civil War Letters of John Bennitt, M. D., Surgeon in the 19th Michigan Infantry*. Detroit: Wayne State University Press, 2004.

Charles W. Bennett. *Historical Sketches of the Ninth Michigan Infantry*. Coldwater, Mich.: Daily Courier Print, 1913.

Martin Bertera and Ken Oberholtzer. *The Fourth Michigan Volunteer Infantry at Gettysburg: The Battle of the Wheatfield*. Dayton, Ohio: Morningside Press, 1997.

Henry Bibb. *Narrative of the Life and Adventures of Henry Bibb, an American Slave*. Madison: University of Wisconsin Press, 2000. Orig. pub. 1849. In one of the finest slave narratives ever published, Babb details his sufferings, various escapes, and the unsuccessful attempt to rescue his family.

George M. Blackburn, ed. *The Diary of Captain Ralph Ely of the Eighth Michigan Infantry: With the Wandering Regiment*. Mount Pleasant: Central Michigan University Press, 1965.

Albert A. Blum and Dan Georgakas. *Michigan Labor and the Civil War*. Lansing: Michigan Civil War Centennial Observance Commission, 1964.

Robert Campbell. "Pioneer Memories of the War Days of 1861-65." *Michigan Pioneer and Historical Collections*, Vol. 30 (1906).

John M. Carroll, ed. *Custer in the Civil War: His Unfinished Memoirs*. San Rafael, Calif.: Presidio Press, 1977.

W. W. Carter. *Little Johnny Clem, The Drummer Boy of Chickamauga*. N.p., 1871.

Bruce Catton. *Waiting for the Morning Train*. New York: Doubleday, 1972. In this gem of a memoir, the Pulitzer Prize-winning historian recalls his youth in northern Michigan, where aging Civil War veterans were treated with a mixture of awe and respect.

William Christen. *Stonewall Regiment: A History of the 17th Michigan Volunteer Infantry Regiment*. Detroit, 1986. Copies of this spiral-bound, limited-circulation history can be found in several libraries around the state.

William Christen. *Pauline Cushman, Spy of the Cumberland*. Roseville, Minn.: Edinborough Press, 2004.

Charles H. Church. "Civil War Letters." Rose City, Mich.: Rose City Area Historical Society, 1987. Correspondence between a member of the 3rd Michigan Infantry Regiment and his parents.

Walter F. Clowes. *The Detroit Light Guard*. Detroit: J. F. Eby & Co., 1900.

David Coe, ed. *Mine Eyes Have Seen the Glory: Combat Diaries of Union Sergeant Hamlin Alexander Coe*. Rutherford, N. J.: Fairleigh Dickinson University Press, 1975.

Maurice F. Cole. *The Impact of the Civil War on the Presbyterian Church in Michigan*. Lansing: Michigan Civil War Centennial Observance Commission, 1965.

Kim Crawford. *History of the 16th Michigan Infantry*. Dayton, Ohio: Morningside Press, 2002.

Daniel G. Crotty. *Four Years Campaigning in the Army of the Potomac: Third Michigan Volunteer Infantry*. Grand Rapids: Dygert Bros. & Co., 1874.

Charles L. Cummings. *The Great War Relic*. N.p., n.d. A quirky pamphlet published by a member of the 28th Michigan Infantry.

O. B. Curtis. *History of the 24th Michigan of the Iron Brigade, Known as the Detroit or Wayne County Regiment*. Detroit: Winn & Hammond, 1891.

Byron M. Cutcheon, comp. *The Story of the Twentieth Michigan Infantry*. Lansing: Robert Smith Printing Co., 1904.

Mildred A. Danforth. *A Quaker Pioneer: Laura Haviland, Superintendent of the Underground*. New York: Exposition Press, 1961.

Carl F. Day. *Tom Custer: Ride to Glory*. Spokane, Wash.: Arthur H. Clark Publishing Co., 2002. The best of a rather thin batch of biographies of "the other Custer."

Judson Leroy Day II. *The Baptists of Michigan and the Civil War*. Lansing: Michigan Civil War Centennial Observance Commission, 1965.

Donald W. Disbrow, ed. "Lincoln's Policies as Seen by a Michigan Soldier." *Michigan History* (December 1961). The views of Captain Henry A. Potter of the 4th Michigan Cavalry regarding emancipation.

Willis F. Dunbar, ed. *Michigan Institutions of Higher Education in the Civil War*. Lansing: Michigan Civil War Centennial Observance Commission, 1964.

Helen H. Ellis. *Michigan in the Civil War: A Guide to the Materials in Detroit Newspapers, 1861-1865*. Lansing: Michigan Civil War Centennial Observance Commission, 1965.

Jean J. L. Fennimore. "Austin Blair: Pioneer Lawyer, Political Idealist, and Civil War Governor." *Michigan History* (March 1964, April 1964, September 1965, December 1965).

Wells B. Fox. *What I Remember of the Great Rebellion*. Lansing: Darius D. Thorp, 1892.

James G. Genco. *To the Sound of Musketry and the Tap of Drum: A History of Michigan's Battery D Through the Letters of Artificer Harold J. Bartlett, 1861-1864*. Rochester, Mich.: Ray Russell Books, 1983.

Mary Karl George. *Zachariah Chandler: A Political Biography*. East Lansing: Michigan State University Press, 1969.

James Greenalch. "Civil War Letters, 1861-1865." Ed. by Knox Mellon Jr. *Michigan History* (June 1960). The correspondence of a sergeant in the 1st Michigan Engineers & Mechanics.

R. Lee Hadden. "The Deadly Embrace: The Meeting of the 24th Regiment Michigan Infantry and the 26th Regiment of North Carolina Troops at McPherson's Woods." *Gettysburg Magazine* (July 1991).

Charles G. Hampton. *Michigan at Vicksburg*. Detroit, 1917.

Robert Charles Harris. "Austin Blair of Michigan: A Political Biography." Ph.D. dissertation, Michigan State University, 1969.

Samuel Harris. *Personal Reminiscences of Samuel Harris*. Chicago: Rogerson Press, 1897. An episodic account of going to war by an officer in the Michigan Cavalry Brigade.

Frank M. Hawthorne. *The Episcopal Church in Michigan During the Civil War*. Lansing: Michigan Civil War Centennial Observance Commission, 1966.

Frederick H. Hayes. *Michigan Catholicism in the Era of the Civil War*. Lansing: Michigan Civil War Centennial Observance Commission, 1965.

Gregory Hayes. "Detroit Hosts a Grand Reunion." *Michigan History* (January/February 2000). An account of the 1914 Grand Army of the Republic national convention.

Raymond J. Herek. *These Men Have Seen Hard Service: The First Michigan Sharpshooters in the Civil War*. Detroit: Wayne State University Press, 1998.

Martin J. Hershock. "Copperheads and Radicals: Michigan Politics During the Civil War Era, 1860-1865." *Michigan Historical Review* (Fall 1992).

Fletcher Willis Hewes, comp. *History of the Formation, Movements, Camps, Scouts, and Battles of the Tenth Regiment Michigan Volunteer Infantry*. Detroit: John Slater's Book and Job Printing, 1864.

Robert W. Hodge, ed. *The Civil War Letters of Perry Mayo*. East Lansing: Michigan State University Museum, 1967.

Karla Jean Husby, comp., and Eric J. Wittenberg, ed. *Under Custer's Command: The Civil War Journal of James Henry Avery*. Dulles, Va.: Brassey's, 2000.

Richard G. Hutchins. *Fowlerville Goes to War, 1861-1865*. Fowlerville, Mich.: R. G. Hutchins, 2001.

Asa B. Isham. *An Historical Sketch of the Seventh Regiment Michigan Volunteer Cavalry*. New York: Town Topics Publishing Co., 1893.

Benjamin C. Johnson. *A Soldier's Life: The Civil War Experiences of Ben C. Johnson*. Kalamazoo: Western Michigan University Press, 1962.

Rodney Howard Joseph. "The Michigan Press and the Coming of the Civil War, 1859-1861: A Study of Editorial Opinion." Ph.D. dissertation, Michigan State University, 1972.

Irving I. Katz. *The Jewish Soldier from Michigan in the Civil War*. Detroit: Wayne State University Press, 1962.

Dennis M. Keesee. *Too Young To Die: Boy Soldiers of the Union Army 1861-1865*. Huntington, W.Va.: Blue Acorn Press, 2001. Of special interest in this comprehensive study of underage soldiers are the sections on Michigan drummer boys Johnny Clem and Robert Hendershot.

James Harvey Kidd. *Personal Recollections of a Cavalryman with Custer's Michigan Brigade in the Civil War*. Ionia, Mich.: Sentinel Press, 1908.

Charles Lanman. *The Red Book of Michigan: A Civil, Military, and Biographical History*. Detroit: E. B. Smith & Co., 1871.

David Lane. *A Soldier's Diary, 1862-1865*. Jackson: David Lane, 1905. Lane served in the 17th Michigan Infantry Regiment.

Coralou Peel Lassen. *Dear Sarah: Letters Home from a Soldier of the Iron Brigade*. Bloomington: Indiana University Press, 1999. The correspondence of John Pardington, a corporal with the 24th Michigan Infantry.

William O. Lee. *Personal and Historical Sketches and Facial History of and by Members of the Seventh Regiment, Michigan Volunteer Cavalry, 1862-1865*. Detroit: 7th Michigan Cavalry Assn., 1902.

Victor Lemmer. *The Impact of the Civil War Upon Mining*. Lansing: Michigan Civil War Centennial Observance Commission, 1966.

Frank A. Lester, comp. *Society of the Ninth Michigan Infantry Veteran Volunteers, 1861-1865*. Lansing : Ripley & Grey Printing Co., 1911.

"Letters from the Front." Plymouth, Mich.: Plymouth Historical Society, 1997. The correspondence of Lt. Lucius Shattuck of the 24th Michigan Infantry, who was killed at Gettysburg.

Don Lochbiler. *Detroit's Coming of Age, 1873 to 1973*. Detroit: Wayne State University Press, 1973. Of interest are the chapters on Emancipation, Elmwood Cemetery (where many soldiers and politicians from the Civil War era rest) and the Grand Army of the Republic, especially the 1891 National Encampment in Detroit.

Edward G. Longacre. *Custer and His Wolverines: The Michigan Cavalry Brigade, 1861-1865*. Conshohocken, Pa.: Combined Publishing, 1997.

Margaret B. MacMillan. *The Methodist Episcopal Church in Michigan During the Civil War*. Lansing: Michigan Civil War Centennial Observance Commission, 1965.

Joseph J. Marks, ed. *Effects of the Civil War Upon Mining*. Lansing: Michigan Civil War Centennial Observance Commission, 1965.

Philip Mason and Paul Pentecost. *From Bull Run to Appomatox: Michigan's Role in the Civil War*. Detroit: Wayne State University Press, 1961.

George S. May. *Michigan and the Civil War Years, 1860-1866: A Wartime Chronicle*. Lansing: Michigan Civil War Centennial Observance Commission, 1964.

George S. May. *Michigan Civil War Monuments*. Lansing: Michigan Civil War Centennial Observance Commission, 1965.

Julia McCune, ed. *Mary Austin Wallace: Her Diary, 1862*. Lansing: Michigan Civil War Centennial Observance Commission, 1964.

Albert H. McGeehan, ed. *My Country and Cross: The Civil War Letters of John Anthony Wilterdink, Company "I," 25th Michigan Infantry*. Dallas: Taylor Publishing Co., 1982.

Norman McRae. *The Impact of the Civil War Upon the Negro*. Lansing: Michigan Civil War Centennial Observance Commission, 1966.

Paul D. Mehney. "Capturing a Confederate." *Michigan History* (May/June, 2000). The experiences of Michigan soldiers in the pursuit and capture of Confederate president Jefferson Davis.

Kenneth Metcalf and Lewis Beeson. *The Effect of the Civil War Upon Manufacturing*. Lansing: Michigan Civil War Centennial Observance Commission, 1966.

Michigan and the Civil War: An Anthology. Lansing: Michigan Department of State, 1999. A compilation of 23 articles previously published in Michigan History magazine.

Michigan Soldiers and Sailors Individual Records. Lansing, 1915. An alphabetical index to the 85,271 names listed in the 46-volume series of "Brown Books" published by the Michigan Adjutant General's Office in 1905.

Minnie D. Millbrook. *Michigan Women in the Civil War*. Lansing: Michigan Civil War Centennial Observance Commission, 1963.

Minnie D. Millbrook. *A Study in Valor -- Michigan Medal of Honor Winners in the Civil War*. Lansing: Michigan Civil War Centennial Observance Commission, 1966.

Minnie D. Millbrook. *Twice Told Tales of Michigan and Her Soldiers in the Civil War*. Lansing: Michigan Civil War Centennial Observance Commission, 1966.

Henry Morrow. "To Chancellorsville with the Iron Brigade: The Diary of Colonel Henry A. Morrow, Part 1." *Civil War Times Illustrated* (January 1976).

Henry Morrow. "The Last of the Iron Brigade. The H. A. Morrow Diary: Conclusion." *Civil War Times Illustrated* (February 1976).

Alan T. Nolan. *The Iron Brigade*. 3rd ed. Berrien Springs, Mich.: Hardscrabble Books, 1983.

Joel J. Orosz. "Lincoln Comes to Kalamazoo." Chronicle: *The Magazine of the Historical Society of Michigan* (Summer 1978).

C. W. Owen. *The First Michigan Infantry: Three Months and Three Years*. Quincy, Mich.: Quincy Herald Printers, 1903.

Nell Irvin Painter. *Sojourner Truth: A Life, A Symbol*. New York: Norton, 1996.

Dominic P. Paris. "The Brothers Died at Gettysburg." *Detroit in Perspective* (Autumn 1973). The story of Michigan volunteers Alfred and John Ryder of Livonia.

Michael Phipps. *"Come On You Wolverines!": Custer at Gettysburg*. Gettysburg, Pa.: Farnsworth House Military Impressions, 1995.

Gerald R. Post, comp. *The Civil War Diary and Biography of George W. Bailey*. Colleyville, Texas: G. R. Post, 1990. Bailey served four years with the 3rd Michigan Infantry Regiment.

Milton M. Quaife, ed. *From the Cannon's Mouth: The Civil War Letters of General Alpheus S. Williams*. Orig. pub. 1959. Lincoln: University of Nebraska Press, 1995.

John L. Ransom. *John Ransom's Andersonville Diary*. New York: Berkley Books, 1994. Sgt. John Ransom of the 9th Michigan Cavalry spent several months in Andersonville before escaping. This edition of Ransom's 1881 self-published prison memoir has an introduction by Bruce Catton.

Record of Service of Michigan Volunteers in the Civil War, 1861-1865. Kalamazoo, Mich.: Ihling Bros. & Everard, 1905. Compiled by the Michigan Adjutant General's Office, this 46-volume set (also known as the "Brown Books") is an invaluable but not infallible resource guide to Michiganians who served in the war.

Marcia Reid-Green, ed. *Letters Home: Henry Madrau of the Iron Brigade.* Lincoln: University of Nebraska Press, 1993.

Jno. Robertson. *The Flags of Michigan.* Lansing: W. S. George & Co., 1877. The story of Michigan's battle flags.

Jno. Robertson, comp. *Michigan in the War.* Lansing: W. S. George & Co., 1882. An excellent resource for facts and figures relating to the state's participation in the war.

Ferdinand L. Sarmiento. *The Life of Pauline Cushman.* Philadelphia: John E. Potter & Co., 1865. An entertaining but untrustworthy biography of the famous Union spy.

Frederick Schneider. " 'Michigan, My Michigan': Origin and History of This Noble State Song...." *Michigan Pioneer and Historical Collections*, Vol. 35 (1907).

John C. Schneider. "Detroit and the Problem of Disorder: The Riot of 1863." *Michigan History* (Spring 1974).

Robert Garth Scott. *Forgotten Valor: The Memoirs, Journals and Civil War Letters of Orlando B. Willcox.* Kent, Ohio: Kent State University Press, 1999.

Stephen W. Sears, ed. *For Country, Cause and Leader: The Civil War Journal of Charles B. Haydon.* New York: Ticknor & Fields, 1993.

Evelyn Sexton. *The Impact of the Civil War Upon the Congregational Church.* Lansing: Michigan Civil War Centennial Observance Commission, 1966.

Charles R. Sligh. *History of the Service of the First Regiment Michigan Engineers and Mechanics During the Civil War, 1861-1865.* Grand Rapids, Mich.: C. R. Sligh, 1921.

Donald Smith. *The Twenty-Fourth Michigan of the Iron Brigade.* Harrisburg, Pa.: Stackpole, 1962.

Thomas I. Starr. *Lincoln's Kalamazoo Address Against Extending Slavery.* Detroit: Fine Book Circle, 1941. This booklet contains the complete text of Abraham Lincoln's 1856 speech in Kalamazoo during his only visit to Michigan.

William Stocking, ed. *Under the Oaks: Commemorating the Fiftieth Anniversary of the Founding of the Republican Party, at Jackson, Michigan, July 6, 1854.* Detroit: Detroit Tribune, 1904.

Mary D. Teal and Lawrence W. Brown. *The Effect of the Civil War on Music in Michigan.* Lansing: Michigan Civil War Centennial Observance Commission, 1965.

"Thank God for Michigan!" *Michigan History* (July/August 1998). This special issue of the state's history magazine features nearly a score of articles on various social, cultural and military aspects of the war.

Marshall P. Thatcher. *A Hundred Battles in the West.* Detroit: M. P. Thatcher, 1884. A history of the 2nd Michigan Cavalry Regiment written by one of its officers.

Leland W. Thornton. *When Gallantry was Commonplace: The History of the Michigan Eleventh Volunteer Infantry, 1861-1864.* New York: Peter Lang, 1991.

Benjamin F. Travis. *The Story of the Twenty-fifth Michigan.* Kalamazoo: Kalamazoo Publishing Co., 1897.

L. S. Trowbridge. *Brief History of the Tenth Michigan Cavalry.* Detroit: Friesema Bros., 1905.

L. S. Trowbridge and Fred E. Farnsworth. *Michigan at Gettysburg.* Detroit: Winn & Hammond, 1889.

Gregory J. W. Urwin. *Custer Victorious: The Civil War Battles of General George Armstrong Custer.* Lincoln: University of Nebraska Press, 1990.

Joseph G. Vale. *Minty and the Cavalry.* Harrisburg, Pa.: Edwin K. Meyers Printer and Binder, 1886. An account of Col. Robert H. G. Minty and his "Saber Brigade," which included the 4th Michigan Cavalry.

Daniel B. Weber, ed. *From Michigan to Murfeesboro: The Diary of Ira Gillaspie of the Eleventh Michigan Infantry.* Mount Pleasant: Central Michigan University Press, 1965.

Wynard Wichers. *The Dutch Churches in Michigan During the Civil War.* Lansing: Michigan Civil War Centennial Observance Commission, 1965.

Roger Wiegand. *Small Arms Used by Michigan Regiments in the Civil War.* Lansing: Michigan Civil War Centennial Observance Commission, 1966.

William Duncan Wilkins. "My Libby Prison Diary August 12 to September 26th 1862." *Detroit in Perspective* (Winter 1979).

Frederick D. Williams. *Michigan Soldiers in the Civil War.* 3d ed. Lansing: Michigan Department of State, 1994.

Benjamin C. Wilson. "Kentucky Kidnappers, Fugitives, and Abolitionists in Antebellum Cass County, Michigan." *Michigan History* (Winter 1976).

Eric J. Wittenberg, ed. At Custer's Side: The Civil War Writings of James Harvey Kidd. Kent, Ohio: Kent State University Press, 2001.

Frank B. Woodford. Father Abraham's Children: Michigan Episodes in the Civil War. Detroit: Wayne State University Press, 1961.

Frank B. Woodford. Lewis Cass: The Last Jeffersonian. New Brunswick, N. J.: Rutgers University Press, 1950.

Resources

A logical starting point for exploring Michigan's role in the Civil War is the **State Archives** (717 W. Allegan, Lansing MI 48918; 517/ 373-1408). As the state's official repository, a rich selection of the expected primary documents is contained here, from military records generated by government agencies during the war to the papers of the Grand Army of the Republic. The archives also has the diaries, letters and discharges of many soldiers who served in the war, as well as a sizable collection of photographs (each of which is available for a nominal fee). Many other libraries and museums house special collections or exhibits of interest to Michigan Civil War buffs. The most comprehensive can be found at the **Bentley Historical Library** (1150 Beal, Ann Arbor MI 48109; 734/764-3482). Its Civil War holdings include more than 400 collections pertaining to the participation of Michigan soldiers, nurses, recruiters and others, ranging from a folder containing a single letter to several volumes of diaries. Also on the University of Michigan campus is the William L. Clements Library (909 S. University, Ann Arbor MI 48109; 734/764-2347), whose **James S. Schoff Collection** contains several hundred regimental histories and the diaries and letters of 350 U. S. and Confederate soldiers from all theaters of action; however, relatively few of the soldiers are from Michigan. The **Springer Collection** housed at the Oakland University Kresge Library (2200 N. Squirrel, Rochester MI 48309; 517/370-4426) is one of the strongest Civil War collections to be found in any state library. It contains 2,000 volumes and a large amount of original materials, including the papers of Fred Black, the attorney Henry Ford hired to investigate the death of John Wilkes Booth. Also of use to researchers are the **Burton Historical Collection** of the Detroit Public Library (5201 Woodward, Detroit MI 48202; 313/833-1483) and the **Clarke Historical Library** (Central Michigan University, Mount Pleasant MI 48859; 989/774-2160).

The African-American perspective of the Civil War era can be gleaned at the **Detroit Historical Museum** (5401 Woodward, Detroit MI 48202; 313/833-1805), which features an Underground Railroad exhibit, and at the nearby **Charles H. Wright Museum of African American History** (315 E. Warren, Detroit MI 48201; 313/494-5800), where a new state-of-the-art core exhibit allows visitors to step inside a simulated slave ship and stand in a slave trade port. At **Michigan's Own Military & Space Museum** (1250 Weiss, Frankenmuth MI 48734; 989/652-8005), where curator Stan Bozich has assembled the largest collection of Medals of Honor in the country, the role of Michiganians in the Civil War (and other wars) is well-represented. The **Monroe County Historical Museum** (126 S. Monroe, Monroe MI 48161; 734/240-7780) features one of the country's largest collections of George Armstrong Custer material, including items pertaining to his brother, Civil War hero Tom Custer, and other family members. In addition to its Civil War holdings, the **Plymouth Historical Museum** (155 S. Main, Plymouth MI 48170; 734/455-8940) features an impressive collection of artifacts and rare books pertaining to Abraham Lincoln, including the ultimate "clip" file—a lock of the president's hair snipped shortly after his death. The **Little Traverse Historical Museum** (100 Depot Court, Petoskey MI 49770; 231/347-2620), housed inside an 1892 train depot on Petoskey's scenic downtown waterfront, features a sizable exhibit dedicated to Civil War historian Bruce Catton, who grew up in Benzonia. One of the buildings owned by the **Marshall Historical Society** (107 N. Kalamazoo, Marshall MI 49068; 269/781-8544) is the 1902 Grand Army of the Republic Hall that now serves as a military museum and archival center. Most displays are from the Civil War era. Every fall, the Sons of the Union Veterans holds an encampment in conjunction with the society's popular home tour.

The **Sons of the Union Veterans of the Civil War (SUVCW)**, formed in 1881, is the legal and spiritual heir to the Grand Army of the Republic, whose last member died in 1956. The fraternal organization boasts nearly 6,400 members in 26 "departments," with each department consisting of one or more states. There are 500 members in 26 posts (called "camps") in the Department of Michigan. Their activities include graves registration, historic preservation, educational programs and "the promotion of good citizenship and patriotism." Associate membership is open to those without lineage to a Union soldier. Contact the SUVCW National Headquarters at P. O. Box 1865, Harrisburg PA 17105; 717/232-7000. Contact the SUVCW—Department of Michigan at 1691 Summerfield S. E., Kentwood MI 49508; 616/827-3369.

The **Daughters of the Union Veterans of the Civil War 1861-1865 (DUVCW)** was organized in Ohio in 1885 and are a bit more selective than their male counterparts in the SUVCW when deciding who to let in. Eligibility for membership "is through lineal descent only and not through adoption." The Department of Michigan, organized in 1914, has chapters (called "tents") currently active in Lansing, Grand Rapids, Detroit and Sunfield. About 175 members are involved in genealogical projects and fundraisers to save Civil War flags and monuments. Contact the DUVCW National Headquarters at 503 S. Walnut, Springfield IL 62704; 217/544-0616. Contact the Department of Michigan—DUVCW at Cynthia Van Antwerp, 9260 17 Mile, Marshall MI 49068; 269/781-4850; JNC77@aol.com.

The first **Civil War Round Table (CWRT)** was founded in Chicago in 1940 as a way for Civil War buffs to get together on a regular basis. The number of CWRTs has fluctuated wildly over the years, but currently stands at about 300 nationally. Although all are locally autonomous organizations, most are loosely affiliated with the **Civil War Round Table Associates (CWRTA)**. This umbrella association coordinates the sponsorship of regional and national conferences and also assists in the organizing of new round tables. Contact the CWRTA at Jerry Russell, P. O. Box 7388, Little Rock AR 72217; 501/225-3996; jrussell@civilwarbuff.com.

There are several CWRTs active in Michigan, most located in the southeastern part of the state. Their ranks include professors, historians, journalists and other professionals, but most members are simply lay people with an active interest in the subject. Annual dues are in the $12-20 range. Members meet one evening each month to discuss the latest books, preservation issues and other topics of interest. Meetings, which are open to the public, usually feature a guest speaker ("Hollywood and the Civil War," "The Naval War on the Mississippi" are typical topics) and refreshments. The **Abraham Lincoln Civil War Round Table of Michigan** gets together one Thursday evening each month at the Plymouth Historical Museum. For more information, contact Liz Stringer, 23959 Brookplace Court, Farmington Hills MI 48336; 248/473-4118; stringerl@aol.com. The **Ann Arbor Civil War Round Table** meets at the Education Center Auditorium, St. Joseph Mercy Hospital at 5305 E. Huron River Drive in Ann Arbor. Contact Tom Nanzig at 734/930-0617 or Pam Newhouse at 734/973-1047. The meetings of the **G. W. Lee Civil War Round Table** are held on the third floor of the First National Bank at the corner of Grand River and Michigan in downtown Howell. Contact Dave Finney at 517/548-3544. Members of the **Kalamazoo Civil War Round Table** gather inside the Westwood Methodist Church at 538 Nichols Rd. in Kalamazoo. Contact Pam Boudreau at 616/349-6195; tmselem2@net-link.net.

The **Michigan Regimental Civil War Round Table**, active since 1960, meets monthly at the Farmington Community Library at 23500 Liberty in Farmington. Each October members travel to a Civil War battlefield for a weekend tour. Contact Jerry Maxwell at 248/363-1710; max82507@msn.com; or visit www.farmlib.org/mrrt.

Since it was founded in 1950, the "aim" of the **North-South Skirmishers Association (NS-SA)** has been to re-create the essence of the Civil War battle experience through the competitive firing of period weaponry at paper targets. About 4,000 members belong to some 200 chapters, each based on an actual unit. There are 13 regions, with the 20 or so Michigan units (including such creatively named outfits as the U.S.S. Michigan Landing Party, founded in 1958) belonging to the North West Territory. Timed shooting competitions, called "skirmishes," are held throughout the summer and can feature everything from muskets and carbines to revolvers and mortars. National matches are held in May and October at the NS-SA home range in Fort Shenandoah, Virginia, where as many as 40 smoothbore and rifled cannon from all over the country send thunder rolling through the picturesque countryside. Skirmishers are required to be authentically dressed in order to participate, though the regulations are slightly less onerous than those governing their costumed cousins in "living history" groups. Newcomers to the NS-SA can either join an existing unit or form one of their own (each requires a minimum of eight members). For information on joining or organizing a Michigan unit, consult the Northwest Territory's web site, www.nwtskirmisher.org.

In the 1950s skirmishers begat re-enactors, who generally prefer the costumed and educational aspects of their hobby to the messy and potentially dangerous firing of weapons. (However, there is considerable overlap between skirmishers and re-enactors in the membership of both groups.) Unlike the NS-SA, there is no state or national association to serve as an organizational umbrella for the many living history groups active in Michigan. These reconstituted units come and go. However, at any given time there may be 25 or more Civil War re-enactment groups active in the state. Typically, each unit is funded by membership fees, donations and fund-raisers. A member can expect to pay roughly $1,000 for his reproduction uniform, weapon and equipment (though not all at once), with the cost of individual items ranging from $35 for a canteen to $400 for a musket. (These costs apply to skirmishers as well.) Unit activities revolve around historically authentic "impressions" (depictions) of military and civilian life at living history encampments, parades, memorial ceremonies and school presentations. A unit may also serve as the honor guard at a wedding or funeral. Over the years many re-enactors who could afford the time off—and more than a few who couldn't—have been hired to work in large-scale battle scenes in such feature films as Gods and Generals and Gettysburg. It's common for several members of the same family to be involved in these costumed activities. In fact, the life cycle of many living history groups coincides with the aging of its founders; if fresh volunteers aren't regularly worked into the ranks as the original members grow old or lose interest, the group eventually disbands.

Among those Michigan units still going strong is **Co. B, 102nd U. S. Colored Troops**, a black history group that since the 1980s has been dedicated to preserving the memory of the state's only African-American unit. More information can be had by contacting Ross Fowler at 313/567-3453. Another veteran outfit, the **2nd Regiment Infantry Michigan Volunteers**, was established in 1986 and is headquartered at Historical Crossroads Village in Flint. Interested recruits can contact the regiment at 316 E. Lexington, Davison MI 48423; 810/653-9153; secondmich@aol.com. The **21st Michigan Volunteer Infantry, Co. H**, has been around since 1979. Contact Bruce Robere at mi21stinf@wideopenwest.com or check out the unit's web site, www.21st

michigan.org. A more recent success, the **4th Michigan Infantry Regiment, Co. A**, was organized in 1996. Contact Ted Barber at 12278 Wisner Hwy., Clinton MI 49236; rbarber@lni.net. The **7th Michigan Volunteer Infantry, Co. B** is one of the sponsors of the annual Cascades Civil War Muster in Jackson. Individual and family memberships begin at $16, an amount typical of most infantry groups. To find out more, write to P. O. Box 16206, Lansing MI 48901, or call 517/332-6632.

In addition to infantry, there also are re-enactors involved with cavalry and artillery units. The cost of purchasing and maintaining horses and equipment necessarily means members should expect to pay more in dues and other costs. To learn more about saddling up with the **1st Michigan Cavalry**, e-mail Jim Dedman at dedman@net66.com. The **3rd Battery, 1st Michigan Light Artillery**, organized in 1987, owns a pair of 10-pounder Parrott cannon and limbers. In addition to its usual schedule of re-enactment events, the battery participates in a long-range live-fire competition each summer at Camp Grayling. Annual dues are $60. Contact the unit at 9703 Verona, Battle Creek MI 49014, or click on www.cwartillery.org/3rdbattery. Another group of artillerists offers interested recruits considerable bangs for their bucks. **Battery D, 1st Michigan Light Artillery** features three 10-pound Parrotts and limbers. Dues are $40 annually. Contact the outfit's recruiter at 1713 Stocker, Flint MI 48503; or visit www.batteryd.com. The **5th Michigan Regimental Band**, which started as a state project for the U. S. Bicentennial, still is going strong three decades later, its members playing marches, waltzes and polkas with antique and replica Civil War-era instruments. Interested parties can contact Carol Smith, P. O. Box 170, Novi MI 48376; gandcsmith@comcast.net. The unit also has an entertaining web site, www.mi5th.org.

Every year since 1985, as many as 2,000 skirmishers and re-enactors have rubbed shoulders at the **Cascades Civil War Muster**, held the weekend before Labor Day at Cascade Falls Park in Jackson. Some 30,000 people attend the event, which features a major re-enactment of a selected battle (with "battle commentary" broadcast over local AM radio) and a slew of related activities, including a bluegrass and acoustical music festival. Contact Cascades Inc., c/o Jackson County Parks, 1992 Warren, Jackson MI 49203; or visit www.civilwar-muster.org.

There are numerous web sites devoted to some aspect of Michigan and the Civil War years. The most comprehensive is Don and Lois Harvey's ever-expanding **Michigan in the Civil War 1861-1866** (www.michiganinthewar .org/cwmireg.htm). It includes regimental histories and the names and units of more than 80,000 Michigan soldiers, as well as a growing photo gallery. For serious researchers, CD's containing the information are available for sale. The best of the regimental web sites are those of the **24th Michigan Infantry** (www.24th-michigan.org) and the **4th Michigan Infantry** (www.4thmichigan .com), managed by Rob Richardson and Dave Prince, respectively. **Michigan's African-American Civil War Soldiers** (www.geocities.com/michhist/civil-war.html) provides information on the members of the 1st Michigan Colored Infantry Regiment, with links to detailed biographies of those soldiers buried in Detroit's Elmwood Cemetery. One of the quirkiest Civil War sites on the internet is artist Lowell Boileu's **Project Plug Ugly** (http://bhere.com/plugugly). This is a multimedia tour of the war from the vantage point of General Alpheus S. Williams and his favorite horse, Plug Ugly.

Although this resource guide is far from exhaustive, a researcher with access to a computer only has to enter the name of a unit or individual into a search engine and let the internet do its work. In fact, simply typing in "Michigan in the Civil War" will produce hundreds of thousands of links. War without end, indeed!

Index

Illustration Credits

A snappy salute to photo researcher Dale R. Niesen for his tireless and expert help in locating and organizing many of the images found in this book. Thanks also to the many individuals and institutions who allowed the use of their photographs and memorabilia, especially collector Bob Coch.

Albion Historical Society: 80 right. Rebecca Amsdill: 12, 204. Sheila A. Beaubien: 190 both. Bentley Historical Library: 41, 56, 66, 81 left. Dave Berry: 90. Dave Bickford: 83, 218 top. Martin Nino Bertera Collection: 43 top. Burton Historical Collection: 10, 11, 19, 24, 28, 29, 33, 34, 40, 48, 54, 63, 82, 91, 103 bottom, 173 bottom, 174 bottom, 175, 177, 192 left, 195, 198, 211 both, 212, 224. Janice Pfluge Cain: 57. Bill and Glenna Jo Christen: 92. Cincinnati Art Museum: 7. Charlie Clark: 130 top. Bob Coch Collection: 37 bottom, 64, 67 left, 74 all, 100 both, 115, 121, 154, 160 both, 171 bottom, 193 both, 197 bottom, 199 top, 200 left, 202 all, 210 bottom left, 213 all, 215 bottom, 216 both, 220, 227 both. Laura D. Cooper: 87 both. Lucille Crooks Family: 149. Louis Cuyler Collection: 99. Dearborn Historical Museum: iv, 52 bottom, 84, 94, 117, 120 bottom, 146, 185. Detroit Historical Museum: 16. Dexter Historical Museum: 222. Jack and Marianne Dibean: 191. Ella Sharp Museum: 180. Luis F. Emilio: 50. Evart Historical Museum: 220. Dave Finney Collection: 116, 118, 131 bottom. Dale Gallon: 122-23. Andy Graves: 113. Dave Gorman: 143. Michael Hogle Collection: 179 left, 215 top. Hudson Historical Museum: 126 left. Darel Kuster and Dan LeBlond: 208, 209. Lenawee County Historical Museum: 27, 43 bottom, 138. Library of Congress: viii, 6, 17 both, 21, 58, 103 top, 110, 125, 148, 168, 200 right. Carol Lindsey and Eleanor Baker: 71 bottom. Allen Marshall: vi. Medal of Honor Society: 158. Paul Mehney Collection: 26. Michigan Capitol Commission/Peter Glendinning: 36 top right, 182 bottom. Monroe County Historical Museum: 1, 23, 47, 68 bottom, 124, 126 right, 172 top, 199 bottom. Sharon Mora: 61. National Archives: 15, 72, 97 right, 135, 194. Trudie Nesbitt: 96. Dale R. Niesen Collection: 36 bottom, 55, 60 both, 62, 65, 69 both, 73, 80 left, 88, 104, 108, 119, 127, 130 bottom, 131 top, 150, 155, 161, 176, 179 center, 201, 203 top, 205, 207, 210 top left, 214 both, 217 left, 218 bottom, 221, 225 left, 228, 229. Theresa Niesen Collection: 86. Dave Parks Collection: 35, 52 top, 70 bottom. Plymouth Historical Museum: 132. Valerie Radee: 98. Alan Rothenberg: 112, 172 bottom. John Sickles Collection: 78 right, 85, 183 right. State Archives of Michigan: 13, 14, 31, 38, 53, 59, 67 right, 71 top, 75 bottom, 78 left, 79, 97 left, 102, 134, 136, 139, 140, 141, 145, 153, 157, 159, 166, 169, 179 right, 183 left, 184, 203 bottom, 210 top right, 226. Rae Swan: 37 top. Robert Thom: 114. Dave Tinder Collection: 49, 196. Painting by Don Troiani: 128. Bill Warnica: 147. Mike Waskul Collection: 36 top left, 45, 75 top, 129, 156, 162, 171 top, 192 top right and bottom, 197 top. George Woodworth: 120 top. Bruce Worden: 106-7. All other illustrations are courtesy of the author or from private collections.